The Major Literary Seminars of Jacques Lacan

"An excellent, thorough and serious work of research on the links between literature and psychoanalysis orientated by the teachings of Jacques Lacan. Written in a highly enjoyable style and tone, this erudite yet accessible work should be a mandatory reference for anyone interested in the latest research in this interdisciplinary area."
Miquel Bassols Puig *Psychoanalyst, A.M.E.,*
Member and Former President of the W.A.P

"Shaped by exquisitely meticulous research on Lacan's 'Literary' seminars, this original volume is a beautiful literary work in itself. To read this book is to dive into the littoral, where the speaking-being's letter and litter rejoin. I hope the book will be translated into other languages. It's definitely worth it."
Gustavo Dessal *Psychoanalyst, A.M.E.,*
Member of the W.A.P., and novelist

The Major Literary Seminars of Jacques Lacan considers the three key phases of Lacan's interest in literary topics.

Santanu Biswas first examines the seminars given between 1955 and 1961, in which Lacan spoke on Edgar Allan Poe's short story "The Purloined Letter", *Hamlet*, Sophocles' *Antigone*, and Paul Claudel's *The Coûfontaine Trilogy*, and where literature is related to meaning. This is followed by an exploration of Lacan's seminar on "Lituraterre" in 1971, wherein Lacan elaborates on the different ways in which literature appeared to turn towards lituraterre. Finally, Biswas considers Lacan's 1975–1976 seminar on James Joyce, who created literature out of "litter" and was concerned with jouissance rather than with meaning.

The Major Literary Seminars of Jacques Lacan will be of great interest to Lacanian psychoanalysts, other mental health practitioners interested in the teachings of Lacan, and academics and students of Lacanian studies, literature, and psychoanalysis.

Santanu Biswas is Professor of English at Jadavpur University in India and a psychoanalyst. He is a member of the Lacan Circle of Australia and an associate member of Réseau Universitaire Européen, Paris. He is an editorial board member of *(Re)-Turn: A Journal of Lacanian Studies* (U.S.A.), *Psychoanalysis Lacan* (Australia), and *Objek želje* (Slovenia), and editorial advisory board member for *The Lacanian Review: Hurly-Burly* (France).

The Major Literary Seminars of Jacques Lacan

Literature, Lituraterre, Litterature

Santanu Biswas

With a Preface by Jacques-Alain Miller

LONDON AND NEW YORK

Designed cover image: Cover Image. Cover Design by Pinaki De

First published 2025
by Routledge
4 Park Square, Milton Park, Abingdon, Oxon OX14 4RN

and by Routledge
605 Third Avenue, New York, NY 10158

Routledge is an imprint of the Taylor & Francis Group, an informa business

© 2025 Santanu Biswas

The right of Santanu Biswas to be identified as author of this work has been asserted in accordance with sections 77 and 78 of the Copyright, Designs and Patents Act 1988.

All rights reserved. No part of this book may be reprinted or reproduced or utilised in any form or by any electronic, mechanical, or other means, now known or hereafter invented, including photocopying and recording, or in any information storage or retrieval system, without permission in writing from the publishers.

Trademark notice: Product or corporate names may be trademarks or registered trademarks, and are used only for identification and explanation without intent to infringe.

British Library Cataloguing-in-Publication Data
A catalogue record for this book is available from the British Library

Library of Congress Cataloging-in-Publication Data
Names: Biswas, Santanu, author. | Miller, Jacques-Alain, writer of preface.
Title: The major literary seminars of Jacques Lacan : literature, lituraterre, litterature / Santanu Biswas ; with a preface by Jacques-Alain Miller.
Description: Abingdon, Oxon ; New York, NY : Routledge, 2025. | Includes bibliographical references and index.
Identifiers: LCCN 2024015489 (print) | LCCN 2024015490 (ebook) | ISBN 9781032748030 (hardback) | ISBN 9781032748009 (paperback) | ISBN 9781003470984 (ebook)
Subjects: LCSH: Lacan, Jacques, 1901-1981—Criticism and interpretation. | Lacan, Jacques, 1901-1981—Knowledge and learning. | Psychoanalysis and literature. | Psychoanalysis—History—20th century.
Classification: LCC BF109.L28 B53 2025 (print) | LCC BF109.L28 (ebook) | DDC 150.19/5—dc23/eng/20240506
LC record available at https://lccn.loc.gov/2024015489
LC ebook record available at https://lccn.loc.gov/2024015490

ISBN: 978-1-032-74803-0 (hbk)
ISBN: 978-1-032-74800-9 (pbk)
ISBN: 978-1-003-47098-4 (ebk)

DOI: 10.4324/9781003470984

Typeset in Times New Roman
by Apex CoVantage, LLC

To Didi, Bubu, and Gublu
with love

Contents

List of Figures   *viii*
Acknowledgements   *ix*
Preface   *x*

Introduction   1

1. "The Purloined Letter"   15

2. *Hamlet*   42

3. *Antigone*   78

4. *The Coûfontaine Trilogy*   116

5. "Lituraterre"   142

6. James Joyce   173

Index   *208*

Figures

3.1	"Eye" (1999).	99
6.1	A Three-Ring Borromean Knot.	193
6.2	A Three-Ring Borromean Knot, Undone.	195
6.3	An Undone Three-Ring Borromean Knot Held Together by a Fourth Ring, the *Sinthome*.	196

Acknowledgements

I am deeply grateful to Jacques-Alain Miller for graciously writing the Preface to the book.

I am especially indebted to Miquel Bassols Puig and Gustavo Dessal for offering their views on the volume.

I express my sincere debt of gratitude to Jean-Luc Monnier, Jean-Michel Rabaté, Sophie Marret-Maleval, Russell Grigg, Dany Nobus, and Fabian Fajnwaks for offering their valuable opinion on different chapters of the book, and to Nancy Blake and Daisuke Fukuda for their views on parts of chapters of the book.

I convey my warm gratitude to István Orosz for generously granting me permission to use his painting in the book.

I express my heartfelt thanks to Pinaki De for designing the cover of the book.

My special thanks to Syamantakshobhan Basu for meticulously copy-editing the manuscript.

My sincere thanks to Jean-Pierre Klotz, Damien Guyonnet, Frank Rollier, and Dibyokamal Mitra for their support.

My deepest thanks to Poppy Biswas for assisting me in various ways in the work of writing the book.

Finally, a special word of thanks to the staff of Routledge for publishing the volume with great care and diligence.

Preface

The Major Literary Seminars of Jacques Lacan is a very comprehensive work that illuminates the Lacanian approach to fiction with mastery in its successive moments. In doing so, Santanu Biswas subtly clarifies a number of Lacan's complex notions. Reading is recommended for an erudite audience.

[Ouvrage très complet, qui éclaire avec maestria l'approche lacánienne de la fiction littéraire, saisie dans ses moments successifs. Ce faisant, Santanu Biswas clarifie subtilement des notions complexes de Lacan. Une lecture recommandée au public cultivé.]

Jacques-Alain Miller
Paris
4th October, 2023

Introduction

The interface between psychoanalysis and literature was inaugurated somewhat fortuitously on 15th October, 1897 when, in a letter addressed to his friend and close confidante, the Berlin-based E.N.T. specialist Wilhelm Fliess, Sigmund Freud touched upon Sophocles' *Oedipus Rex* and Shakespeare's *Hamlet* in order to explain his own Oedipus complex, which he had discovered through his self-analysis[1] (Freud, 1950/1954, pp. 223–224). In addition to the interpretations of *Oedipus Rex* and *Hamlet* in his letters to Fliess in 1897 and in *The Interpretation of Dreams* in 1899, Freud produced the following ten treatises on literature—two lectures, seven essays and a book—between 1905 and 1930 to illustrate different aspects of psychoanalysis: "Psychopathic Characters on the Stage" (1905 or 1906), *Delusion and Dream in Jensen's Gradiva* (Freud, 1907), "Creative Writers and Day-Dreaming" (1907), "The Theme of the Three Caskets" (1913), "Some Character-Types met with in Psychoanalytic Work" (1916), "A Childhood Recollection From *Poetry and Truth*" (1917), "The Uncanny" (1919), "Humour" (1927), "Dostoevsky and Parricide" (1927), and "Address Delivered in the Goethe House at Frankfurt" (1930).[2] Freud's French follower Jacques Lacan was just as strongly dependent on literature for the grasping and teaching of psychoanalysis. Lacan not only considered the study of literature essential for the "formation" or training of psychoanalysts like Freud but referred to literature as often as him. He had psychoanalytically deliberated upon, with different levels of intensity and interest, the works of Homer, Sophocles, Euripides, Aristophanes, Plautus, Ovid, Dante, Rabelais, Shakespeare, Molière, Racine, Defoe, Sade, Goethe, Wordsworth, Coleridge, Hoffmann, Stendhal, Heine, Balzac, Hugo, Poe, Dostoevsky, Flaubert, Carroll, Mallarmé, Maupassant, Chekhov, Wedekind, Claudel, Gide, Valéry, Apollinaire, Joyce, Giraudoux, Eliot, Breton, Aragon, Prévert, Queneau, Beckett, Genet, Blanchot, Anouilh, and Duras, as well as upon the genres of tragedy and comedy and other matters of literary importance, like rhetoric, psycho-biography, literary criticism, nonsense, "lituraterre", and so on, in important addresses, essays, book reviews and especially in his annual public seminar. At the earliest stage, Freud felt compelled to illustrate his discovery of the sexed unconscious with reference to works of literature rather than to his own unconscious or to the unconscious of his patients because he wanted to protect himself and his patients in whom he had identified such unconscious from the scrutiny of others. Thus, literature helped Freud convey the meaning of the sexed unconscious to others without revealing too much about any real human being. By choosing widely-read works like *Oedipus Rex* and *Hamlet*, Freud was moreover able to illustrate the Freudian unconscious to a very large audience and, at the same time, claim its universal validity in a way that case histories of real patients would not have enabled him to do. Lacan's reasons for turning to literature as a teacher of psychoanalysis were more or less similar to those of Freud.

Freud had a great deal of respect for creative writers from an early age. While his favourite author was Goethe, he had read European literature fairly extensively and knew a lot of Greek and Latin classics by heart by the time he completed his schooling. As a psychoanalyst, he argued that creative writers had the ability to anticipate psychoanalysis. For instance, while speaking on *Hamlet* he stated that playwrights like Shakespeare unconsciously, as in intuitively, understood psychoanalytic concepts like the Oedipus complex long before they had been formally discovered: "Shakespeare's . . . own unconscious understood that of his hero" (ibid., p. 224). Lacan not only agreed with Freud on this, stating in his seminar of 1961 that in Sophocles' *Antigone,* both Creon and Antigone speak of the "other's *Atè*" exactly in the manner in which he did, "even though neither of them attended my Seminar"[3] (Lacan, 1991/2015, p. 278), but held creative writers in even higher regard than Freud by often proclaiming that they understood psychoanalysis better than the psychoanalysts themselves. For instance, while speaking on Poe's short story "The Facts in the Case of M. Valdemar" in his seminar of 1955, Lacan praises Poe's poetic imagination, contrasting it with the feeble imagination of psychoanalysts: "This is fine poetical imagination, which ranges much further than our timid medical imaginations, although we all try hard along that road" (Lacan, 1978/1993, p. 231). Not only that, in his 1965 "Homage to Marguerite Duras", Lacan says that Duras already knew what he taught in his seminar without any need on her part to attend any of it: "Marguerite Duras knows, without me, what I teach" (Lacan, 1965/1987, p. 124). Furthermore, in his 1971 essay and seminar on "Lituraterre", Lacan says that James Joyce had nothing to gain from psychoanalysis because he had been able to achieve on his own, without any help from psychoanalysis, the best result that one can achieve from reaching the end of an analysis (Lacan, 2007, p. 113). Notably, although Joyce had no need to be psychoanalysed, Lacan needed to refer to *Finnegans Wake* in order to be able to frame his views on the psychoanalytic concept of the *sinthome*. Jacques-Alain Miller rightly points out that Lacan's approach to literature was "[i]nspiring no contempt for artists. Inviting analysts, rather, to learn from the example" (Miller, 1987/2012, p. 5). Despite all these broad similarities in their respective attitudes toward literature, the nature of Lacan's psychoanalytic engagement with literature[4] is highly different from that of Freud on several counts.

An important difference between the psychoanalytic approaches of Freud and Lacan to literature is that whereas Freud tended to read literature or aspects of the lives of writers as allegorical representations or faithful illustrations of his theory, thereby reducing literature to psychoanalysis, and literature and psychoanalysis to one, Lacan, unless he sought illumination on psychoanalysis from literature, read literature and psychoanalysis in terms of each other, keeping their difference alive so that each is able to reflect on the other without losing its individual essence. This is evident in his studies on "The Purloined Letter" and the subject's determination by the signifier; desire and jouissance and Jean Genet's *The Balcony*; desire and its interpretation in *Hamlet* and the same in Freud; *Antigone* and the ethics of psychoanalysis (and Immanuel Kant's *Critique of Practical Reason* and Marquis de Sade's *Philosophy in the Bedroom* within it); *The Coûfontaine Trilogy* and transference; *Alice's Adventures in Wonderland* and *Through the Looking-Glass* and the nature of sublimation in a work of art (and *Alice's Adventures in Wonderland* and Darwin's *On the Origin of Species* within it); Frank Wedekind's *Spring Awakening* and the awakening of sexuality in boys; letter-literal-literature and litter-littoral-lituraterre; *Finnegans Wake* and Borromean knots; poetry and the clinic; and so on, never letting the two collapse into one. Lacan effectively read two difficult texts together, making the difficulties collide—or have their edges touch each other—to produce a creative spark that would illuminate both texts at their limits. Thus, far from closing down literary texts with psychoanalytical interpretations like Freud, Lacan learnt aspects of psychoanalysis from literature and served psychoanalysis and literary criticism in return. In this, Lacan seems to have been implementing a strategy recommended by Freud himself in *The Interpretation of Dreams*:

> When in the course of a piece of scientific work we come upon a problem which is difficult to solve, it is often a good plan to take up a second problem along with the original one—just as it is easier to crack two nuts together than each separately.
>
> (Freud, 1899/2001, pp. 135–136)

Following Miller, who speaks of Lacan's procedure of reading "X with Y" in his essay "Joyce with Lacan", this method of reading two different types of texts in terms of each other may also be described as a "way of reading via interference" that was Lacan's preferred and habitual mode of reading (Miller, 1987/2012, p. 2). It is somewhat akin to the psychoanalyst's act of listening fleetingly to the speech of the analysand at times or to Freud's act of doodling while listening to his patients, which has a special clinical efficacy. The nature of Lacan's engagement with literature may be said to bear out at the broadest level the "X with Y" pattern mentioned by Miller in terms of its "early with later" structure. Briefly put, Lacan devoted large parts of several early seminars to reading Edgar Allan Poe's "The Purloined Letter", *Hamlet*, Sophocles' *Antigone,* and Paul Claudel's *The Coûfontaine Trilogy* in order to shed light on the concepts of the subjects' determination by the signifier, desire and its interpretation, between two deaths, and transference in psychoanalysis respectively, which constitute Lacan's early teachings on literature. This is followed by a break of almost a decade during which Lacan spoke on Lewis Carroll and wrote on Marguerite Duras and others but did not engage with literature in the same serious and sustained manner as before. Lacan resumed his serious engagement with literature in 1971 by speaking and writing on "Lituraterre" which marked a radical shift of focus from the signifier in the symbolic to the letter in the real. Following "Lituraterre" as the pivot, Lacan devoted a good part of his 1975–1976 seminar on *The Sinthome* to James Joyce and spoke on the Irish writer at the fifth international Joyce Symposium in Paris in 1975, which constituted Lacan's later teachings on literature. These two sets of teachings offer, very broadly speaking, a signifier-based conceptualisation of literature and a litter-based conceptualisation of literature, respectively. Evidently, therefore, the two cannot be reduced to one. They must be read one with the other or one against the other.

Another major difference between the psychoanalytic approaches of Freud and Lacan to literature is that whereas Freud took a psycho-biographical approach to literature, Lacan sought to break free from it in terms of an approach to literature concerned with the holes in the text. For instance, Freud writes in his analysis of *Hamlet*:

> I observe in a book on Shakespeare by Georg Brandes (1896) a statement that *Hamlet* was written immediately after the death of Shakespeare's father (in 1601), that is, under the immediate impact of his bereavement and, as we may well assume, while his childhood feelings about his father had been freshly revived. It is known, too, that Shakespeare's own son who died at an early age bore the name of "Hamnet", which is identical with "Hamlet".
> (Freud, 1899/2001, pp. 265–266)

Lacan, by contrast, categorically stated, "[I]t is out of question to analyse dead authors" (Lacan, 1978/1993, p. 152). In order to prevent literary criticism from falling into the psycho-biographical trap, Lacan suggested that a proper psychoanalytic reading of literature ought to compare the holes made by the letter in literary and psychoanalytic discourses, respectively—a goal that cannot be reached along the psycho-biographical route. Once again, while Freud sought to erroneously reduce literature to the events of the life of the author, which was the dominant mode of literary criticism in the 19th and early 20th centuries, Lacan, by and large, sought to focus on the text rather than on the life of the author, and more specifically on the holes made by the letter in literary and psychoanalytical writings. By shifting the focus to the holes rather than to the statements made by the letter and by giving equal importance to two different kinds of holes made by the letter in two different types of discourses, Lacan tried to rule out the possibility of any reductive readings.

For an example of a letter making a hole in psychoanalytic discourse, one may turn to the letter "*a*" which denotes the object small *a* in Lacan. Lacan described the object *a* in terms of a cut as early as in his 1958–1959 seminar on *Desire and Its Interpretation*, where, as the "object involved in weaning", it is "the object involved in the cut [or: object cut off, *objet de coupure*]" (Lacan, 2013/2019, p. 383). In other words, the object *a* is an inadequacy. It is that which we do not get even when the demand for an object has been otherwise fulfilled. Later, in his

1965–1966 seminar on *The Object of Psychoanalysis*, in the course of explaining how the divided subject is sustained in the fantasy by the object *a* as something falling and vanishing, Lacan states that although there can be no subject without the support of the object, as brought out by the formula for fantasy, ($ \lozenge a$) the object *a* is nevertheless an impossible object for the subject. This is so not only because the object *a* is a pure lack, in that the primordial object is lost forever, but also because the object *a* is the subject's counterpart situated on the other side of the surface, on the other side of the lozenge as a hole,[5] thereby making it impossible for the subject and the object to encounter each other directly. In the same seminar, Lacan moreover makes a slightly different point that he had started to develop from the seminar on *The Four Fundamental Concepts of Psychoanalysis* onward, namely that the cut of the object *a* is the frame through which the barred subject sees, as well as the frame that frames the barred subject. Continuing from there in the seminar on *The Object of Psychoanalysis*, Lacan compares the object *a* to the frame of a window, or to the slit between the eyelids acting as a window, or the edge of a hole through which all images are viewed by the barred subject but which itself is never clearly visible: "It is in so far as the window, in the relationship of the look to the seen world is always what is elided, that we can represent for ourselves the function of the object *a*, the window" (Lacan, 2002, p. 241). He argues that the window frame at the top right-hand corner of Diego Velázquez's "Las Meninas", through which light enters and illuminates the entire scene of the painting, has the function of the object *a*. In the session on "Lituraterre" of the seminar on *On a Discourse that Might not be a Semblance*, as well as in the essay based on it cited here, Lacan goes on to describe the letter that is hollowed out and reduced to a frame, to the edge of a hole: "The edge of the hole in knowledge, isn't this what the letter outlines?" (Lacan, 1971/2013, p. 329).

In literature, there are plenty of examples of the letter making different kinds of holes in the writing to which it belongs, even if we were to confine ourselves entirely to the works and authors discussed by Lacan. For instance, the letter makes a hole in the narrative of "The Purloined Letter" in terms of the irrevocable elision of the message or the contents of the letter. Somewhat differently, the letter as litter creates holes rather than meaning in the text of Joyce's *Finnegans Wake*. In the case of André Gide, he is severely tormented when his enraged wife Madeleine burns all the letters he had written to her, although they were most precious to her and there were no copies (Lacan, 1958/2006). And the emptiness or vacuity Lol falls into towards the end of Duras's *The Ravishing of Lol Stein* is described in terms of an absence-word:

> What she does believe is that she must enter it, that that was what she had to do, that it would always have meant, for her mind as well as her body, both their greatest pain and their greatest joy, so commingled as to be undefinable, a single entity but unnamable for lack of a word. I like to believe—since I love her—that if Lol is silent in her daily life it is because, for a split second, she believed that this word might exist. Since it does not, she remains silent. It would have

been an absence-word, a hole-word, whose center would have been hollowed out in a hole, the kind of hole in which all other words would have been buried. It would have been impossible to utter, it would have been made to reverberate. Enormous, endless, an empty gong, it would have held back anyone who wanted to leave, it would have convinced them of the impossible, it would have made them deaf to any other word save that one, in one fell swoop it would have defined the moment and the future themselves. By its absence, this word ruins all the others, it contaminates them, it is also the dead dog on the beach at high noon, this hole of flesh.

(Duras, 1964/1966, pp. 37–38)

Referring to the incident of young Lol's abandonment by her fiancé, Michael Richardson, for the older lady, Anne-Marie Stretter, at a ball in a seaside resort, an incident that Lol had to recreate in a different form ten years later in order to come to terms with it, the narrator states that if there existed a word for Lol's undefinable and unnameable feeling for which there is none, it would have been a hollowed out word, like an empty gong. It would have been an unutterable hole-word that would have absorbed all other words and made people deaf to them. But the absence of this word, like the hollow created by the flesh of the dead dog on the beach, infects and destroys all other words.

Even though Lacan's references to Joyce's father, John Stanislaus Joyce, and to Joyce's wife, Nora Barnacle, in his reading of the Irish author seem to offer the reading a psycho-biographical bent, Lacan's main focus is rather on the specificities of Joyce's writing than on these familial references that serve merely as points of departure. Lacan's central argument about Joyce—that he composed his last novel with his *lalangue* that at once gave him jouissance and enabled him to construct his *sinthome*—would not be affected too much even if the biographical references to Joyce's family were reduced to a minimum. Besides, the "father" invoked is not so much the father in the family as the father in the complex, which is a name and a metaphor, as we shall see. Was Lacan possibly suggesting in terms of his reading of Joyce that bits and pieces of psycho-biography cannot seriously affect readings that are principally motivated by Borromean knots as a form of topology? After all, topology offers another instance of how writing makes holes in the written, as Lacan stated with reference to Aristotle's *Prior Analytics*: "There is no topology without writing. . . . [T]opology . . . consists precisely in making holes in what is written" (Lacan, 2007, p. 81). A few years later, he would go on to discuss "[t]he hole of the [Borromean] knot" itself (Lacan, 2005/2016, p. 60) by stating that "[t]he hole is something that the most basic experience [of the Borromean ring] dictates" (ibid., p. 67) because "in a circle there is a hole" (ibid., p. 91).

Yet another significant difference between Freud and Lacan as psychoanalytic readers of literature is that, whereas Freud treated literary characters as individuals and often as individuals suffering from psychopathological conditions, Lacan rightly treated them as literary creations. For instance, Freud discusses Norbert Hanold's delusion and its successful treatment by his childhood friend and neighbour

Zoe Bertgang in *Delusion and Dream in Jensen's* Gradiva as though they were real human beings (Freud, 1907/2001). Similarly, Freud conflates real clinical cases with literary constructs in "Some Character-Types met with in Psychoanalytic Work", treating them as exact equivalents (Freud, 1916/2001). Taking the opposite route as it were, Lacan categorically states in the seminar on *Hamlet* that Hamlet is not a clinical case because he is not a real person: "Hamlet is not a clinical case. Hamlet, of course—this is all too obvious, and there is no need to recall it to mind—is not a real being" (Lacan, 2013/2019, pp. 289–290). Accordingly, Lacan clarifies that Hamlet does not "have" a neurosis like real human beings do, but rather that his character "demonstrates" some neurosis to the psychoanalysts, which is completely different from being a neurotic: "Hamlet does not have a neurosis; he demonstrates neurosis to us, which is something altogether different than to be neurotic" (ibid., p. 295). Despite not dealing with a clinical case or a real person, the play is of interest to psychoanalytically-oriented readers because, as a place or hub of desire, the character of Hamlet allows them to comprehensively situate desire in "all" its traits: "Hamlet is, if you will, a sort of hub where a desire is situated, and we can find all the features of desire in him" (ibid., p. 290). As a matter of fact, the character of Hamlet is able to demonstrate "all" the features of neurotic desire precisely because he is a poetic creation, not a real person, for while a real person can either be an obsessional or a hysteric, never both at once, a poetic creation can easily display signs of both these forms of neurosis, as Hamlet, in fact, does:

> Hamlet, as I told you, is not this or that, is neither an obsessive nor an hysteric. Why? Because he is first and foremost a poetic creation.
>
> (Ibid., p. 295)

> People have said that Hamlet's desire is an hysteric's desire. This is perhaps quite true. Other people have said that it is an obsessive's desire. That, too, might be argued, for it is a fact that he is full of psychasthenic symptoms, even severe ones. But that is not the point. In truth, Hamlet is both. He is purely and simply the place of desire.
>
> (Ibid., p. 289)

One more major difference between the psychoanalytic approaches to literature of Freud and Lacan, respectively, stemmed from the latter's new realisation concerning the interdisciplinary domain of "Literature/Art and Psychoanalysis" following his engagement with the works of Joyce. Lacan says in his "Yale University Interview with Students, Answers to Their Questions" on 24th November, 1975: "Explaining art through the unconscious seems to me to be highly suspect, though this is what analysts do. Explaining art through the symptom seems more serious to me" (Lacan, 1975b/2022, p. 67). Art ought to be explained in terms of the symptom because the symptom is what art explicitly targets, and the truth imposed in the form of a symptom is what it tends to undo, as Lacan had indicated only a few days ago, on 18th November, 1975, while speaking on his own act of "examination of art" in the seminar on *The Sinthome*: "In what way is artifice expressly able to target what presents itself in the first instance as a symptom? In what way can art . . . foil, as it were, what imposes as a symptom? Namely, truth" (Lacan, 2005/2016, p. 14). Apart from being the target of art and the bearer of truth, the symptom is also equivalent to the father by way of the Oedipus complex: "[A]ll in all, the father is a symptom . . . The Oedipus complex is, as such, a symptom" (ibid., pp. 11–13).

Elucidating art through the unconscious is "highly suspect" because the unconscious, though an extremely precise concept, has been reduced to a highly general idea owing to the imprecise and flawed nature of the term itself. In his reply to Miller's first question, on the unconscious, in the *Television*, Lacan says:

> The disadvantage of this word is that it is negative, which allows one to assume anything at all in the world about it, plus everything else as well. Why not? To that which goes unnoticed, the word everywhere applies just as well as nowhere. It is nonetheless a very precise thing.
>
> (Lacan, 1974/1990, p. 5)

The unconscious can, moreover, be conceived entirely theoretically. Since an approach to art or literature through the unconscious neither demands precision in interpretation nor requires the interpreter to have grasped psychoanalysis well enough, it tends to slip into the university discourse far too easily. Elucidating art through the symptom, by contrast, is a "serious" exercise because it compels the reader to be precise and enables him to make meaningful observations. Symptom-formation is a precise kind of unconscious-formation that cannot be confused with other things easily. Besides, while almost anything can be interpreted as pertaining to the unconscious by a novice, a symptom usually bears a very precise message that can only be uncovered by a correct interpretation—one that must account for all the details involved. At times, the greater part of a psychopathological act is accounted for by the symptom rather than by the unconscious. For instance, the obsessional symptom of the thirty-year-old female patient of Freud mentioned in the *Introductory Lectures on Psychoanalysis*, who would run into a room that had a table at its centre, take up a particular position beside the table and summon the housemaid for no apparent reason. This otherwise harmless symptom enabled the patient to let her present maid see the prominent, old, red stain of tomato ketchup on the tablecloth and thus fulfil her old unconscious wish to save the honour of her husband in the eyes of their maid after her wedding night, since her husband, who proved to be impotent that night, was anxious to hide the truth from the maid who was to make the bed in the morning by trying to pour red ink on the bed sheet, but due to his anxiety had poured the ink at the wrong place. Thus, in terms of the ketchup stain at the right place on the table cloth that substitutes for the blood stain missing at the right place on the bed sheet, the patient was able to portray the sexual competence of her impotent husband before the maid, albeit a different maid. The precise aim of the symptom, therefore, was to give the patient the satisfaction of saving her husband's honour in the eyes of her maid, although she had no idea of this before she discovered the meaning of her symptom (Freud, 1916–1917/2001, pp. 261–264). Here, only the patient's act of summoning her maid without knowing the reason for it pertains to her unconscious, while the rest of the details related to the act pertain to her symptom. Deciphering the symptom is important because, as Lacan said in 1975, a symptom is a form of truthful saying and a form of resistance at one and the same time: "Symptoms also say something. A symptom says something, and it is another form of truthful saying. . . . Symptoms resist" (Lacan, 1976/2022, p. 79). The ability to explain art or literature in terms of the symptom requires the reader to have a fairly good command over clinical psychoanalysis, including the ability to make a distinction between the symptom and the *sinthome* in practise, which tends to bring the explanation closer to the psychoanalyst's discourse.[6]

While Lacan must have had Freud's works on art and literature on his mind when he spoke of how "analysts" usually approach art and literature, since in his "Yale University: Kanzer Seminar", delivered earlier on the same day, he had explicitly stated with reference to Freud's psychoanalytic works on these fields, and especially to the latter's essay on Jensen's *Gradiva* that "Freud tried . . . to see in art a kind of testimony of the unconscious" (Lacan, 1975a/2022, p. 51) the plural "analysts" indicates that Lacan may well have been thinking of the works of Freudians like Jones, Bonaparte, Rank, and others on literature in addition to those of Freud. However, since Lacan himself explained "The Purloined Letter" in 1955, *Hamlet* in 1958–1959, *Antigone* in 1960, and *The Coûfontaine Trilogy* in 1960–1961 through the unconscious, the need to approach literature and art through the symptom rather than through the unconscious must have been a new realisation of his, one that had dawned on him only after he had practised both types of reading of art sufficiently. The fact that Lacan was able to state this only a few months after explaining Joyce's art through the symptom in two papers on "Joyce the Symptom", and only a few days after the first session of his public seminar on Joyce's *sinthome* in Paris, unmistakably indicates that this realisation was facilitated by his engagement with the works of Joyce. Even Lacan's use of the word "art" to denote "literature" seems to have been influenced by Joyce's use of the word "artist" to denote a writer. More pertinently, since the letter has turned to litter, the literal has turned to the littoral, literary language has turned to *lalangue*, meaning has been replaced by jouissance, literature has started to tend towards lituraterre, and literature has turned to "litteringture" (Joyce, 1939/1975, p. 570), all predominantly thanks to Joyce, psychoanalytic literary criticism ought to correspondingly change from being unconscious-centric to becoming symptom-centric or *sinthome*-centric in order to match the advancement made in the field of literature. It is a change in this interdisciplinary area that Joyce had rendered obligatory, and a change that no one before Lacan had been able to identify, let alone introduce.

Not only that, Freud and Lacan radically differed from each other even on the nature of their literary approach to psychoanalysis. Thus, whereas Freud approaches the infantile sexual drive in terms of the Oedipus complex based on the tragedy of

Oedipus, Lacan thinks that "[w]hat matters in the sexual is the comic", because while man aspires to his object as a woman, and therefore "loves" as a woman, he desires with the support of his erection, and therefore "desires" as a man (Lacan, 1977–1978, p. 6. My translation).[7] This makes man's love, his sexual desire, and their combination essentially comical in nature. Accordingly, Lacan concludes the first Session dated 15th November, 1977 of the seminar on *The Moment to Conclude* [*Le Moment de Conclure*] with the observation:

> Life isn't tragic, it's comic, and yet it's rather curious that Freud could think of nothing better than the 'Oedipus complex', that is to say a tragedy, in order to name what was in question. It is hard to see why he designated what he was dealing with in this relationship that links the Symbolic, the Imaginary and the Real, by anything other than a comedy that would have allowed him to take a shorter route.
>
> (Ibid., p. 6. My translation)

In keeping with this view, Lacan discusses the works of Aristophanes, Dante's *The Divine Comedy*, Genet's *The Balcony*, and other comedies in different seminars, alongside the Oedipus trilogy, *Hamlet, The Coûfontaine Trilogy*, and other tragedies. In other words, whereas Freud took the longer literary approach of tragedy to psychoanalysis, Lacan recommended the shorter literary approach to the same offered by comedy, even though he explored both approaches.

The focus of this volume is on the six major seminars on literature given by Lacan in three phases that began when he spoke on Poe in his annual public seminar of March 1955 and ended when he spoke on Joyce in his annual public seminar of May 1976. In the period from 1955 to 1961, constituting the first phase, Lacan spoke on "The Purloined Letter", *Hamlet, Antigone*, and *The Coûfontaine Trilogy*, where the letter, related to meaning, is in its "literal" condition, and the works produced by it deserves to be described as "literature". Lacan returned to literature in his seminar after a long break with his seminar on "Lituraterre" in 1971, which constitutes the second phase, where the letter as an "edge" that separates knowledge from jouissance brings out the "littoral" condition of the letter, and the works produced by it ought, therefore, to be described as "lituraterre". The third and last phase of Lacan's sustained engagement with literature took place in 1975–1976, in the form of his seminar on Joyce. In this phase, in which Lacan explains how Joyce turns the letter into litter, we encounter the "litteral" condition of the letter, where the letter as litter produces jouissance instead of meaning, and the works created with its help are best described as "litterature". Broadly speaking, Lacan turned to literature for a better understanding of certain psychoanalytical concepts, like the subject, the signifier, the object, the phallus, desire, interpretation, transference, the letter, semblance, *lalangue*, the *sinthome*, et cetera, and he served literary studies by shedding psychoanalytic light on vexed literary issues like Antigone's *Kommos*, Hamlet's behaviour, Joyce's language, the upper case Û with a circumflex accent in Claudel's spelling of the name of his protagonist "COÛFONTAINE", to name a few. It seems Lacan had compensated for his not having written a single psychoanalytical case history by speaking and writing extensively on works of literature. Further light will be shed on these and other aspects of Lacan's psychoanalytic engagement with literature in the six chapters on his major literary seminars that follow.

Notes

1 Freud and his childhood friend Eduard Silberstein together read Miguel de Cervantes' 1613 novella *El coloquio de los perros* (*The Dialogue of the Dogs*) that dealt with the conversation of the two dogs, Cipión and Berganza, and corresponded on it. In a letter dated 7th March, 1875, Freud suggested to his friend that from then on, they should always call themselves "perros" (dogs) (Freud, 1989/1990, p. 99) even though, right from one of his earliest published letters to his friend dated 12th December, 1871 to his last published letter to him dated 24th January, 1881, Freud predominantly signed his letters "Cipion" and addressed Silberstein as "Berganza". Freud also read *Don Quixote* in 1875 and wrote to Silberstein about the novel (ibid., pp. 81, 87). Based on this, Jean-Michel Rabaté argues that Freud had taken Cervantes, and not Sophocles or Shakespeare, as a main paradigm for literature. Referring to their correspondence on the novella in particular, he states that the "spirit of burlesque, whimsy, and satire" displayed in the "droll and sad poem" called "Epithalamium" that Freud had composed under the pen name "a Homerian of the Academia Espanola" and sent to Silberstein in a letter dated 1st October, 1875, (ibid., pp. 135–138) when he came to know that his pretty young neighbour and object of adoration, Gisela Fuss, was to get married, "derives its ultimate inspiration from Cervantes's tale". Following from this, Rabaté claims that Freud's discovery of a "writing cure" with the help of this poem, together with the "transferential friendship" indicated by his correspondence in which may be recognised the "practice of self-analysis via dialogue with an intimate friend", or "the idea of a confidential exchange between two persons who will discuss everything that they have experienced to extract a truer meaning", i.e., "talking cure", "anticipate" psychoanalysis. Most pertinently, he implies that Freud had thus effectively launched the interdisciplinary domain of "psychoanalysis and literature" via Cervantes as early as in October 1875 (Rabaté, 2014, pp. 9–17). In my opinion, Freud may at best be said to have touched upon something of the nature of "ur-psychoanalysis and literature" in terms of the kind of "writing cure" and "talking cure" he had identified by the mid-1870s in course of his correspondence with Silberstein on Cervantes, because, in order for him to have inaugurated the field of "psychoanalysis and literature", the praxis of "psychoanalysis" itself ought to have been first of all discovered as an essential prerequisite, a discovery that required the identification of repression, the unconscious, infantile sexuality, Oedipus complex, resistance, and transference as a set of interrelated concepts at the very least, which he had not been able to accomplish before 1896, which also happens to be the year he introduced the term "psychoanalysis".

2 Some of the important works in the interdisciplinary field of literature and psychoanalysis by Freud's contemporaries following Freud are: Ernest Jones's "The Œdipus-complex as an Explanation of Hamlet's Mystery: A Study in Motive" (1910), "A Psychoanalytic Study of *Hamlet*" (1922), an expanded version of it bearing the same title (1923), and *Hamlet and Oedipus* (1949); Otto Rank's *The Incest Theme in Literature and Legend: Fundamentals of a Psychology of Literary Creation* (1912), and *Art and Artist: Creative Urge and Personality Development* (1932); Ella Sharpe's unfinished papers of (1929) and (1947) on *Hamlet* posthumously published as *Collected Papers on Psychoanalysis* (1950); (some of the other early psychoanalytic readings of *Hamlet* came from Otto Rank, Theodor Reik,

Kurt Robert Eissler, Erik Erikson, Alfred Adler, the Adlerian Philippe Mairet, and the Jungians Maud Bodkin and Peter Dow Webster); Marie Bonaparte's *The Life and Works of Edgar Allan Poe: A Psychoanalytic Interpretation* (1933); Van Wyck Brooks's psychoanalytical biography *The Ordeal of Mark Twain* (1920); and René Laforgue's *The Defeat of Baudelaire: A Psychoanalytical Study of the Neurosis of Charles Baudelaire* (1931). Some of the important early attempts by academics and scholars to read literature with aspects of psychoanalysis are Robert Graves' *Poetic Unreason and Other Studies* (1925); William Empson's *Seven Types of Ambiguity* (1930), *"Alice in Wonderland*: The Child as Swain" (1935), *English Pastoral Poetry* (1938), and *Essays on Shakespeare* (1986); Sir Herbert Read's *Form in Modern Poetry* (1932); Edmund Wilson's "The Ambiguity of Henry James" (1934) and *The Wound and the Bow* (1941); Kenneth Burke's "Freud—and the Analysis of Poetry" (1939); Lionel Trilling's "The Legacy of Sigmund Freud: An Appraisal" (1940), the second part of which was reprinted as "Freud and Literature" (1959); Northrop Frye's critical work *Anatomy of Criticism: Four Essays* (1957); William Phillips's edited volume *Art and Psychoanalysis* (1957); Simon O. Lesser's *Fiction and the Unconscious* (1957); Norman Holland's *Psychoanalysis and Shakespeare* (1966), *The Dynamics of Literary Response* (1968), *Poems in Persons: An Introduction to the Psychoanalysis of Literature* (1973), the co-edited *Shakespeare's Personality* (1989), and *Holland's Guide to Psychoanalytic Psychology and Literature-and-Psychology* (1990); Harold Bloom's *The Anxiety of Influence: A Theory of Poetry* (1973), *A Map of Misreading* (1975), and *Poetry and Repression: Revisionism from Blake to Stevens* (1976); and Steven P. Marcus's *Dickens: From Pickwick to Dombey* (1961), *The Other Victorians* (1966), *Representations: Essays on Literature and Society* (1975), and *Freud and the Culture of Psychoanalysis* (1984). The attitude of creative writers towards Freud and/or psychoanalysis has been a mixed one. James Joyce, Thomas Stearns Eliot, and David Herbert Lawrence were critical of Freud and psychoanalysis to different degrees. Although Leonard Woolf held Freud in very high regard and took a huge financial risk to publish the latter's complete works in English, and several members of the Bloomsbury group respected Freud a lot, Virginia Woolf was initially sceptical about Freud but later on, was less resistant toward him. And Thomas Mann, Stefan Zweig, Romain Rolland, Herbert George Wells, Eugene O'Neill, William Faulkner, Wystan Hugh Auden, Saul Bellow, Samuel Beckett, and others were appreciative of Freud and/or psychoanalysis to different degrees.

3 The only exception is the depiction of something akin to the Oedipus complex in the play *Crusts* written by Freud's contemporary Paul Claudel that Lacan attributes more to the spirit of the times than to the playwright's insight: "something common to one and the same era connects it from one creator to another, from a reflective thinker [Freud] to a creative one [Claudel]" (Lacan, 1991/2015, p. 286).

4 Lacan's non-psychoanalytic engagements with literature should include his reading of stories, fables, plays and poems as a school boy, poems like Guillaume Apollinaire's "Le Pont Mirabeau", even though Lacan would later read the line, "Under the Mirabeau Bridge there flows the Seine" (*Sous le pont Mirabeau coule la Seine*) from this poem in his "Lesson on Lituraterre" psychoanalytically by calling the river "*Seine* primitive" so as to invoke the Freudian notion of "Scène primitive" or "primal scene" (*Urszene*) (Lacan, 2007, p. 123); his writing of a poem in August 1929 that was published under the title "Hiatus Irrationalis" in the surrealist journal *Le Phare de Neuilly* in 1933; his discussions with his patient Marguerite Pantaine on the unpublished autobiographical fiction that she had written during her treatment for self-punitive paranoid psychosis at the Sainte-Anne Hospital (L'Hôpital Sainte-Anne) in Paris, as her psychiatrist from May 1931 (when she was sent there by court orders for her treatment, following her imprisonment in April 1931 for trying to stab the famous actress Huguette Duflos); his nicknaming of Pantaine as "Aimée" (Beloved), after the name of the heroine of one of her own works of autobiographical fiction, in his doctoral thesis on "Paranoid Psychosis and its Relation to the Personality"; and other such instances.

5 For the meaning of the logical symbol of the lozenge or *poinçon* (◊) a coinage of Lacan, see Biswas, 2011.
6 Shedding further light on why the symptom is more important than the unconscious in psychoanalysis, Lacan states in Session 1 dated 16th November, 1976 of the 1976–1977 seminar on *L'insu que sait de l'une-bévue s'aile à mourre*, that since the symptom, which is one's own, which one knows the best, and which one can ultimately know what to do with, is more authentic than the unconscious that forever remains the Other, an analysis ends not when one identifies with one's unconscious but only when one identifies with one's symptom (Lacan, 1976–1977, p. 4. My translation). Due to homophony and allusions, the title of the seminar may be variously translated as The Non-known that Knows about the One-blunder Chances Love; Love is the Failure of the One-blunder; The Non-known Knew it was a Mistaken Moon on the Wings of Love; The Unknown that Knows of the One-blunder that Flies in the Game of Guessing; et cetera.
7 Not only is the sexual comic, but comedy is dependent on the phallus. Pointing to Plato's reference to "the genital organ as such in a discourse concerning . . . love", Lacan had stated in 1960 that "[t]his confirms what . . . was essential to the mainspring of comedy, which is always, in the end, a reference to the phallus" (Lacan, 1991/2015, p. 94).

References

Biswas, Santanu (2011). The Poinçon (◊) in Lacan. In Ellie Ragland (Ed.), *(Re)-Turn: A Journal of Lacanian Studies*, Vol. 6, University of Missouri, Spring, 135–147. Available at https://return.jls.missouri.edu/ReturnVol6/Biswas_ThePunch.pdf (Accessed on 7th January, 2024).
Brandes, Georg (1905). *William Shakespeare: A Critical Study*. In William Archer, Mary Morison and Diana White Trans. William Heinemann (Original work published 1896).
Duras, Marguerite (1966). *The Ravishing of Lol Stein*. In Richard Seaver Trans. Pantheon (Original work published 1964).
Freud, Sigmund (1954). *The Origins of Psychoanalysis. Letters to Wilhelm Fliess, Drafts and Notes: 1887–1902*. In Marie Bonaparte, Anna Freud and Ernst Kris (Eds.). Basic Books, Inc. (Original work published 1950).
Freud, Sigmund (1990). *The Letters of Sigmund Freud to Eduard Silberstein, 1871–1881*. In Walter Boehlich (Ed.) and Arnold J. Pomerans Trans. The Belknap Press of Harvard University Press (Original work published 1989).
Freud, Sigmund (2001). Delusion and Dream in Jensen's Gradiva. In James Strachey (Ed.), *The Standard Edition of the Complete Psychological Works of Sigmund Freud*, Vol. IX. Vintage, Hogarth Press and the Institute of Psychoanalysis, 1–95 (Original work published 1907).
Freud, Sigmund (2001). The Interpretation of Dreams. In James Strachey (Ed.), *The Standard Edition of the Complete Psychological Works of Sigmund Freud*, Vol. IV. Vintage, Hogarth Press and the Institute of Psychoanalysis (Original work published 1899).
Freud, Sigmund (2001). Introductory Lectures on Psychoanalysis. In James Strachey (Ed.), *The Standard Edition of the Complete Psychological Works of Sigmund Freud*, Vol. XVI. Vintage, Hogarth Press and the Institute of Psychoanalysis (Original work published 1916–1917).
Freud, Sigmund (2001). Some Character-Types met with in Psychoanalytic Work. In James Strachey (Ed.), *The Standard Edition of the Complete Psychological Works of Sigmund Freud*, Vol. XIV. Vintage, Hogarth Press and the Institute of Psychoanalysis, 309–333 (Original work published 1916).
Joyce, James (1975). *Finnegans Wake*. Faber and Faber (Original work published 1939).
Lacan, Jacques (1976–1977). *Le Séminaire de Jacques Lacan. Livre XXIV. L'insu que sait de l'une-bévue s'aile à mourre, 1976–1977*. Partly published in *Ornicar? Bulletin*

périodique du champ freudien, Lyse, N°12–13, 1977, 21–32; N°14, 1978, 33–39; N°15, 1978, 49–68; and N°17–18, 1978, 69–74. Available at http://staferla.free.fr/S24/S24%20 L%27INSU . . . . pdf (Accessed on 11th January, 2024).

Lacan, Jacques (1977–1978). *Le Séminaire de Jacques Lacan. Livre XXV. Le Moment de Conclure, 1977–1978*. First session published in *Ornicar? Bulletin périodique du champ freudien*, Lyse, N°19, 1979, 5–9. Available at http://staferla.free.fr/S25/S25.htm (Accessed on 11th January, 2024).

Lacan, Jacques (1987). Homage to Marguerite Duras, on Le ravissement de Lol V. Stein. In Peter Connor Trans. *Marguerite Duras by Marguerite Duras*. City Lights Books, 122–129 (Original work published 1965).

Lacan, Jacques (1990). *Television: A Challenge to the Psychoanalytic Establishment*. In Denis Hollier, Rosalind Krauss (Eds.) and Annette Michelson Trans. W.W. Norton (Original work published 1974).

Lacan, Jacques (1993). *The Seminar of Jacques Lacan. Book II. The Ego in Freud's Theory and in the Technique of Psychoanalysis, 1954–1955*. In Sylvana Tomaselli Trans. W.W. Norton (Original work published 1978).

Lacan, Jacques (2002). *The Seminar of Jacques Lacan. Book XIII. The Object of Psychoanalysis, 1965–1966*. Unofficially translated by Cormac Gallagher from the unedited French typescripts of the unpublished seminar *Le Séminaire de Jacques Lacan. Livre XIII. L'objet de la psychanalyse, 1965–1966*. Karnac Books.

Lacan, Jacques (2006). The Youth of Gide, or the Letter and Desire. In Bruce Fink Trans., in collaboration with Héloïse Fink and Russell Grigg, *Écrits: The First Complete Edition in English*. W.W. Norton, 623–644 (Original work published 1958).

Lacan, Jacques (2007). Leçon Sur Lituraterre. In *Le Séminaire de Jacques Lacan. Livre XVIII. D'un discours qui ne serait pas du semblant, 1971*. Texte Établi par Jacques-Alain Miller, Seuil, 113–127.

Lacan, Jacques (2013). Lituraterre. In Dany Nobus Trans. *Continental Philosophy Review* Vol. 46, N°2. Springer, 327–334 (Original work published 1971).

Lacan, Jacques (2015). *The Seminar of Jacques Lacan, Book VIII: 1960–1961: Transference*. In Bruce Fink Trans. Polity Press (Original work published 1991).

Lacan, Jacques (2016). *The Seminar of Jacques Lacan, Book XXIII: 1975–1976: The Sinthome*. In Adrian Price Trans. Polity Press (Original work published 2005).

Lacan, Jacques (2019). *The Seminar of Jacques Lacan. Book VI. Desire and Its Interpretation, 1958–1959*. In Bruce Fink Trans. Polity Press (Original work published 2013).

Lacan, Jacques (2022, April). Columbia University Lecture on the Symptom. In Russell Grigg Trans. *The Lacanian Review: Hurly-Burly: Journal of the New Lacanian School and the World Association of Psychoanalysis. American Lacan*, Issue 12, 75–84 (Original work published 1976).

Lacan, Jacques (2022, April). Yale University: Kanzer Seminar. In Philip Dravers Trans. *The Lacanian Review: Hurly-Burly: Journal of the New Lacanian School and the World Association of Psychoanalysis. American Lacan*, Issue 12, 39–61 (Original work published 1975a).

Lacan, Jacques (2022, April). Yale University Interview with Students, Answers to Their Questions. In Philip Dravers Trans. *The Lacanian Review: Hurly-Burly: Journal of the New Lacanian School and the World Association of Psychoanalysis. American Lacan*, Issue 12, 63–68 (Original work published 1975b).

Miller, Jacques-Alain (2012). Joyce with Lacan. In Santanu Biswas (Ed.) and Russell Grigg Trans. *The Literary Lacan: From Literature to Lituraterre and Beyond*. Seagull Books, 1–7 (Original work published 1987).

Rabaté, Jean-Michel (2014). *The Cambridge Introduction to Literature and Psychoanalysis*. Cambridge University Press.

Chapter 1

"The Purloined Letter"

Lacan spoke on Edgar Allan Poe's 1844 short story "The Purloined Letter" in session 15, a "Complement" to session 15, and session 16, between 23rd March and 27th April, 1955, of his 1954–1955 seminar on *The Ego in Freud's Theory and in the Technique of Psychoanalysis* (*Le Moi dans la théorie de Freud et dans la technique de la psychanalyse*) (Lacan, 1978/1993, pp. 175–205).[1] He also wrote the essay "The Seminar on 'The Purloined Letter'" ("*Le séminaire sur 'La lettre volée'*") between June and mid-August 1956, which was published in *Le Psychanalyse* in 1957 (Lacan, 1957). A revised version of the essay was published in 1966 as the opening chapter of Lacan's collection of essays called *Écrits*, breaking the more or less chronological sequence of the essays in the collection (Lacan, 1957/2006). The present chapter is predominantly based on the 1966 essay as it offers the latest and most detailed version of Lacan's discussion. In this seminar, Lacan takes the help of Poe's story to shed light on the intersubjectivity of the Freudian unconscious, the relation between the insistence of the signifier and the ex-sistence of the subjects, the determination received by the subject from the signifier, aspects of the signifier of lack in the Other, and other psychoanalytical concepts of importance, while illuminating aspects of the story psychoanalytically.

Primal Scene and Its Repetition

Lacan thinks that, at the broadest level, Poe's story is about the repetition of a primal scene. He says that the story unfolds around two scenes, the first of which is the primal scene and the second its repetition. The first scene takes place in the royal boudoir, where we find the Queen alone with a secret letter. The unexpected entrance of the King creates an awkward situation for her as the King's knowledge of the letter would jeopardise her "honor and peace" (Poe, 1844/1938, p. 209). Taking advantage of the King's inattentiveness, she leaves the letter on the table, turned face down, "address uppermost" (ibid., p. 210). At this moment, the Minister D— enters the scene, notices the Queen's distress, fathoms her secret, and decides to steal the letter. As a daring political opponent of the King and the Queen, the Minister D— wanted to steal the letter to blackmail the Queen for political gains. Accordingly, the Minister takes out a similar letter from his pocket, pretends to read it, and then places it next to the letter belonging to the Queen. After a bit more conversation, he deliberately picks up the Queen's letter and leaves, while the Queen, who noticed everything, does not intervene out of fear of drawing the attention of the King to the letter. Since no one expressed any hesitation in the course of the entire set of actions, the act of theft might easily have escaped the notice of an ideal spectator. The quotient of the operation is that the Minister possessed the letter while the Queen knew that he did so and with mala fide intention. A remainder of the operation is the letter left behind for the Queen by the Minister.

The second scene is set in the Minister's office in the Ministerial hotel. We know from the account that the Prefect of Police gave to the private detective Le Chevalier C. Auguste Dupin that the police had thoroughly searched the office and its surroundings for the last three months but in vain, although the Minister must have kept the letter within easy reach. Dupin, a royalist who knew the Minister personally, visits him in his office and inspects the premises through his green spectacles, which prevented his gaze from being seen. When he saw a very chafed letter carelessly thrust in a card-rack hanging in the middle of the mantelpiece, he knew he had found the letter, especially because, barring the size of the letter, which matched the description of the stolen letter, every other detail contradicted the description. Dupin left, leaving behind his gold snuff-box on the table as if by mistake so that he could return to claim it, which he does the following day, armed with a facsimile of the letter seen in the Minister's office. When the loud noise of a musket fired by Dupin's accomplice upon his instruction outside the window of the Minister's office draws the Minister to the window, Dupin snatches the letter from the card-rack, replaces it with the facsimile, and makes a normal exit thereafter. The quotient of this operation is that the Minister no longer possessed the letter, though he knew nothing about it and did not suspect that Dupin had stolen it from him. Moreover, when the Minister tries to make use of it, he will be able to read the following words from Crébillon's *Atrée*, inscribed in Dupin's handwriting, with which the Minister was familiar: "So fatal a scheme,/If not worthy of Atreus, is worthy of Thyestes" (ibid., p. 222) (Lacan, 1957/2006, pp. 7–9).[2]

That the second scene is a repetition of the first scene is evident from three details in particular. First, just as the Queen is able to prevent the King from noticing the letter by casually leaving it upside down on the table, in full view of everyone, but unable to prevent the cunning Minister D— from stealing it from right under her nose, so is the Minister D— able to prevent the Prefect of Police from detecting the letter by hiding it in open view in his office, but unable to prevent the clever detective Dupin from stealing the letter from there and that too when he was present close at hand. Second, just as the remainder of the first scene is the Minister's letter with which he had exchanged the letter belonging to the Queen in the royal boudoir, so is the remainder of the second scene Dupin's facsimile letter with which he had exchanged the letter belonging to the Queen in the Minister's office. And third, both acts of theft are carried out in the course of inane conversations by the perpetrator. Thus, in the primal scene, the letter is lost by the Queen, while in the second scene, in the form of its repetition, the letter is lost by the Minister.

Above all, the repetition of the primal scene is indicative of the insistence of the purloined letter or the insistence of the signifier. Notably, Lacan did not make any clear distinction between the letter and the signifier at this stage, and he did not do so until the 1970s. In the present seminar, the letter is really the signifier of lack in the Other, or the phallus, as Lacan will spell out in 1971. In the 1970s, Lacan continued to relate the signifier to the symbolic order as before, but he began to relate the letter to the real order.

The Act of Narration: From Signifier to Speech and from Speech to Signifier

Lacan rightly points out that the story is narrated in terms of two dialogues. Of these, the first dialogue is primarily between the Prefect of Police and Dupin, though the latter's friend, the narrator, too, briefly takes part in it. In terms of this dialogue, the Prefect describes the theft of the letter by the Minister and the nature of the investigation undertaken by his force to recover it. The second dialogue is between Dupin and his narrator-friend that took place after Dupin had returned the letter to the Prefect and the latter had left with it, in the course of which Dupin explains to his friend how he procured the letter that the Prefect couldn't. Lacan states that, although it is obvious that both the dialogues are narrated to us by Dupin's friend, these dialogues, by making opposite uses of speech, convert the original drama that was meant to be narrated into a new drama in the course of the narration, one that is about the symbolic order itself, insofar as it sheds light on the relation between speech and the signifier (ibid., 12).

Lacan says three things about the first dialogue. First, making a distinction between the drama or the action and its narration in speech, marked by the conditions of narration, Lacan says that the drama, in this case, is a primal scene that is not possible to know about without the narration or commentary embodying it. In other words, the *mise-en-scène* is made possible by the commentary that doubles the drama in the course of representing it. In fact, the audience's attention is drawn to the theft not by the Minister's act of stealing the letter but by the Queen's commentary on it in the course of describing the act to the Prefect later on. Thus, the most significant act in the scene, that of the theft of the letter, is brought into existence in terms of its narration by one of the actors—first the Queen and later on the Prefect—who narrates while playing her or his part in the scene. Second, Lacan described the first dialogue as one between a deaf man and one who hears. Communication, Lacan contends, can give the impression of conveying only one meaning in its transmission, which is a false impression, for this impression ignores the highly significant context into which he who can hear it integrates it. While communication is integrated into a context by he who hears properly, the context is unperceived by he who does not hear. Communication conveys more than one meaning owing to its context, which is heard by some and not heard by others. Simply put, in this dialogue, the Prefect does not hear the implications of his own words, while his interlocutor Dupin does.[3] And third, Lacan explains that if we regard the dialogue's meaning as the Prefect's report to Dupin, then "its verisimilitude will appear to depend on a guarantee of accuracy", i.e., its verifiability would depend on its accuracy. In the story, however, the accuracy of the first scene is impossible for us to judge because it comes to us through a triple subjective filter. The first dialogue is a narration by Dupin's close friend of the account by which the Prefect reveals to Dupin the version the Queen gave him of it, whereby, as Lacan points out, the original narrator, the Queen, is so extremely reduced in the narrative that the possibility of her altering any of the events is precluded. Lacan states that Poe deliberately wanted to transmit the message in this circuitous way so as to indicate that the message belongs to the dimension of language rather than to this or that subject. Thus, in the first dialogue, there is a movement from the signifier to speech, or a rendition of the signifier in speech, which is one use of speech (ibid., pp. 12–13).

Lacan says that in the second dialogue, we shift from the "field of accuracy to the register of truth", that is to say, from the field of accuracy or inaccuracy of the Prefect's account to the symbolic order as the register of truth situated at the "very foundation of intersubjectivity", where the letter is truly situated (ibid., p. 13). According to Lacan, truth is situated at the foundation of intersubjectivity in terms of the relation between the signifier and speech. In other words, Dupin understood that the letter had to be sought not in the Prefect's statements about it, according to which the police had looked *everywhere* for the letter, but rather in the Prefect's enunciation of the letter, according to which the police hadn't looked at the *other side* of the letter that they must have encountered in the Minister's office. In the second dialogue, therefore, there is a movement from the signifier of the statement to the signifier of the enunciation beyond the statement. Lacan invokes Freud's famous joke to illustrate the difference between statement and enunciation: "Yes, why are you lying to me by saying you're going to Cracow in order to make me believe you're going to Lemberg, when in reality you *are* going to Cracow?" (ibid., p. 13). Here, the sentence "I'm going to Cracow" makes the false claim that "I'm going to Lemberg" at the level of the statement but points to the truth that "I'm going to Cracow" at the level of enunciation. In short, insofar as it is the Prefect's oral narrative on the letter as a signifier, or words spoken on a missing signifier, and insofar as it is deliberately articulated through a triple subjective filter in order to tell us that the message truly belongs to the field of language, the first dialogue concerns the movement from the signifier to speech, which comprises one use of speech. Whereas, insofar as Dupin discerns that speech posits the signifier of the truth at the level of enunciation even as it deceives with false signifiers at the level of the statement, the second dialogue concerns the movement from speech to the signifier of truth, which is another use of speech (ibid., pp. 13–14). In the context of such extensive discussion on the narration of Poe's story, what are we to make of Derrida's complaint that Lacan had ignored the question of the narration of "The Purloined Letter"? Derrida writes, "But what the 'Seminar' treats is only the content of this story, what is justifiably called its history, what is recounted in the account, the internal and narrated face of the narration. Not the narration itself" (Derrida, 1975/1987, p. 427).

The Insistence of the Signifier Is Correlated to the Ex-sistence of Subjects

As we have seen, the insistence of the signifier is borne by the repetition of the primal scene. But how is the insistence of the signifier related to the ex-sistence of the subjects? Well, the insistence of the signifier is related to the ex-sistence of the subjects insofar as sets of subjects—including esteemed and powerful ones, such as royal personages, eminent ministers, and police commissioners—are compelled to occupy predetermined positions by a stolen letter, as well as to act in accordance with the precise dictates of that position, irrespective of their innate nature or personal wish. In the story, the purloined letter creates three interrelated positions—real, imaginary, symbolic—whereby the occupant of the first position shall be unable to see or act with the letter; the occupant of the second position shall be able to see the letter, able to see that the occupant of the first position failed to see the letter, but unable to act with the letter; while the occupant of the third position shall be able to both see everything and act with the letter. Thus, in the first scene, the King sees nothing and is unable to act with the letter, the Queen sees the King's failure to see the letter but cannot act with the letter, and Minister D— sees the most, carries out a set of acts, and ends up possessing the letter. In the second scene, the Prefect of Police sees nothing and is unable to act with the letter, Minister D— sees the Prefect's inability to see but cannot act with the letter, and Dupin sees the most and ends up possessing the letter in terms of a set of acts. There is, in fact, the germ of a third scene, or a second repetition, at the end of the story where Minister D— sees nothing, as in he is blind to the fact that he does not possess the letter anymore. Lacan calls this interplay of three subjects in tandem an "intersubjective complex" involving three partners that are akin to "the technique legendarily attributed to the ostrich when it seeks shelter from danger". Describing the technique, Lacan states: "The technique is distributed among three partners in such a way that the second believing himself invisible because the first has his head stuck in the sand, all the while lets the third calmly pluck his rear" (Lacan, 1957/2006, p. 10).[4] The three ostriches manifestly behave in this odd manner only when a detoured letter finds its place among them. Therefore, the letter is the most important character in the story. All the other characters receive their "major determination" from nothing but "its itinerary" (ibid., p. 7). Lacan indicates by pointing to the title that the letter is "the true subject of the tale" (ibid., p. 21).

Lacan ratifies that what confirms for us that this is repetition-compulsion or insistence of the signifier and nothing else is that the subjects "relay each other in course of the intersubjective repetition" owing precisely to their displacement determined by a pure signifier, the purloined letter, in their midst (ibid., p. 10). Accordingly, each character behaves exactly as the first occupant of a place soon after occupying it subsequently, no matter what he or she really was or how he or she really wanted to behave. For example, "to protect the letter from inquisitive eyes, he [the Minister] cannot help but employ the same technique he himself already foiled: that of leaving it out in the open", as Lacan points out (ibid., p. 22).

In addition, just as the Queen hid the letter by leaving it upside down on the table, so does the Minister hide the letter by turning it inside out and getting his address written on it. Not only that, Lacan states that in his new place, which is but the old place of the Queen, the Minister is unable to see the very things he was able to see in the previous scene when he occupied a different place with respect to the purloined letter. He is:

> [C]aught in the trap of the typically imaginary situation of seeing that he is not seen, leading him to misconstrue the real situation in which he is seen not seeing. And what does he fail to see? The very symbolic situation which he himself was able to see, and in which he is now seen seeing himself not being seen.
>
> (Ibid., p. 22)

Lacan indicates that, in playing the game of the one who hides, the Minister is "obliged to don the role of the Queen, including even the attributes of woman and shadow, so propitious for the act of concealment" (ibid., p. 22). Furthermore, like the King who could not read the letter in the first scene, the police who replaced him in the second scene failed to read the letter "because that *place entailed blindness*" (ibid., p. 27), while the Minister, the occupant of the same place, failed to read Dupin's facsimile letter in germinating the third scene. Similarly, just like the Queen, who was engrossed with deceiving the King in the first scene, the Minister is engrossed with deceiving the police in the second scene, and Dupin is engrossed with the fact that he had deceived the Minister in the third scene. Furthermore, just like the Queen, who was marked by inaction in the first scene in which she lost the letter, the Minister, who was perfectly active in that scene, is paralysed in relation to the letter in the second scene in which he occupied the place belonging to the Queen in the first scene. He is, moreover, completely unable to see or act with the letter in the third scene in which he occupies the place originally belonging to the King. Therefore, when Lacan says in the session on "Odd or even? Beyond intersubjectivity" in the seminar on *The Ego in Freud's Theory and in the Technique of Psychoanalysis*, that "[t]he subject adopts a mirror position, enabling him to guess the behaviour of his adversary", (Lacan, 1978/1993, p. 180) he is at once referring to how a player in the game of odd or even try to fathom the thoughts of his adversary by simulating his appearance, and how the characters in Poe's story behave exactly like the first occupant of a position they find themselves in. Speaking on the way in which sets of subjects relay each other in this drama governed by the signifier, that is to say, how the insistence of the signifier is related to the ex-sistence of the subjects, Lacan asserts:

> [I]t is the letter and its detour which governs their entrances and roles. While the letter may be *en souffrance*, they are the ones who shall suffer from it. By passing beneath its shadow, they become its reflection. By coming into the letter's possession—an admirably ambiguous bit of language—its meaning possesses them.
>
> (Lacan, 1957/2006, p. 21)

The case of Minister D——, who moves from the position of seeing the most and being able to act in the first scene to the position of seeing a little and being unable to act in the second scene to finally the position of seeing nothing and being unable to act in the third scene, best reveals how the subject's action, inaction, behaviour, role, et cetera, are all determined by his or her relation to the repressed and insisting signifier. Since the word "*lettre*" (letter) is similar to the expression "*l'être*" (being), both phonetically and in the use of a similar set of letters, the letter may be said to have a relation to being at the level of speech and writing. Lacan goes on to claim that, in fact, almost everything of importance about the subject is determined by the signifier:

> If what Freud discovered . . . has a meaning, it is that the signifier's displacement determines subjects' acts, destiny, refusals, blindnesses, success, and fate, regardless of their innate gifts and instruction, and irregardless of their character or sex; and that everything pertaining to the psychological pregiven follows willy-nilly the signifier's train, like weapon and baggage.
>
> (Ibid., p. 21)

Thus, the trajectory of the letter determines the subjects. Repetition is also evident in the form of the return of the repressed in that, although the Minister forgot the letter, the letter remembered him so well as to transform him:

> Like the man who withdrew to an island to forget—to forget what? he forgot—so the Minister, by not making use of the letter, comes to forget it. . . . But the letter, no more than the neurotic's unconscious, does not forget him. It forgets him so little that it transforms him more and more in the image of her who offered it up to his discovery, and that he now will surrender it, following her example, to a similar discovery. The features of this transformation . . . might legitimately be compared to the return of the repressed.
>
> (Ibid., pp. 24–25)

In other words, although the Minister could not act with the letter, the letter continued to act on him. In these two ways, repetition compulsion is based on the insistence of the signifying chain, which is a correlate of the ex-sistence of the subject. Therefore, Lacan contends that the story not only illustrates the Freudian truth that the symbolic order is constitutive for the subject, but also something more gripping still. Whereas Freud teaches us that the subject follows the channel of the symbolic, Poe showed us—and well before Freud, too—that "[i]t is not only the subject, but the subjects, caught in their intersubjectivity, who line up . . . and who . . . model their very being on the moment of the signifying chain that runs through them" (ibid., p. 21).

Lacan moreover contends that the three terms (real, imaginary, symbolic) derive their privileged status from the fact that they correspond to the three logical moments through which the decision is precipitated and, as we have seen, to the three places which this decision assigns to the subjects that it separates out (ibid., p. 9). Lacan had shown at length in his 1945 essay "Logical Time and the Assertion of Anticipated Certainty: A New Sophism" that subjective decision is not only taken collectively by the three prisoners but more pertinently is precipitated by the organisation of three logical moments in such a way that the first moment—that of the glance—already includes the germ of the second and the third moments to follow—that of comprehension and conclusion, respectively—as presuppositions (Lacan, 1945/2006). Thus, in Poe's story, the comprehension of the true meaning and value of the letter, including the decision of both the Minister and Dupin to seize it in the respective scenes, takes place right at the moment of seeing the letter, at the moment of the glance itself. Lacan writes that the moment is prolonged in the necessary manoeuvres that follow, and, in the second scene, the manoeuvres that took place over a day deferred the opportunity and apparently disrupted the unity of the moment of the glance (Lacan, 1957/2006, p. 9). However, the manoeuvres add nothing to the decision arrived at in the moment of the glance in either of the scenes because that decision to steal the letter in a particular method already includes the decisions of the moments of comprehension and conclusion that follow.

Lacan clarifies that the decision "separates out" the "three moments, ordering three glances, sustained by three subjects, incarnated in each case by different people" (ibid., pp. 9–10). The first glance sees nothing (King; Prefect). The second glance sees that the first sees nothing and thereby deceives itself into believing that what it hides is covered (Queen; Minister). The third glance sees that the first two glances have uncovered for whoever would seize it what should have been kept hidden (Minister; Dupin) (ibid., p. 10). In the final analysis, then, the story is about the specificities of the interrelations of the real, imaginary, and symbolic orders in terms of the three moments ordering three glances of the occupants of three places sustained by three subjects, but in the form of different people: King/Prefect/Minister and Queen/Minister/Dupin.

Finally, it may be argued that the two scenes constitute the two signifying chains, S_1 and S_2, presided over by the master signifier, the letter, while the subjects, the lacking subjects, are produced and captured in their intersubjectivity in the gap between the two signifying chains.

Attributes of the Purloined Letter

Of the numerous attributes of the purloined letter isolated by Lacan, seven seem to stand out. Let us examine them one by one. To begin with, the letter has a location and an "odd" relation to it, for the letter will be and will not be in its place at the same time. This can be understood in terms of the curious fact that, although the police had looked everywhere, had exhausted the space in and around the Minister's apartment, they failed to locate the letter that was nevertheless present in that very apartment all the time, i.e., within the space under their scanner. Lacan asks:

> Are we not then within our rights to ask how it happened that the letter was not found *anywhere*, or rather to observe that nothing we are told about a higher

caliber conception of concealment ultimately explains how the letter managed to escape detection, since the field exhaustively combed did in fact contain it, as Dupin's discovery eventually proved?

(Ibid., p. 16)

According to Lacan, the police did not find the letter because what they handled "*did not fit* the description they had been given of it".[5] The "seeming scrap of waste paper they were handling did not reveal its other nature" because it was half torn, had a different cipher on a seal of another colour, and had the mark of a different handwriting.[6] Above all, the police, like the King, had stopped on the reverse side of the letter that bore these marks. "The letter had for them no other side but this reverse side", said Lacan (ibid., p. 18).

More importantly, as Lacan explains, the police did not think that the letter was such that it could *be and not be* in its place:

[W]hat is hidden is never but what is *not in its place*, as a call slip says of a volume mislaid in a library. And even if the book were on an adjacent shelf or in the next slot, it would be hidden there, however visible it may seem there. For it can *literally* be said that something is not in its place only of what can change places—that is, of the symbolic.

(Ibid., p. 17)

This is the reason that Lacan says, "we cannot say of the purloined letter that, like other objects, it must be *or* not be somewhere but rather that, unlike them, it will be *and* will not be where it is wherever it goes" (ibid., p. 17). That apart, Lacan describes the letter or the signifier as "the symbol of but an absence" (ibid., p. 17), which denotes the simultaneous presence of the symbol and the absence of what it symbolises. In short, because the purloined letter is situated in the symbolic order where absence and presence necessarily coexist—which makes the letter's relation to its own location "odd"—the police failed to locate it even when they handled it, and the King failed to notice it even though it was situated right in front of his eyes.

In addition, the materiality of the letter is singular. Lacan explains this by saying, "Cut a letter into small pieces, and it remains the letter that it is" (ibid., p. 16). In other words, even if a letter is cut into, say, ten pieces, then, one the one hand, we will still have one letter and not ten, and on the other hand, each piece of the letter will still represent nothing but the one and only original letter. Simply put, the materiality of the letter is indivisible; it does not "allow of partition" (ibid., p. 16). Therefore, borrowing words from the story, Lacan said the singularity of the letter is "simple and odd" (ibid., p. 21). The police, whose method of detection consisted of breaking up the whole into a number of small units, fail to identify the letter because, instead of looking for this singular document holistically, which is the only approach that would have led them to this undividable letter, they looked for it in terms of its constituents. No wonder then that they missed the wood for the trees.

Moreover, the letter has a path, which, in the case of the purloined letter, is detoured. The Middle English word "purloin", possibly used for the first time in the first half of the 15th century, means "[to] put far away", "[to] put at a distance", "[to] misappropriate". Although the word thus had connotations of both theft and deferral, the word "purloin" has been subsequently taken only to mean to appropriate wrongfully and often by a breach of trust, to take dishonestly, or to steal, in a formal or humorous sense. However, the etymology of the word suggests a slightly different meaning. The Middle English word "purloined" is derived from the Anglo-French word "*purloigner*". Comprising "*pur*", meaning "forward" or "forth", and "*luin*" or "*loign*", meaning "far" or "at a distance", "*purloigner*" means "[to] prolong", "postpone", "put away", "put off", "retard", "remove", "delay", "set aside", et cetera. The Anglo-French word is moreover derived from the Latin words "*pro*", meaning "forth", "in front of", "before", "on behalf of", "for", and "*longe*" meaning "far", which is derived from "*longus*" meaning "long". In other words, etymologically speaking, the word purloined primarily means delayed, though its modern meaning focuses on misappropriation, which is but one way of delaying the return of an object to its owner.

Lacan stresses the etymology of the word in his seminar. He duly mentions with reference to the O.E.D. that "purloin" is an Anglo-French word comprising the prefix "pur", and the Old French words "*loing*", "*loinger*", "*longé*", and explains that the prefix "pur" is derived from the Latin "*pro*", which means, "in front of", or "before", as opposed to behind, and which is the opposite of the Latin "*ante*", meaning "prior" or "earlier":

> We recognize in the first element the Latin *pro-*, as opposed to *ante*, insofar as it presupposes a back in front of which it stands, possibly to guarantee it or even to stand in as its guarantor (whereas *ante* goes forth to meet what comes to meet it).
>
> (Ibid., p. 20)

Simply put, *pro* is what is at the front, and *ante* is what is at the back. In psychoanalysis, the *pro* is what has arrived or appeared and must be accounted for, and the *ante* is the background to the *pro* that has to be reconstructed in order to account for the *pro*. Lacan further clarifies that since the Old French word "*loinger*" is a verb that means "alongside", to "purloin" is "to set aside"; and a "purloined" letter is a letter that has been "detoured", one whose trajectory has been "prolonged", or, in the language of the post office, "a letter *en souffrance* (awaiting delivery or unclaimed)" (ibid., pp. 20–21). Lacan thus stresses two aspects of the word "purloined": the "before" aspect that requires an *ante* to explain it and the aspect of being "prolonged", "delayed", or "detoured". In this way, Lacan corrects Baudelaire's somewhat simplistic French translation of "purloined" as "stolen" (*volée*).

Not only that, the letter is that of a woman. This is so in a number of ways. To begin with, in French, the word for letter (*lettre*) is a feminine noun. In addition, the letter belongs to the Queen. Moreover, partly following the French sociologist Marcel

Mauss's study of the sociology of gift-exchange in archaic societies in his famous 1925 book *The Gift*, which is based on his own 1925 essay called "An Essay on the Gift", Claude Lévi-Strauss argues in his 1949 book *The Elementary Structures of Kinship* that kinship systems are based on the exchange of women between groups. This implies that women, as objects of exchange, circulate like signifiers between kinship groups, somewhat like Poe's letter, so as to ensure the existence of the groups (Lévi-Strauss, 1949/1969). Accordingly, in the chapter on "Language and the Analysis of Social Laws" of the first volume of *Structural Anthropology*, Lévi-Strauss speaks of "the circulation of women" (Lévi-Strauss, 1958/1963, p. 60). And finally, in Poe's story, the letter, which belongs to the Queen, effeminises each of its subsequent holders. Thus, the Minister had his address written in "a diminutive female hand" (Poe, 1844/1938, p. 220) so as to indicate that "the letter which the Minister addresses to himself, ultimately, is a letter from a woman" (Lacan, 1957/2006, p. 25); he exudes "the oddest *odor di femina*", (ibid., p. 25) though Éric Laurent considered the Minister dandified and not effeminised by his possession of the letter (Laurent, 1999/2007, p. 32); the Prefect described him as one "who dares all things, those unbecoming as well as those becoming a man" (Poe, 1844/1938, p. 209); and Dupin felt a rage of a feminine kind and unexpectedly declares himself "a partisan of the lady" (ibid., p. 222). Following this, Lacan compares Dupin's act of identifying the letter in the Minister's apartment to the uncovering of a female body with his eyes. He states that, as in the game of identifying a name on the map mentioned by Poe, where the name that a novice would find difficult to spot is the one "in large letters spaced out widely across the field of the map, the name of an entire country", so does the purloined letter "like an immense female body, sprawl across the space of the Minister's office when Dupin enters it", who expects to find it there, "having only to undress that huge body, with his eyes veiled by green spectacles" (Lacan, 1957/2006, pp. 25–26).

Furthermore, since the letter can be used only once, it must be used in terms of its non-use, and since the letter must be used in terms of its non-use, the very possession of the letter imposes a state of inaction on the possessor. Apropos of the narrator's remark that the letter's "power" would depart as soon as it is used, Lacan writes, "this remark concerns only its use for ends of power—and simultaneously that the Minister will be forced to use it in this way" (ibid., p. 23). To use the letter "in this way" is to not use the letter, which is precisely how the Minister used it. Lacan thinks that it is the letter's "effect of this non-use alone" (ibid., p. 23) that should concern us because letters such as these—namely, a signifier that signifies the cancellation of what it signifies—tend to get destroyed if they are not delayed by non-use:

> [F]or it is clear that while the Minister will be forced to make use of the letter in a non-significant way, its ends of power can only be potential, since it cannot become actual without immediately vanishing. Hence the letter exists as a means of power only through the final summons of the pure signifier—either by prolonging its detour . . . or by destroying the letter, which would be the only

sure way, as Dupin proffers at the outset, to be done with what is destined by nature to signify the cancellation of what it signifies.

(Ibid., p. 23)

Since the letter cannot be used by its possessor, its possession moreover imposes a state of inaction on its possessor. Anyone who possesses the letter and is thereby possessed by it remains inactive and imbecile as long as he or she possesses the letter. Both the Queen, for a few moments at the time of the theft of the letter, and the Minister, for a long period of time after he had stolen the letter, were, as long as they possessed the letter, unable to act with the letter. Even Dupin—for whom the purloined letter is no longer the letter he had stolen from the Minister's apartment but the one he had left there—must necessarily be inactive in relation to this new purloined letter created by him. Indeed, as Lacan states:

> There must be a very odd *noli me tangere* in this sign for its possession to, like the Socratic stingray, make its man so numb that he falls into what unequivocally appears in his case to be a state of inaction.
>
> (Ibid., pp. 31–32)

"*Noli me tangere*" or "Touch me not" are the words that Jesus promptly said to Mary Magdalene as soon as she recognised him and made a move towards him when he appeared before her immediately following his resurrection (John 20:17) (*King James Version of the Holy Bible*, 1611/2004, p. 624). The reference to the "Socratic stingray" comes from Plato's *Meno*:

> At this moment I feel you [Socrates] are exercising magic and witchcraft upon me and positively laying me under your spell until I am just a mass of helplessness. If I may be flippant, I think that not only in outward appearance but in other respects as well you are exactly like the flat sting ray that one meets in the sea. Whenever anyone comes into contact with it, it numbs him, and that is the sort of thing that you seem to be doing to me now.
>
> (Plato, 385 BC/1956, *Meno*, 80 a—b)

While the possessor of the letter appears as though struck numb by a stingray by the very fact of his or her possession of the letter, the letter appears to say to anyone who wants to use it, "*Noli me tangere*", do not touch me.

On top of that, the "address" of the letter is the locus of the Law. In the story, the letter finally returns to the Queen as its "holder" via Dupin and the Prefect of Police. What is the "address" of the purloined letter? Its address is, in Lacan's words, "the place previously occupied by the King, since it is there that it must fall back into the order based on the Law" (Lacan, 1957/2006, p. 27). In other words, the letter will have completed its journey and become well and truly neutralised, once it fell into the hands of the King. But more importantly, Lacan's stress is on the place of the law rather than on the occupant of the place. Accordingly, Lacan further indicates that the effectiveness of the letter is exhausted when, at the end of the story, it fell into the hands of the Prefect who represents the Law, and who had significantly not purloined but purchased the letter, that is to say, acquired the letter lawfully by paying the price for it. The Prefect is situated in the locus of the law also in the sense that he occupies in the second scene the exact position that the King occupies in the first scene, as well as in the sense that he is the keeper of the law of the King. In a word, the "address" of the letter is the Law or the King; the "holder" of the letter is the Queen; and the destination or final receiver of the letter is its sender, the Duke of S—.

And finally, what remains of the letter when it leaves the Minister's hand, that is to say, when it has been relieved of its message for the Queen and its text thus invalidated? According to Lacan:

> The only thing left for it to do is to answer this very question: what remains of a signifier when it no longer has any signification? This is the very question asked of it by the person [Minister] Dupin now finds in the place marked by blindness.
> (Ibid., p. 28)

Lacan writes that the signifier that has completed its journey tells anyone who questions what remains of it: "Eat your *Dasein*!" What does this mean? *Dasein* is an everyday German term for "being" or "presence", or, better still, for someone's being there in the universe. It is a term that has been used in German philosophy by others before Heidegger, notably by Hegel, to denote "existence" in general. However, Heidegger uses the term narrowly to denote the Being or existence of persons. Although we live in the present, not in the future, we do tend to go ahead of ourselves and exceed our situation in the present, for instance, in terms of thoughts of career, marriage, children, et cetera, as matters belonging to the future. This being-there, existing in a future time, anticipatorily ahead of the self that is situated in the present, is one of the connotations of the term "*Dasein*" in Heidegger, who gave the term a central place in his philosophy. In Heidegger, who at times hyphenates the term *Da-sein*, "*Da*" or "there" stands for the locus of the "*sein*" or "Being". *Dasein* is moreover *Das Sein*, or "the Being" (Heidegger, 1927/2001). In Lacan's rendition, however, the "there" of the "being-there" does not mean a future time only. It can easily refer to one's being-there in the past, such as in the cases of Thyestes and the Minister. In Lacan, "there" stands for an *other* place or time relative to "here".

Lacan said in his seminar on *The Ego in Freud's Theory and in the Technique of Psychoanalysis* that if the Minister were to use the facsimile letter without checking it first, the letter would tell him, "*Eat your Dasein*!": "all the Minister will be capable of doing is to follow the order of the day which I ironically threw out in Zurich, in answer to Leclaire—*Eat your Dasein*! That is Thyestes's dish *par excellence*" (Lacan, 1978/1993, p. 205). Let us note that the letter would say this to the Minister in any case, even if he were to check the letter before producing it. If the Minister checked the letter first, then the letter would speak to him in private, and the meal would be a private one. But if he were to produce the letter before others, presumably triumphantly, before first checking it, then the letter would direct him to eat his *Dasein* publicly, and the meal would be a far more awkward one. That's the only difference.

But what does it mean to eat one's being-there? Why is it Thyestes's dish *par excellence*? In Greek mythology, Atreus and Thyestes were the two sons of Pelops. Following a curse upon the house of Pelops, Thyestes seduced Atreus's wife, Aethra, for which Thyestes was banished and later recalled and served the flesh of his own children by Atreus (Harvey, 1937/1969, p. 311). The two lines cited by Dupin in the facsimile letter—"*Quel qu'en soit le forfait, un dessein si funeste,/S'il n'est digne d'Atrée, est digne de Thyeste.*" ["So fatal a scheme,/If not worthy of Atreus, is worthy of Thyestes."]—appear in a soliloquy by the character of Atreus in Prosper Jolyot de Crébillon's 1707 play *Atrée Et Thyeste, Tragédie*. The two lines—lines 13 and 14 of Act 5, Scene 5 of the play, to be precise—refer to Atreus's scheme for avenging himself on Thyestes for having seduced his wife by serving him the flesh of the son born out of that unlawful union (Crébillon, 1707/2015, p. 46). Thus, in Crébillon's version of the myth referred to by Dupin, the revenge is far more precise than it is in its Greek prototype, insofar as Atreus does not serve Thyestes the flesh of Thyestes's children in the French play but serves him the flesh of his son, Plisthenes, born out of the very illicit union that he sought to punish. Thyestes is thus compelled to consume the fruit of his action in the literal sense of the term. Dupin cited Crébillon's words in the fake letter to tell the Minister that it was he and not the Queen who deserved to be the victim of a treacherous deception such as that.

In Greek mythology, and more particularly in Crébillon's play, Atreus forced Thyestes to neutralise the symbolic excess he had created by making him consume the flesh of his son who resulted from his illegitimate union. Therefore, for Thyestes to eat his being-there meant to consume the flesh of his son at a future time, to counterbalance the crime of having produced him unlawfully in the past. This is the reason that *Dasein* is Thyestes's dish *par excellence*. In this case, the word "there" in the expression "being-there" means there where you were the deceiver. By placing the plate before Thyestes, Atreus implied: Eat your seducer being-there that is now on the plate before you. This is the essence of the message that Atreus conveyed to Thyestes in Crébillon's play, and the same message shall be conveyed to the Minister by the hidden face of the facsimile letter as and when he opens it because, for the Minister confronted with the lines inscribed by Dupin, it shall be a question of eating and digesting his duping and duped being-there.

Moreover, a little like Heidegger's notion of *Dasein* that has a relation to death— "Death is Dasein's *ownmost* possibility" (Heidegger, 1927/2001, p. 307)—eating one's *Dasein* in Lacan is related to the subject's submission to the law of the symbolic order that subordinates his being to the signifier. In the final analysis, eating one's *Dasein* is variously a question of settling one's symbolic debts; of neutralising the excesses produced in course of one's existence; of knowingly situating oneself at the receiving end of the return of the arrow one had sped; of facing the truth at the hour of reckoning; of acknowledging castration; of arriving at the destination. Above all, "eat your *Dasein*" is an invitation to comprehend one's finiteness.

Most probably a few years after the seminar, Lacan had said the same thing to Umberto Eco in a different context, as reported by Elisabeth Roudinesco in her 1993 biography, *Jacques Lacan*:

> At a dinner party he [Lacan] said something to Eco that changed his life. "Eat your *Dasein*," he had exclaimed (literally, "Eat your being-there," a play on the resemblance between the German word and the French *dessert*, or "dessert" in English). [Roudinesco quotes Eco] "With his animal flair for devouring souls, he had understood that in speaking of other things I was really speaking of myself, and he, also speaking of other things, said what he did in order that his meaning might strike home". [Eco, in *L'Ane*, 14].
> (Roudinesco, 1993/1997, p. 323)

In his seminar, Lacan moreover identifies a number of important psychoanalytic lessons contained in Poe's story. Let us briefly discuss the most important ones among them.

Truth Offers Itself in Hiding

In his 1930 work, *The Essence of Truth*, Heidegger made an attempt to understand truth in a new way by approaching it through an etymological analysis of the lost Greek word for it, "*aletheia*", meaning, dis-concealment, or disclosure or truth (Heidegger, 1930/2002). *Aletheia* is the opposite of "*Lethe*", the name of a mythical river, meaning forgetfulness. Heidegger's attempt to understand truth in this way constituted a radical departure from tradition. Since the time of Socrates, truth has been defined in terms of statements that either correspond to the state of affairs or cohere with a system taken as a whole. Instead of focusing on the statements bearing the truth, Heidegger focused on the meaning of truth, and instead of defining truth in terms of its correspondence or coherence to something beyond it, Heidegger defined truth in terms of its very revelation. By doing so, Heidegger radically departed from nearly the entire Western philosophical tradition since Socrates on the definition of truth.

Heidegger's definition of truth as *aletheia* implies that, for something to qualify as true, it must be in a position to appear before us. It also implies that untruth, or falsity is something that is impossible to dis-conceal or reveal. Heidegger had already given an important place to the concept of truth as *aletheia* in his 1927 *Being and Time*, and he would develop the concept further in his 1953 *Introduction to Metaphysics*. Moving somewhat away from this position in his posthumously published *Poetry, Language, and Thought*, Heidegger regarded art as a means for the revelation of truth. However, in his 1962 lecture *On Time and Being*, Heidegger changed his long-held opinion radically and considered it a mistake to regard *aletheia* as truth:

> To raise the question of *aletheia*, of disclosure as such, is not the same as raising the question of truth. For this reason, it was inadequate and misleading to call *aletheia*, in the sense of opening, truth.
> (Heidegger, 1969/1972, pp. 69–70)

When Lacan wrote on Heidegger's notion of *aletheia*, Heidegger himself still believed that it meant the truth or an opening that revealed the truth, not just any opening. According to Lacan, Heidegger interpreted *aletheia* as that which is not hidden or not forgotten or as he who does not hide or does not forget. Therefore, Heidegger's essence of truth, according to Lacan, is what Heidegger called the "openness of the open". Following this, Lacan states that truth reveals itself most truly only from the position of being concealed:

> Thus, when we are open to hearing the way in which Martin Heidegger uncovers for us in the word *alethes* the play of truth, we merely rediscover a secret to which truth has always initiated her lovers, and through which they have learned that it is in hiding that she offers herself to them *most truly*.
> (Lacan, 1957/2006, p. 15)

Since truth offers itself in hiding, the letter offered its truth first to the Minister and then to Dupin even as it remained hidden from the King and the Prefect, respectively. For the same reason, Dupin would have to identify the letter in the Minister's office, in Lacan's words, by undressing or dis-concealing it. In the contexts of the words "letter" and "purloined" in Poe's story, let us note that, like the word "*lettre*", "*vérité*", meaning "truth" in French, is a feminine noun. In the story, the letter and truth are inextricably interrelated. Whenever we encounter a "front", we already know it has an unknown "back" as its truth, even though we may not know what the truth is. The other side of any discourse, the truth side of it, is hidden from view, like the Queen's letter lying upside down on the table in the royal boudoir before the King or the same letter turned inside out hanging before the Prefect. Like a piece of paper that will always have an other side to it, there is always a truth side to every discourse that remains hidden by virtue of its being situated on the invisible side.

The Signifier "Money" Neutralises the Responsibility of Transference

Lacan thinks that Dupin's possible act of withdrawal "from the letter's symbolic circuit" after handing over the letter to the Prefect against the "check" can justifiably make the psychoanalyst feel "implicated" because, quite like Dupin, who was a temporary custodian of the letter after having recovered it from the Minister's office, and who returned the letter to its owner through the Prefect in exchange for the owner's money paid as his reward, thereby setting the letter gone astray on its correct path towards its rightful owner, the psychoanalysts make themselves "the emissaries of all the purloined letters which, at least for a while, remain *en souffrance* [awaiting delivery of unclaimed], with [them] in the transference", and they neutralise the responsibility that this transference entails, "by equating it with the signifier that most thoroughly annihilates every signification—namely, money" (ibid., pp. 26–27). The analysands address their own "purloined letters", as in their own signifiers from which they are alienated, to the analyst under transference, that then remain *en souffrance* with the analyst. While the responsibility for holding the analysand's purloined letters in the transference, as their temporary address, is neutralised by the analyst's receipt of fees from the analysand, the latter's purloined letters themselves are neutralised through analysis and interpretation at an appropriate time in the course of the analysis. Such letters are neutralised when they are returned by the analyst to the analysands, their true owners, in an inverted form so that they can recognise and own up the message contained on the other side of their own signifiers. As no longer the address of the analysand's purloined letters following this, the analyst may be said to have exhausted his role of a temporary holder in the letter's symbolic circuit and may withdraw from it.

Money is a very special signifier whose range of impact is extremely wide. For instance, unlike most other objects, money freely circulates across almost all kinds of symbolic domains. Besides, the universal belief that it would be accepted enables it to transcend individual beliefs and notions about it. Not only that, although as pieces of paper or as promises, money does not exactly look like wealth, it is nevertheless believed to be so by almost everyone. More pertinently, money opens up the possibility of exchanging it with most material things, and as soon as money enters the scene, almost everything else tends to take a back seat. Therefore, money or fees have the ability to annihilate the responsibility of transference for the psychoanalyst. Simply put, the psychoanalyst neutralises his responsibility for the analysand's transference towards him by the fees that he accepts. By charging a remuneration for listening, the psychoanalyst converts the dialogue into a mostly professional exchange from his side, even though he is thoroughly immersed in it. The unworthy motives that can be imputed to the psychoanalyst's act of listening by the analysand in the transference if the psychoanalyst were to listen for free, the advent of certain types of negative transference, and the reinforcement of the analysand's symptoms involving mistrust of Others are all prevented or nullified by the money received by the psychoanalyst by way of fees.

The importance of paying fees to the psychoanalyst became quite clear to Freud fairly early in the history of psychoanalysis, especially with regard to his treatment of the Russian patient Sergei Konstantinovitch Pankejeff, better known as the "Wolf Man", whom Freud initially saw between 1910 and 1914. Freud not only treated him for a few months for free but, as Muriel Gardiner points out, "collected a sum of money [from the circle of psychoanalysts in Vienna in 1919], for this former patient, who had served the theoretical ends of analysis so well, and repeated this collection every spring for six years" (Gardiner, 1971, p. 266). The effect of this well-intended financial assistance was not at all beneficial for his analysis, as it problematised his transference. His unresolved transferential problems with Freud came up during his subsequent analysis with Ruth Mack Brunswick (Brunswick, 1928/1971). The Wolf Man himself had an adverse view of the assistance forever, as is evident from what he went on to tell his interviewer, the young journalist Karin Obholzer, towards the end of his life many years later:

> W [WOLF-MAN]: And I receive free treatment. A whole number of dependencies arise, and that's harmful, of course. It harms the ego, I'd say.
> O [OBHOLZER]: The motive is incomprehensible to me. What interest would they have in keeping you dependent?
> W: That's easy to understand. E. wants to keep track of the case that has become so famous—Freud's most famous case—and see how it ends.
> (Obholzer, 1980/1982, p. 126)

It is not at all surprising, therefore, that Freud categorically mentions in his 1913 "On Beginning the Treatment: Further Recommendations on the Technique of Psycho-Analysis I" that "Points of importance at the beginning of the analysis are arrangements about *time* and *money*" (Freud, 1913/2001, p. 126). Lacan specifies in a 1975 lecture that "the analyst—even if he [the analysand] doesn't come—will demand his fee" (Lacan, 1976/2022, p. 76).

Thus, the effect of money on the transference is extremely significant in psychoanalysis. Money helps the analyst create a gap between himself and the analysand's transference and thus insulate himself from the effects of the analysand's transferential love towards him without depersonalising the analytic act, however. In this way, money helps the analyst neutralise transference by allowing him to question and thus disarm the responsibility it entails for him. Besides, the security of the analysand's purloined signifiers temporarily kept in the custody of the psychoanalyst is guaranteed by the signifier money that thoroughly annihilates every signification, as money is the universal signifier of exchange for all objects. That apart, a psychoanalytically proper resolution is purchased with effort and appropriate remuneration and not purloined because to purloin is to create a fresh symbolic debt at the very moment of resolving an older one through analysis. Furthermore, as Žižek correctly summarises, a psychoanalyst or a detective ought to be paid his fees if he has been made to do a job so as to prevent him from getting involved in the libidinal circuit of the analysand or client respectively:

> [W]hat is at stake here is not the classical detective's simple greed or his callousness toward human suffering and injustice—the point is much finer: the payment enables him to avoid getting mixed up in the libidinal circuit of (symbolic) debt and its restitution. The symbolic value of payment is the same in psychoanalysis; the fees of the analyst allow him to stay out of the "sacred"

domain of exchange and sacrifice, i.e., to avoid getting involved in the analysand's libidinal circuit.

(Žižek, 1991, pp. 60–61)

Accordingly, "reward" is very important to both the Prefect and Dupin in the story, and the word is mentioned several times in it. That the check was important to Dupin is indicated by three details in the story, namely, that he was a pauper at that time, that he did not produce the letter before the check was written and handed over to him, and that he made it impossible for the Prefect to not mention the reward by citing the words of the English surgeon John Abernethy: "why, take advice to be sure" (Poe, 1844/1938, p. 214). That is, seek paid advice.

There Is No Winning Formula in the Game of Odd or Even

The case of the schoolboy mentioned by Dupin, who was a champion at guessing correctly in the game of odd or even, is suspicious on several counts. First of all, the method he employed of reading people's minds by emulating their facial expressions is an imaginary and completely unconvincing method of reading other people's minds. It has no support of reason or science whatsoever. That the boy could moreover use this method to infer as precise things as thoughts of odd or even in his opponent's mind make the method and the claimed results sound fantasmatic and absurd. Referring to Dupin's description of the schoolboy, who managed to defeat all his classmates in the game of odd or even, Lacan cautions us by stating that "he [the boy] cannot reach the first level of its mental elaboration—namely, the notion of intersubjective alternation—without immediately being tripped up by the stop of its recurrence". This is because he will confront "the impasse implied by every purely dyadic intersubjectivity, which is . . . of having no recourse against an absolute Other" (Lacan, 1957/2006, p. 14). An absolute Other as one who is capable of guessing just anything and has a mind that is almost impossible to read.

Lacan explains the matter further in the seminar on *The Ego in Freud's Theory and in the Technique of Psychoanalysis* where he mentions that there can be three ways of playing the game: playing like a simpleton, who guesses whatever comes to mind, playing like the boy referred to by Dupin, who tried to fathom his opponent's guesses by imitating their external appearance; and deliberately playing like a simpleton, that is to say, guessing at random as a deliberately chosen strategy (Lacan, 1978/1993, pp. 180–181). Lacan says that although the third way collapses into the first, it thereby nullifies the effectiveness of the second way. In other words, if one's opponent deliberately guesses like an idiot, one would find it impossible to figure out his guesses, no matter how smart one is. He shall become one's "absolute Other" in the imaginary, capable of guessing anything. Besides, contrary to Dupin's claim that "[o]f course he had some principle of guessing; and this lay in mere observation and admeasurement of the astuteness of his opponents" (Poe, 1844/1938, p. 215), "astuteness" of individuals is not measurable in any precise way, certainly not with the help of the method employed by the boy of mimicking the expressions of the other.

At a broader level, Lacan moreover thinks that rather than being able to master the game of odd or even as claimed by Dupin, the human subject is, in fact, converted into an element of the game as soon as he begins to play, and the laws of the game tend to situate him on several crisscrossing levels at once. Thus, he says in the session on "The Purloined Letter" in his seminar on *The Ego in Freud's Theory and in the Technique of Psychoanalysis*:

> By itself, the play of the symbol represents and organizes, independently of the peculiarities of its human support, this something which is called a subject. The human subject doesn't foment this game, he takes his place in it, and plays the role of the little pluses and minuses in it. He is himself an element in this chain which, as soon as it is unwound, organizes itself in accordance with laws. Hence the subject is always on several levels, caught up in crisscrossing networks.
> (Lacan, 1978/1993, pp. 192–193)

This is evident from the manner in which the characters of Poe's story are offered symbolic determination by the game of repetition compulsion orchestrated by the purloined letter. Lacan further clarifies that the game will eventually compel the players to give up on imaginary identification and resort to symbolic rules instead:

> [since] such a purely imaginary identification generally fails . . . each player, if he reasons, can only resort to something beyond the dyadic relationship—in other words, to some [symbolic] law which presides over the succession of the rounds of the game.
> (Lacan, 1957/2006, p. 44)

In other words, any reasoning player will eventually give up random guessing or other imaginary modes of figuring out the other's guesses and look for symbolic traits, such as patterns or repetitions in the opponent's guesses, statistics, probability, et cetera. In short, if this game is played seriously in practice, it will invariably bring in symbolic laws, such as the conventions in Bridge or the kinds of attack or defence in chess, excluding the kind of imaginary principles mentioned by Dupin. In fact, Lacan thinks that if we take probability seriously, then there is no such thing as a game of pure chance. Quite appropriately, he defines the Freudian unconscious itself, which cryptically bears the story of an individual's life, in terms of recollection and probability underlying chance and randomness in the session on "Homeostasis and insistence" of the seminar on *The Ego in Freud's Theory and in the Technique of Psychoanalysis*:

> Think of that very strange game Freud mentions at the end of *The Psychopathology of Everyday Life*, which consists in inviting the subject to say numbers at random. The associations which then come to him bring to light significations

which reverberate so neatly with his remembrance, his destiny, that, from the point of view of probabilities, what he chose goes well beyond anything we might expect from pure chance.

(Lacan, 1978/1993, p. 56)

Shedding further light on how, in the case of a series of guesses, symbolic chains will always emerge from the real, Lacan demonstrates in breathtaking detail in the note added to the essay in 1966, using a chain of randomly chosen pluses and minuses, that no matter how randomly one guessed in the game of odd or even, any finite chain of guesses will inevitably be marked by symbolic lack in terms of the probability of exclusion; certain gaps in the chain; and the introduction of grammatical interval in the form of retroaction and future anterior time (Lacan, 1957/2006, pp. 35–40). Therefore, a close study of a series of random guesses will invariably reveal that its symbolic determinations "predate any real observation of randomness" (ibid., p. 45). This is also the reason that, in order for a letter to be effective, it is enough for it to be organised in a "symbolic system" rather than for it to mean something. Lacan argues in the 1953–1954 seminar on *Freud's Papers on Technique*, no one needed to understand the meaning of the hieroglyphics in order to decide that it was a language. Its evident organisation in a symbolic system alone was sufficient to indicate that it was a language (Lacan, 1975/1991, pp. 244–245). Similarly, we do not need to know the content of the letter at all in order to be able to appreciate Poe's story.

However, the important Lacanian lesson here is, although any series constructed at random shall inevitably prove to have been structured by the symbolic laws from the outset, laws that are moreover knowable, there are no winning formulae in the game of odd or even. And conversely, because the symbolic laws structuring a random series are knowable, though only in retrospect, human beings erroneously tend to imagine that there must be a winning formula in the game of odd or even that must, therefore, be knowable in advance.

A Letter Always Arrives at Its Destination

Lacan concludes the essay and the seminar with the remark, "a letter always arrives at its destination" (Lacan, 1957/2006, p. 30; Lacan, 1978/1993, p. 205). Objecting to it, Derrida writes, "letter can always not arrive" (Derrida, 1975/1987, pp. 443–44). In Lacan, however, the return of the repressed comes first, and the repressed is subsequently reconstructed retroactively at another time and place in the form of a chain of signifiers, in order to explain the return and thus remove the oddity. In other words, whereas Derrida is concerned with a letter that is on the way to its destination and might, therefore, equally well miss the destination, Lacan is concerned with the puzzle of the arrival of a letter following the event of its arrival. Differently put, if repression is verifiable only by the return of the repressed, then it is possible to say that the repressed always returns. It is the certainty regarding the ending that any retroactive reading entails.

Lacan's axiom begs a question, though. Since Lacan had said before, "it [the letter] will be *and* will not be where it is wherever it goes", does that mean that the letter will be *and* will not be at its destination when it reaches there? In a way, yes, because, at the end of the story, the letter is in the hands of the Queen and, at the same time, it is hanging from the card rack in the Minister's office in another form. Similarly, the locus of the law for the letter is the Prefect and the King. And as far as the phallus is concerned, it is separately embodied by the letter and by the King at the same time.

Unlike Derrida, both Barbara Johnson and Slavoj Žižek took Lacan's remark seriously, claiming moreover that it had many possible meanings. For instance, Johnson writes in her 1977 essay, "The Frame of Reference: Poe, Lacan, Derrida":

> The sentence "a letter always arrives at its destination" can thus either be simply pleonastic or variously paradoxical: it can mean "the only message I can read is the one I send," "wherever the letter is, is its destination," "when a letter is read, it reads the reader," "the repressed always returns," "I exist only as a reader of the other," "the letter has no destination," and "we all die." It is not any one of these readings, but all of them and others in their very incompatibility, which *repeat* the letter in its way of reading the act of reading. Far from giving us the Seminar's final truth, these last words enact the impossibility of any ultimate metalanguage.
>
> (Johnson, 1977/1989, p. 503)

Several commentators who subsequently sought to interpret Lacan's remark have often done so by elucidating one or the other interpretation made by Johnson. For instance, Joseph Valente effectively elucidated in 2003 Johnson's interpretation "wherever the letter is, is its destination", or, more precisely, "wherever the letter arrives, is its destination" by invoking the signifier's restorative and preemptive powers:

> For Lacan, the letter always arrives at its destination precisely on account of the recuperative power of the signifier which, in preempting the very signified that it promises, perpetually turns arrival into destination, contingency into ratio.
>
> (Valente, 2003, p. 170)

Žižek, too, amplifies Johnson's remark, "wherever the letter is, is its destination" in his 1992 *Enjoy your Symptom!* but he does so in order to explain why the destination of the letter is the very place it arrives at:

> The letter always arrives at its destination . . . not because of an unshakeable belief in teleology, in the power of a message to reach its preordained goal: Lacan's exposition of the way a letter arrives at its destination *lays bare the very mechanism of teleological illusion.* . . . A letter always arrives at its destination—especially when we have the limit case of a letter *without* addressee,

of what is called in German *Flaschenpost*, a message in a bottle thrown into the sea from an island after shipwreck. This case displays at its purest and clearest how a letter reaches its true destination the moment it is delivered, thrown into the water—its true addressee is namely not the empirical other which may receive it or not, but the big Other, the symbolic order itself, which receives it *the moment the letter is put into circulation*, i.e., the moment the sender "externalizes" his message, delivers it to the Other, the moment the Other takes cognizance of the letter and thus disburdens the sender of responsibility for it.

(Žižek, 1992, pp. 9–10)

In other words, as soon as a letter is dispatched, it may be said to have reached its destination in the form of the symbolic order as the Other. Žižek thus questions those readings of Lacan's remark that imagine the letter's destination in terms of a specific individual addressee and the letter's arrival at its destination in terms of teleology. Žižek also amplifies Johnson's interpretation, "we all die", when he writes that the letter could be the one that bears our death warrant:

A common pretheoretical sensitivity enables us to detect the ominous undertone that sticks to the proposition 'a letter always arrives at its destination': the only letter that nobody can evade, that sooner or later reaches us, i.e. the letter which has each of us as its infallible addressee, is death. We can say that we live only in so far as a certain letter (the letter containing our death warrant) still wanders around, looking for us.

(Ibid., p. 21)

Johnson's otherwise brilliant reading is somewhat marred by one remark, however. While Lacan's remark does have "various" possible "incompatible" meanings at one level, Johnson seems to have gone slightly off the mark in "simply" viewing the remark as "pleonastic" or "paradoxical" for the reason that "these last words" of Lacan, contrary to Johnson's claim, do offer us "the Seminar's final truth" at another level; namely, there is no final truth except that there is no final truth; the letter has no destination other than its destination; there is no big Other of the big Other; or, simply, there is no metalanguage.

Somewhat like Johnson, Žižek too gives us a list of different possible meanings of Lacan's remark in *Enjoy your Symptom!*: "The sender always receives from the receiver his own message in reverse form, . . . the frame itself is always being framed by part of its content, we cannot escape the symbolic debt, it always has to be settled" (ibid., p. 12). While readers like Johnson and Žižek have read a great deal into this remark, at times departing from Lacanian principles, and readers like Derrida refused to read it adequately, Lacan himself would go on to clarify in the seminar *On a Discourse that Might not be a Semblance* that the letter always arrives at its destination simply because of the message it carries (Lacan, 2007, p. 102).

From the clinical point of view, the letter stands for the speech of the analysand and, in that sense, it has two destinations: the analyst, who is the supposed addressee, the temporary holder, and the proper destination of the letter; and the analysand himself or herself who is the sender, the reader of the false side of the letter, and the true destination of the letter. Therefore, in order to enable the analysand's own speech to arrive at its true destination with its face bearing the message uppermost, the analyst returns the analysand's speech to the latter in an inverted form so that the latter can hear what the signifier has to say on the other side of the words. The sender of the letter can, in fact, be the letter's final destination even outside analysis and in everyday reality, for example, when an ex-lover demands his or her own love letters to be returned to him or her. The letter arrives at its destination, at last, in such cases, when the sender reclaims his or her own letters following a detour through a holder of the letter. Such a letter could well act like a boomerang, and reading it can easily produce the effect of eating one's *Dasein*. Žižek, too, described the arrival of the letter at its destination in relation to eating one's *Dasein*, although the hypothetical subject in Žižek's narrative, like Thyestes before him, does not seem to be ready for the meal:

> In other words, . . . the letter that the subject put into circulation "arrives at its destination," which was from the very beginning the sender himself: the letter arrives at its destination when the subject is finally forced to assume the true consequences of its activity. . . . when, in other words, he gets back from the other his own message in its inverted, true form, i.e., when the true dimension of his own "letter" (teaching) reaches its proper addressee, namely himself—he is shaken and shrinks back from the consequences of his words, unprepared to recognize in them his own truth.
>
> (Žižek, 1992, p. 13)

Lacan completed writing the first version of "The Seminar on 'The Purloined Letter'" in San Casciano, the birthplace of Machiavelli. Departing from this detail, Elizabeth Roudinesco points to a relation between the letter's destination and the subject's destiny:

> [Lacan] also constructed what amounted to a "political" logic of the signifier: a letter always arrives at its destination because the *letter*—i.e., the *signifier*, as inscribed in the unconscious—determines, as *fortuna* did for Machiavelli, the subject's fate in its various orientations.
>
> (Roudinesco, 1993/1997, p. 269)

Since the letter always arrives at its destination, as does human life caught up in the route of the letter's journey, it is ethical and economical to quietly eat one's *Dasein* when the chickens come home to roost.

Notes

1 An earlier version of this chapter has been published as Biswas, 2009.
2 Based on some of the resemblance between Dupin and the Minister who knew each other well—such as the common first letter of their surnames, the fact that both were poets and mathematicians, and the final reference to the two brothers Atreus and Thyestes engaged in revenge—the French linguist Jean-Claude Milner claimed in his 1985 book, *Détections fictives* (Fictitious Detections) that Dupin and Minister D—were brothers (Milner, 1985). Like Atreus, who sought to avenge the seduction of his wife by Thyestes, Dupin inscribed the lines from Crébillon's play in the facsimile letter in order to avenge an "evil turn" done him by the Minister in Vienna (Poe, 1844/1938, p. 222). Since revenge was extremely important for Dupin, he was curious to know the Minister's reaction to his letter: "I should like very well to know the precise character of his thoughts, when, . . . he is reduced to opening the letter which I left for him in the card-rack" (ibid., p. 222). Although there are other resemblances between the two men that have not been pointed out by Milner, such as that both of them could easily see the hidden letter, unlike the other characters in the story, and that both of them used the letter for personal benefit, political and/or economic, they could nevertheless well be each other's alter egos rather than brothers.
3 Armchair detectives tend to take this notion of communication to its limit insofar as they solve a mystery entirely on the basis of the verbal accounts of someone else who visits the site of crime on their behalf, such as their assistant, who himself remains unable to fathom the mystery. Inspector Brasig and his assistant Karl, mentioned in the second chapter of Freud's *The Interpretation of Dreams*, offer a very good example of this type of detection.
4 The expression "*l'autruiche*" (Lacan, 1957/2006, p. 10) used by Lacan is a coinage through condensation. It is the result of the combination of three terms: the ostrich (*l'autruche*); [imaginary] others (*autrui*); and [the politics of] Austria (*Autriche*) in the form of the politics of the Freudian association. The more complex coinage, the expression "*autruicherie*" (ibid., p. 22), combines all of that with the notion of deception (*tricherie*).
5 All emphases are in the original.
6 "'A letter, a litter': in Joyce's circle, they played on the homophony of the two words in English" (Lacan, 1957/2006, p. 18). Lacan's description of the relation between a letter and a litter in Joyce is entirely restricted to the phonetic similarity between the two words, to the play on words that this similarity enabled Joyce to engage in, and to the playing with sounds of words in general that Joyce's lead encouraged among his followers. He makes no attempt to engage with the meanings of the words. The expression "Joyce's circle" refers to the group of writers and scholars, including Samuel Beckett, Stuart Gilbert, William Carlos Williams and several others, who produced the 1929 volume on Joyce's *Work in Progress*, entitled *Our Exagmination Round His Factification for Incamination of Work in Progress*, as Lacan mentions in a footnote (ibid., p. 47, fn. 11). The essays in the volume extensively discuss Joyce's wordplay, often with the help of a play on words, as the very title of the volume testifies. From this volume, Lacan must have particularly had in mind the "letter" of protest dated 9th February, 1929, addressed to Joyce by Vladimir Dixon, who described his own letter as "A Litter", and referred to Joyce as "Mister Germ's Choice" and "mysterre Shame's Voice" in it (Beckett, et al., 1929/1961, p. 89). By doing so, Dixon, Joyce's reader, had played on this very homophony eight years before Joyce himself. Although several scholars, such as Stuart Gilbert, Richard Ellmann, John Slocum, Herbert Cahoon and others, have surmised or claimed that Dixon was Joyce himself, Goldwasser, Whittier-Ferguson and others have subsequently established that Dixon was not Joyce (Goldwasser, 1979; Whittier-Ferguson, 1992). Dixon's father was an American, his mother was a Russian, and he worked in Paris during the 1920s. The detail provided by Lacan that it was not Joyce alone but a circle of people ("they") who played on this homophony implies that at first there was the one, named

Joyce, and then there were many, a "circle". The playing was thus not the effort of a single swallow but an indication of the arrival of summer, as Lacan would go on to say about his own teaching in 1970, following the publication of the first two books on it by Anthony Wilden and Anika Lemaire. In any case, this is a limited commentary on Joyce's expression compared to what Lacan shall go on to state on it later in the 1970s.

References

Beckett, Samuel, Brion, Marcel, Budgen, Frank, Gilbert, Stuart, Jolas, Eugene, Llona, Victor, McAlmon, Robert, McGreevy, Thomas, Paul, Elliot, Rodker, John, Sage, Robert, Williams, William Carlos, Slingsby, G.V.L. and Dixon, Vladimir (1961). *Our Exagmination Round His Factification for Incamination of Work in Progress*. Faber and Faber (Original work published 1929).

Biswas, Santanu (2009). Lacanian Lessons in Edgar Allan Poe's 'The Purloined Letter'. In Malabika Sarkar (Ed.), *Moneta's Veil: Essays on the Nineteenth Century*. Pearson, 121–143.

Brunswick, Ruth Mack (1971). Supplement to Freud's 'History of an Infantile Neurosis'. In Gardiner (Ed.), *The Wolf-Man by the Wolf-Man*. Basic Books, 263–307 (Original work published 1928).

Crébillon, Prosper Jolyot de (2015). *Atrée Et Thyeste, Tragédie*. Théâtre Classique (Original work published 1707). Available at https://theatre-classique.fr/pages/pdf/CREBILLON_ATREETHYESTE.pdf (Accessed on 25th July, 2023).

Derrida, Jacques (1987). Le Facteur de la Verité. In Jacques Derrida's (Ed.) and Alan Bass Trans. *The Post Card*. The University of Chicago Press, 411–496 (Original work published 1975).

Freud, Sigmund (2001). On Beginning the Treatment: Further Recommendations on the Technique of Psycho-Analysis I. In James Strachey (Ed.), *The Standard Edition of the Complete Psychological Works of Sigmund Freud*, Vol. XII. Vintage, Hogarth Press and the Institute of Psychoanalysis, 121–144 (Original work published 1913).

Gardiner, Muriel (Ed.) (1971). *The Wolf-Man by the Wolf-Man*. Basic Books.

Goldwasser, Thomas A. (1979). Who Was Vladimir Dixon? Was He Vladimir Dixon? *James Joyce Quarterly*, *16*, 219–222.

Harvey, Sir Paul (Ed.) (1969). *The Oxford Companion to Classical Literature*. Clarendon Press (Original work published 1937).

Heidegger, Martin (1972). *On Time and Being*. In Joan Stambaugh Trans. Harper and Row (Original work published 1969).

Heidegger, Martin (2001). *Being and Time*. In John Macquarrie and Edward Robinson Trans. Blackwell (Original work published 1927).

Heidegger, Martin (2002). *The Essence of Truth. On Plato's Cave Allegory and Theaetetus*. In Ted Sadler Trans. Continuum (Original work published 1930).

Johnson, Barbara (1989). The Frame of Reference: Poe, Lacan, Derrida. In Shoshana Felman (Ed.), *Literature and Psychoanalysis: The Question of Reading: Otherwise*. The Johns Hopkins University Press, 457–505 (Original work published 1977).

King James Version of the Holy Bible (2004). Pdf Version, www.holybooks.com (Original work published 1611). Available at www.holybooks.com/wp-content/uploads/2010/05/The-Holy-Bible-King-James-Version.pdf (Accessed on 21st July, 2023).

Lacan, Jacques (2006 [1957]). Le séminaire sur la lettre volée. *La Psychanalyse*, *2*, 1–44.

Lacan, Jacques (1991). *The Seminar of Jacques Lacan. Book I. Freud's Papers on Technique, 1953–1954*. In John Forrester Trans. W.W. Norton. (Original work published 1975).

Lacan, Jacques (1993). *The Seminar of Jacques Lacan. Book II. The Ego in Freud's Theory and in the Technique of Psychoanalysis, 1954–1955*. In Sylvana Tomaselli Trans. W.W. Norton (Original work published 1978).

Lacan, Jacques (2006). Logical Time and the Assertion of Anticipated Certainty: A New Sophism. In Bruce Fink Trans., in collaboration with Héloïse Fink and Russell Grigg, *Écrits: The First Complete Edition in English*. W.W. Norton, 161–175 (Original work published 1945).

Lacan, Jacques (2006). Seminar on 'The Purloined Letter'. In Bruce Fink Trans., in collaboration with Héloïse Fink and Russell Grigg, *Écrits: The First Complete Edition in English*. W.W. Norton, 6–48 (Original work published 1957).

Lacan, Jacques (2007). Leçon Sur Lituraterre, *Le Séminaire de Jacques Lacan. Livre XVIII. D'un discours qui ne serait pas du semblant, 1971*. Texte Établi par Jacques-Alain Miller, Seuil, 113–127.

Lacan, Jacques (2022, April). Columbia University Lecture on the Symptom. Russell Grigg. In *The Lacanian Review: Hurly-Burly: Journal of the New Lacanian School and the World Association of Psychoanalysis. American Lacan*, Issue 12, 75–84 (Original work published 1976).

Laurent, Éric (2007). The Purloined Letter and the Tao of the Psychoanalyst. In Véronique Voruz and Bogdan Wolf (Eds.) and Marc Thomas and Victoria Woollard Trans. *The Later Lacan: An Introduction*. State University of New York Press, 25–52 (Original work published 1999).

Lévi-Strauss, Claude (1963). *Structural Anthropology*, Vol. I. Claire Jacobson and Brooke Grundfest Schoepf Trans. Basic Books (Original work published 1958).

Lévi-Strauss, Claude (1969). *The Elementary Structures of Kinship*. In James Harle Bell, John Richard von Sturmer and Rodney Needham Trans. Beacon Press (Original work published 1949).

Milner, Jean Claude (1985). *Détections Fictives*. Seuil.

Obholzer, Karin (1982). *The Wolf-Man Sixty Years Later: Conversations with Freud's Controversial Patient*. In Michael Shaw Trans. Continuum International Publishing Group (Original work published 1980).

Plato (1956). *Protagoras and Meno*. In W. K. C. Guthrie Trans. Penguin (Original work published 385 BC).

Poe, Edgar Allan (1938). The Purloined Letter. In *The Complete Tales and Poems of Edgar Allan Poe*, The Modern Library, 208–222 (Original work published 1844).

Roudinesco, Elisabeth (1997). *Jacques Lacan*. In Barbara Bray Trans. Columbia University Press (Original work published 1993).

Valente, Joseph (2003). Lacan's Marxism, Marxism's Lacan (from Žižek to Althusser). In Jean-Michel Rabaté (Ed.), *The Cambridge Companion to Lacan*. Cambridge University Press, 153–172.

Whittier-Ferguson, John (1992). The Voice behind the Echo: Vladimir Dixon's Letters to James Joyce and Sylvia Beach. *James Joyce Quarterly*, *29*(3), 511–531.

Žižek, Slavoj (1991). *Looking Awry: An Introduction to Jacques Lacan through Popular Culture*. MIT Press.

Žižek, Slavoj (1992). *Enjoy Your Symptom! Jacques Lacan in Hollywood and Out*. Routledge.

Chapter 2

Hamlet

Between 4th March and 29th April, 1959, Lacan devoted sessions 13 through 19 of his 1958–1959 seminar on *Desire and Its Interpretation* (*Le désir et son interprétation*) to discussing the play *Hamlet*, making the seminar on *Hamlet* Lacan's longest discourse on a literary work. In Freud's psychoanalytic writings and letters combined, there are fifty or so published references to *Hamlet*, dated between 1897 and 1938, that is to say, spanning Freud's entire career as a psychoanalyst, out of which forty-four or so are passing mentions. Even in the six relatively longer discussions on the play, a large number of details pertaining to the play were completely ignored by Freud.[1] Lacan's discussion of *Hamlet*, by contrast, is quite comprehensive. Thus, Lacan speaks about the first performance of the play, the first copies of the play, the first quarto edition, the first folio edition, et cetera. He remarks on the significance of the fact that *Hamlet* was written in the same year as the execution of the Earl of Essex, 1601. Not only that, Lacan discusses the earlier versions of *Hamlet*, such as the versions of Saxo Grammaticus and François de Belleforest, the lost *Ur-Hamlet*, possibly by Kyd, and a first draft of the play possibly by Shakespeare. In the course of his commentary on these versions, Lacan highlights the original contributions, additions, extensions, and innovations introduced by Shakespeare to the saga of "Hamlet" as he found it, such as the graveyard scene, the extended role of Ophelia, et cetera, as well as the significance of these. Lacan situates *Hamlet* at a turning point in Shakespeare's life and literary career, one that is marked by the death of his father and other events, as well as by his transition from Comedies and Histories to Tragedies. Lacan duly refers to the psychoanalytic readings of *Hamlet* by Freud, Jones, Rank, and Sharpe, as well as to a wide variety of other types of readings of *Hamlet*, such as those by Julius Leopold Klein, Karl Werder, Goethe, Coleridge, Hazlitt, Georg Brandes, Edward Vining, Richard Loening, Dover Wilson, Otto Luitpold Jiriczek, Thomas Stearns Eliot, Wilbraham Fitzjohn Trench, Hume, and so on. Nor does Lacan ignore the great Hamlet actors, like David Garrick, Edmund Kean, and Sir Johnston Forbes-Robertson, discussing at length the question of the image and the unconscious the actors lent to the characters. Lacan duly comments on the blank verse and the rhyming couplets, and he even provides a summary of the play.

Lacan chose *Hamlet* to frame his discussion on the psychoanalytic interpretation of human desire for a number of reasons. Such as, the play helps understand the elaboration of the castration complex in the course of an analysis; it depicts the opposition between unconscious and defence, the opposition between the ego and the id, and the imperatives of the superego in a simplified manner; its structure rigorously delineates human desire in terms of the precise Freudian coordinates of desire, which Lacan thinks is the reason for the play's exceptional effect; its structural equivalence with *Oedipus*; and its structure enables him to articulate the function of the object in psychoanalysis in an exemplary fashion, in the main.

Hamlet's Desire Is Troubled by the Desire of Gertrude

According to Lacan, *Hamlet* is dominated by the mother as Other and by Gertrude as the "primordial" as well as "omnipotent" Other of Hamlet, especially in terms of the hold of her desire on Hamlet's desire. He states:

> [W]e cannot fail to realize that what Hamlet is constantly dealing or grappling with is a desire which is far from being his own. As it is situated in the play, it is the desire, not *for* his mother but *of* his mother—that is, it is his mother's desire. That alone is what is at work.
>
> (Lacan, 2013/2019, p. 280)

Reiterating this a little later, Lacan says:

> The first step we took along this pathway was thus to articulate to what degree the play is the drama of desire insofar as desire is related to the Other's desire.
>   I showed you to what degree this play is dominated by the Other whose desire we are talking about here. She is unambiguously the mother—that is to say the primordial subject to whom demands are addressed.
>
> (Ibid., pp. 307–308)

Lacan further clarifies that "it is . . . indisputable that the fact that his desire is fixated on her affects him; this is what is most certain and apparent in Hamlet's role" (ibid., p. 279). Therefore, in order to understand Hamlet's desire, we must necessarily understand the desire of Gertrude that determines it and through which it works. In Hamlet's own words, the desire of his mother is an "appetite" (Shakespeare, 1603/1997, p. 188) stemming from her need for the phallus, which is in consonance with the Ghost's description of it as her "luxury" (ibid., p. 220). In Act 3 Scene 4, by holding up a mirror to her in order to reveal her sexual appetite to Gertrude—"You go not till I set you up a glass/Where you may see the inmost part of you" (ibid., p. 319)—Hamlet clearly spells out how he viewed his mother's desire, which, going by her replies, Gertrude herself seems to accept:

> O shame! where is thy blush?
> Rebellious hell,
> If thou canst mutine in a matron's bones,
> To flaming youth let virtue be as wax,
> And melt in her own fire: proclaim no shame
> When the compulsive ardour gives the charge,
> Since frost itself as actively doth burn
> And reason panders will.
>
> *GERTRUDE*
>
> O Hamlet, speak no more:
> Thou turn'st mine eyes into my very soul;
> And there I see such black and grained spots
> As will not leave their tinct.
> (Ibid., pp. 323–324)

Gertrude acknowledges here that Hamlet's attempt to hold up a mirror to her has been effective, for she is able to see the black and grained spots inside her soul that will not lose their colour. Hamlet continues:

> *HAMLET*
>
> Nay, but to live
> In the rank sweat of an enseamed bed,
> Stew'd in corruption, honeying and making love
> Over the nasty sty,—
>
> *GERTRUDE*
>
> O, speak to me no more;
> These words, like daggers, enter in mine ears;
> No more, sweet Hamlet!
> (Ibid., p. 324)

Here, Hamlet speaks of his mother's desire as "rebellious" because it was able to take over the bones of an old woman, and he describes the same desire as "hell". He says that acting impulsively is not shameful anymore because desire rules over reason. It is clear that in this passage, Hamlet views his mother's desire as her sexual passion. Hence, the expressions "flaming youth" and "compulsive ardour" are used in continuation of the expression "the heyday in the blood" used shortly before. The expression "rebellious hell" is linked to the word "mutine" in the next line, where the rebellion or mutiny consists of Gertrude's unabashed expression of her sexual desire at a matured age.[2] And the most direct description of the sexual nature of Gertrude's desire is: "making love/Over the nasty sty". Hamlet further says to her, "Good night. But go not to my uncle's bed" (ibid., p. 328), and he urges her to begin to abstain from that night onward, which will make it easy for her to abstain the next night, and so on:

> Refrain to-night,
> And that shall lend a kind of easiness
> To the next abstinence: the next more easy.
> (Ibid., p. 329)

When Gertrude asks Hamlet toward the end of the scene, "What shall I do?" Hamlet urges her not to reveal the truth about his madness to Claudius under the spell of his erotic touch:

> Not this, by no means, that I bid you do:
> Let the bloat king tempt you again to bed;
> Pinch wanton on your cheek; call you his mouse;
> And let him, for a pair of reechy kisses,
> Or paddling in your neck with his damn'd fingers,
> Make you to ravel all this matter out,
> That I essentially am not in madness,
> But mad in craft.
> (Ibid., p. 330)

Here, Hamlet's allegation is clearly aimed at Gertrude's need for Claudius' phallus or at the excess of her sexual desire at an inappropriate age. The important point for us to note is that Hamlet's desire of the Other is Gertrude's troublesome sexual desire related to her lack. In terms of her consent to marry "brother" Claudius within a month of the shocking death of her admirable husband, she betrayed the urgency of her need for the phallus. This desire of the mother problematised Hamlet's own desire. Lacan states that Gertrude's desire, more precisely the incomprehensible aspect of her lack, is responsible for putting Hamlet's desire out of joint. Hamlet had unfortunately stared at the abyss of the barred A, of the lacking mother, whose incomprehensible aspect troubled him and kept him fixated to it. He is stunned and paralysed by the enigma of his mother's lack. Lacan says, "the value of the play is that it allows us to accede to the meaning of $S(A)$" (Lacan, 2013/2019, p. 297). He describes $S(A)$ as "the signifier that is missing at the level of the Other" (ibid., p. 298) and explains its meaning by stating that "The hidden signifier, the one that is not at the Other's disposal, . . . there is only one and not dozens of them . . . [is] what we call the phallus" (ibid., pp. 299–300). We must bear in mind, however, that in general, the Other's lack, according to Lacan, is not merely the mother's lack; it is more importantly a structural lack primordially but not solely represented by the mother that the subject must traverse on the way to reaching his fantasy-regulated desire.

That Gertrude's desire problematised Hamlet's desire is evident from a number of details. To begin with, Hamlet's complaint against his mother is that, given the easiest choice on earth she had to make between an ideal man and a despicable man, she did not choose the right man. This is also to be understood in the sense that she did not choose the right man alone. That is to say, after choosing the right man, she went on to choose the wrong man, and thereby, she had chosen both of them, which means that she had not chosen between them. In Lacan's words, Hamlet's mother's desire

> essentially presents itself as a desire that cannot tell the difference between an eminent, idealized, and exalted object, Hamlet's father, and a disparaged object worthy only of scorn, Claudius, the criminal and adulterous brother . . . because of . . . instinctual voracity.
>
> (Ibid., p. 308)

Similarly, every time Hamlet faced Gertrude's desire, he failed to execute his resolve to separate her from Claudius because his own resolve is overridden by Gertrude's desire for Claudius' phallus. Thus, he, too, failed to choose between his father and Claudius for his mother insofar as he sent her back to Claudius. Lacan said:

> Hamlet's plea to his mother vacillates. I showed this to you in the scene in which, when face to face with her, Hamlet calls on her to become abstinent, in the crudest and cruelest terms, moreover, at the moment at which he communicates to her the essential message that the ghost, his father, charged him with transmitting. Suddenly this plea collapses, and Hamlet send his mother back to Claudius' bed, back to the caresses of a man who will not fail to make her yield yet again.
>
> (Ibid., p. 308)

In the play, Hamlet first asks Gertrude to abstain. He even teaches her how to gradually refrain from going to his bed, one night at a time, as we have seen. And after all that he said to her, go to his bed and be caressed by him—by implication, make love even—but do not tell him the truth about my madness. Thus, Hamlet's zest for his aim fades whenever he confronts his mother's desire, and he is unable to understand why. Lacan states that this sort of "collapsing or caving in" at the end of his plea indicates "a waning [*retombée*] of his own desire" (ibid., p. 308). Seeing this as consenting to his mother's desire, Lacan states:

> We are following the oscillating motion we see in Hamlet here. He storms, he insults, he implores, and then his discourse collapses—he gives up. We see in his very words a disappearance or vanishing of his appeal when he consents

to his mother's desire, laying down his arms before something that seems ineluctable.

His mother's desire here takes on anew for him the value of something that can in no way be dominated, moved, or eliminated.

(Ibid., p. 282)

Thus, confronted by his mother's desire, Hamlet's own desire that she should abstain from sex with Claudius collapses, and he eventually acts in perfect consonance with her desire rather than with his own desire. In addition, Lacan thinks that Gertrude's failure to observe the usual conventions of mourning disrupts Hamlet's experience of mourning and poisons it with the despair of sexual loathing and contempt. Simply put, Hamlet couldn't mourn his father's death adequately and was full of contempt for sex instead because Gertrude had chosen to shorten her mourning by getting married to Claudius too soon. Moreover, Gertrude's sexual appetite destroyed the sexual desire of Hamlet. Hamlet scorns sex and childbirth from the time he is disturbed—as in from the time his character begins to demonstrate a pathological hysteria—by his mother's apparently excessive sexual desire. Ophelia became the symbol of Hamlet's repudiation of desire as a result. Lacan says Hamlet's encounter with the unanticipated excess of feminine desire in the form of his mother's sexual desire gave him his psychopathic predisposition. Furthermore, Hamlet generalises feminine desire in terms of his impression of his mother's desire. Please note that, in response to his mother's frailty, Hamlet does not say: "Frailty, thy name is Gertrude!" He says, "Frailty, thy name is woman!" More problematically, he mistreats Ophelia as a despicable object worthy of living in a brothel for no reason other than the influence of Gertrude's sexual desire on his understanding of feminine desire in general. These indicators together bring out the nature and extent of the shaping influence of Gertrude's desire on the desire of Hamlet.

Lacan's argument is a revision of Freud's interpretation of the play on two counts. First, unlike Freud, who considered Hamlet's desire to be his own desire, Lacan shows us the extent to which Hamlet's desire is conditioned by his mother's desire. And second, unlike Freud, who argued that Hamlet is not psychopathic from the beginning but becomes one in the course of the action in the play, Lacan maintains that it is his confrontation with Gertrude's desire at the very beginning of the play that predisposed Hamlet to his illness, even before his encounter with the Ghost. The originality of Lacan's argument lies in his understanding that Gertrude's sexual desire for Claudius rather than the need to avenge Senior Hamlet's death has the strongest influence on Hamlet's psyche. In fact, Lacan thinks that it is only against the backdrop of the intemperance of Gertrude's desire and the violation of the mourning custom that the Ghost's imperative for revenge must be assessed.

Hamlet's desire is moreover regulated by the desire of the Other in general. Thus, the influence of his mother's desire makes him let his mother return to the arms of Claudius despite his own opposition to it; his dead father's desire requires Hamlet to take revenge; Claudius' and Gertrude's desires make Hamlet decide to stay on instead of going back to his school in Wittenberg; Fortinbras' desire arouses his sense of honour and makes him decide to act; Laertes' grief for Ophelia arouses Hamlet's grief for her; and Claudius' desire makes him take part in the final fatal duel with Laertes. Thus, Hamlet is marked by "his being fundamentally open to whatever comes along" (ibid., p. 329), as Lacan puts it later, or by his being someone who is at the beck and call of everyone, who appears to exist for the Other's sake.

Hamlet Is Suspended in the Time of the Other

In addition to his desire being conditioned by the desire of his mother, Hamlet is suspended in the time of the other. Lacan says, "Hamlet is always suspended in the other's time [*suspendu à l'heure de l'autre*], and this is true right up until the end of the play" (Lacan, 2013/2019, p. 315. Translation modified). Owing to this, we get the impression that Hamlet will do things only at the time of the other: "[W]hatever Hamlet does, it is only and always on the other's time that he does it. He puts up with anything and everything" thrown at him by the other (ibid., p. 316). Hamlet's suspension in the time of the other is a constant factor throughout the play. To begin with, in Act 1 Scene 2, even before the Ghost had spoken to Hamlet, the latter draws our attention to the problem afflicted on his desire by the desire of Gertrude when he begins his first soliloquy with the words:

> O, that this too too sullied flesh would melt,
> Thaw and resolve itself into a dew!
> (Shakespeare, 1603/1997,
> p. 187)

Hamlet claims that his flesh is "sullied", or "solid" in a different edition, and he goes on to explain the reason for this toward the end of the same soliloquy as follows:

> Within a month,
> Ere yet the salt of most unrighteous tears
> Had left the flushing in her galled eyes,
> She married. O, most wicked speed, to post
> With such dexterity to incestuous sheets!
> (Ibid., p. 189)

Since he is suspended in the time of his mother despite not wanting to, Gertrude's haste in getting married to Claudius brought about Hamlet's hesitation and his inability to act. Conversely, immediately after Gertrude's death at the end of the play, Hamlet is able to act in haste and, at last, complete his task of killing Claudius.

Moreover, there are plenty of direct examples of Hamlet's suspension in the time of the other to be found all throughout the play until we come to the very end. For instance, Hamlet initially wanted to go back to his school in Wittenberg because he was disgusted with his mother's hasty remarriage. But when his mother and his stepfather ask him not to, he agrees:

CLAUDIUS

For your intent
In going back to school in Wittenberg,
It is most retrograde to our desire,
And we beseech you, bend you to remain
Here in the cheer and comfort of our eye,
Our chiefest courtier, cousin, and our son.

GERTRUDE

Let not thy mother lose her prayers, Hamlet.
I pray thee, stay with us; go not to Wittenberg.

HAMLET

I shall in all my best obey you, madam.
(Ibid., p. 186)

By deciding to stay on, Hamlet enters the time of his parents in the form of the time of Claudius and Gertrude. He enters his parents' time also in the sense that, by staying on, Hamlet allows himself to be gripped by his mother's desire for incest and his dead father's desire for revenge. Speaking on Hamlet's suspension in his parents' time, Lacan says:

> Let us not forget, all the same, that at the outset of the play—disgusted as he was already, even before his encounter with the ghost and the unveiling of the crime, by his mother's remarriage—he was thinking of one thing and one thing alone: leaving for Wittenberg.... It is owing to his parents' agenda [*heure*] that he stays put.
>
> (Lacan, 2013/2019, p. 316)

Similarly, Hamlet decides not to kill an unprepared and unarmed Claudius, who was not even aware of his presence—in other words, when he had the best opportunity to take revenge by killing him—because he did not consider it the right time for Claudius to die. He thought that by killing Claudius when he was praying, he could be sending the latter straight to heaven while his father, who was cut off at the blossoms of his sin, suffered in hell. Lacan states:

> [During] the play scene, ... [t]he king gets upset about what is happening onstage, and visibly betrays his own crime in front of everyone, proving that he

cannot bear the sight of it. Hamlet triumphs, exults, and scorns the man who has thus given himself away. Then he goes to the rendezvous with his mother that he had scheduled before the play scene. . . .

On the way to the rendezvous, Hamlet comes across the king, who is praying. Shaken to his very foundations by the scene that has just shown him the visage of his own actions, his own scenario, Claudius prays. Hamlet stands there before the king, and everything seems to suggest that the latter is not only disinclined to defend himself, but that he does not even perceive the threat that hangs over him. Hamlet stops at that point because it is not the right time [*heure*].

It is not the other's time [*heure*]. It is not the right moment [*heure*] for him to account for himself to God. To kill him now would be too good for him and too bad for Hamlet's father. It would not sufficiently revenge the latter's death because, owing to Claudius' repentance in his prayer, salvation might be open to him. Be that as it may, one thing is clear, which is that, having just caught the king's conscience as he had hoped—"The play's the thing/Wherein I'll catch the conscience of the king" [II, ii, 590–1]—Hamlet stops. Not for a single instant does he think this is the right time. Whatever may happen afterward, this is not the other's time, and he refrains from acting.

(Ibid., pp. 315–316)

Differently put,

[I]t is because he is concerned with the eternal 'to be' of the said Claudius that, at that precise moment, in a way that turns out to be altogether coherent, he does not even draw his sword from its scabbard.

(Ibid., p. 264)

In fact, Lacan explains how most of the acts of Hamlet are situated in the time of the other, using the word "*heure*" or "hour" for the purpose:

It is owing to his parents' agenda [*heure*] that he stays put. It is in accordance with the other's schedule [*heure*] that he puts his crime on hold. It is owing to his stepfather's plans [*heure*] that he departs for England. It is owing to Rosencrantz and Guildenstern's mission [*heure*] that he is led to send them to their deaths, thanks to the rather prettily executed trick that so impressed Freud. And it is all the same owing to Ophelia's time, the time at which she commits suicide, that the tragedy finds its terminus at a moment at which Hamlet—who has just, it seems, perceived that it is not so difficult to kill someone, the time "to say 'one'"—will not even have time to say "Phew!"

(Ibid., p. 316)

The hour of her suicide is Ophelia's time. Hamlet's passage through the time of Ophelia in terms of his scuffle with Laertes inside her grave proves to be absolutely crucial for him insofar as it enables him to renew his desire whose track he had lost, as we shall see.

Even toward the end of the play, when Claudius and Laertes set up a trap for Hamlet and invite him to a duel where he is required to fight on Claudius' behalf, he agrees to participate for no good reason at all. Thus, he is suspended in the time of Claudius even toward the end of the play. He wears Claudius' colours even while unknowingly taking his first step towards his own time:

> People propose that he do something that in no way resembles an opportunity to kill Claudius—namely, fight in a very pretty fencing contest. . . . But it is still essentially on the other's time, and far more ridiculously, in order to win the other's bet for him—recall that it is not Hamlet's possessions that are wagered—that he agrees to fight this battle for his stepfather's benefit and as his advocate. . . . Right up till the end—right up until the final hour [*heure*], an hour that is so determinate that it will be his own hour, for he will be mortally wounded before he can strike his enemy—it is always by the other's watch [*heure*] that the plot of the tragedy proceeds and is brought to an end.
> (Ibid., pp. 316–317)

Since every hour traversed by Hamlet is, in fact, the hour of the other, Hamlet, strictly speaking, has only one hour, his own hour, which is the hour of his destruction. The rest of the play consists of Hamlet's progression toward this hour of his own. The final hour of the play belongs to Hamlet. It is Hamlet's own time at last, following his prolonged suspension in the time of others, but it is also the time in which he is mortally wounded. Differently put, Hamlet is suspended in the time of others up to the very last moment until he is mortally wounded and is aware of it, which is when he enters his own time. Immediately upon entering his own time at last, Hamlet promptly kills not only his own killer but, more importantly, his father's killer and thus fulfils the task given to him by his father's ghost. Thus, Hamlet's time, his only time, is the time of his destruction as well as the time of the fulfilment of his mission. Everyone's appointment with the hour of his death is meaningful in his destiny. But, as Lacan explains, Hamlet's appointment with the hour of his destruction is of such great importance due to a distinguishing sign relating to the phallus in his fate. We will come to that later.

There is one more way in which we can think of Hamlet's suspension in the time of the other. Describing this very tendency to be suspended in the other's time as the "foundation of neurotic behavior", Lacan further clarifies that "[t]he subject always seeks to find his moment [*heure*] in his object. One might even say that he learns how to tell time from it" (ibid., p. 315). Precisely put, the very basis of the neurotic subject's relation to his desired object in his fantasy is time. For the obsessional, the object arrives too late, while for the hysteric, it arrives too soon:

> In neurosis, the object takes on a signification that must be sought out in what I call "the moment [*heure*] of truth." The object there is always an hour ahead of

schedule or an hour behind.... This phenomenon constantly arises and manifests itself in the obsessive's procrastination, which is moreover founded on the fact that he always prepares himself for things when it is too late [*anticipe trop tard*]. Similarly, the hysteric always repeats what initially occurred in her trauma—namely, something that came too soon, a fundamental unreadiness [*immaturation*].

(Ibid., p. 315)

Even though Hamlet's character predominantly demonstrates the traits of an obsessional, such as in terms of his characteristic procrastination, it also demonstrates certain traits of a hysteric,[3] which is the reason that, at times, the object arrives too soon for him, such as the exceptional haste with which he first kills Polonius and later on deals with Rosencrantz and Guildenstern that Freud had paid so much attention to.[4] As a subject suspended in the time of the other, Hamlet's appointment with his act is either too late or too soon. Hamlet's hesitation and haste, and the impression he gives of forever being at the beck and call of others, are thus the two overlapping indicators of his suspension in the time of the other.

Hamlet's Inaction

Hamlet himself asks why he can't act in Act 4 Scene 4, lines 43–44:

> I do not know
> Why yet I live to say this thing's to do.
> (Shakespeare, 1603/1997,
> p. 345)

Lacan states that there were two tendencies that should have made Hamlet act, but oddly enough, together, they produced no result whatsoever:

> We see him actuated in the end by two different impulses: an imperative impulse, commanded doubly by his father's authority and by the love Hamlet bears his father, and the impulse to defend his mother and keep her for himself, both of which must drive him in the same direction—to kill Claudius. How could two positive things zero out? It is quite odd.
>
> (Lacan, 2013/2019, pp. 279–280)

Lacan offers several explanations for Hamlet's inaction. To begin with, he says Hamlet had every reason to act with urgency, and yet he does not act because of some problem with his desire:

> If Hamlet leaves him unscathed, it is because, we are told, of his scruples of conscience. But how much weight do they carry with respect to what is forced on him once the ghost has literally ordered him to take revenge on Claudius for him? From the moment of this initial encounter, Hamlet, in order to take action

against his father's murderer, who is also the usurper who dispossessed him, is armed with all the necessary feelings—a feeling of having been usurped, of rivalry, and of vengeance—as well as with the explicit order received from a father who is above all admired. Surely, everything in Hamlet is aligned for him to act, and yet he does not act.

... there is clearly something wrong with Hamlet's desire.

(Ibid., pp. 243–244)

In the same session, Lacan says Hamlet cannot act because both his father and he knew about the murder: "The mainspring that constitutes the whole difficulty of the problem Hamlet faces in assuming responsibility for his action [*assumer son acte*], is the fact that both the father and son know—for both of them, their eyes have been opened" (ibid., p. 247). In this session, Lacan moreover attributes Hamlet's inaction "to the relations between Hamlet and the *conscious* object of his desire" in the form of Ophelia (ibid., p. 244).

Lacan furthermore states in this very session that in order for Hamlet to act, he must be mortally wounded:

Hamlet can neither pay in his father's stead nor leave the debt unpaid. In the final analysis, he must get the debt paid, but, in the conditions in which he finds himself, the blow strikes him. Following a dark plot, which we will discuss at length, it is only after Hamlet has been wounded that he can strike, with the very weapon from which he has received his mortal wound, the criminal who is there within range namely, Claudius. . . . It is . . . not before having been dealt a mortal blow himself, that Hamlet can stab Claudius.

(Ibid., p. 247)

In other words, Hamlet will be able to deliver the blow only after he has entered his own time in terms of his destruction and received from the other the weapon with which he shall kill. In a subsequent session, Lacan says Hamlet finds it difficult to act because, unknown to him, his action is not disinterested in the Kantian sense—as in, he did not wish to carry it out for its own sake—that is, his desire is not pure:

There is something that makes Hamlet's action difficult for him, that makes his task repugnant to him, and that thrusts him into a problematic position with respect to his own action; and this something, this x, is his desire. The impure nature of this desire plays an essential role, but it does so unbeknownst to Hamlet. In some sense, it is inasmuch as his action is not disinterested, not motivated in some Kantian way, that Hamlet cannot carry it out.

(Ibid., p. 280)

In the same session, Lacan reiterates Freud's overlapping explanations that Hamlet's repressed desire for his mother prevented him from acting against Claudius, who possessed her, and that Hamlet was unable to kill Claudius as he had to punish himself first before doing so since Claudius had done no more than fulfilled Hamlet's own Oedipal desire to kill the father and marry the mother:

> What does the psychoanalytic tradition tell us about this? It says that everything in this case depends on his desire for his mother. Being repressed, this desire makes it such that the hero cannot move forward to take the action he is ordered to take, namely to take revenge on a man who is the current—and oh so illegitimate, because criminal—possessor of the maternal object. And if Hamlet cannot strike he who is designated as the target of his revenge, it is because he himself had in short already committed [in fantasy] the crime for which he was supposed to wreak vengeance.
>
> (Ibid., p. 278)

Repeating in the next session what he had already said in an earlier session, Lacan states that Hamlet is unable to kill Claudius because in order to do so, his own death must not be too far away as its essential precondition:

> Why doesn't Hamlet go straight for it? Instead, he tarries. . . . We are told [by Freud] that the action in question, the action of putting someone to death—an action that is so pressing and that in the final analysis takes such a short time to execute, we not knowing why it takes the hero so long—encounters an obstacle in Hamlet, that of desire. . . . this desire should, good Lord, go in the same direction as the action. What, then, can it mean if desire serves to obstruct action here? . . . what we immediately see when we read the text is *the close link between this murder*, whose necessity he does call into question, *and his own death*.
>
> This murder is not committed until Hamlet has already been given a fatal blow, in the short space of time remaining to him between the death blow and the moment at which he will be no more.
>
> (Ibid., p. 293)

In the same session, Lacan says that Hamlet waits because his character is marked by the traits of an obsessional. Due to this obsessional trait, his desire tends to delay the moment of the desired encounter:

> [S]pecific sentences make him [Hamlet] appear to have something bordering on obsessive structure. This has to do with the element that reveals structure in the obsessive, the element that is highlighted maximally by obsessive neurosis—namely, that the major function of desire consists here in keeping at bay and awaiting the hour of the desired encounter.
>
> (Ibid., p. 295)

Finally, in a later session, Lacan says Hamlet couldn't strike Claudius because he had to strike what was not there—i.e., the phallus—as we shall see. Hamlet's hand is stayed because "what he must strike is something other than what is there" (ibid., p. 353).

The Changing Relationship between Hamlet and Ophelia in Hamlet's Fantasy

Unlike Freud, who had kept quiet on Ophelia, Lacan considers her character absolutely crucial for the play. Lacan first points out that Shakespeare had introduced a shift in the plot of the play that distinguishes it from the earlier treatments of the legend by Saxo Grammaticus in about 1200 AD and François de Belleforest in 1570. The shift involves an extension of the function of Ophelia in the plot so as to capture Hamlet's secret by surprise. Lacan points out that in Belleforest's text, the equivalent of Ophelia is a prostitute who draws Hamlet into the depths of the woods in order to get him to reveal his innermost thoughts so that an eavesdropper is able to know about his thoughts better. But the strategy fails, Lacan thinks, due to the girl's love for him (Lacan, 2013/2019, p. 303). Lacan then says that in Shakespeare's play, by contrast, Ophelia has the much more serious function of questioning the secret of Hamlet's desire:

> Shakespeare takes to a new level what he finds in Belleforest's work. In the legend, as it is related by Belleforest, the courtesan is the bait designed to rip Hamlet's secret away from him—that is, the dark designs he is mulling over—and the goal is to get him to confess them within earshot of those around him who are not too sure how far he might go. Shakespeare transposes this to the upper level where the true question resides: Ophelia, too, is asked to investigate a secret, but, . . . it is the secret of desire.
>
> (Ibid., p. 304)

In the versions of Saxo Grammaticus and Belleforest, "Ophelia is a trap into which Hamlet does not fall". Shakespeare, however, deepens her role in the plot and makes her one of the "innermost elements" in the way of Hamlet's desire, which is crucial in the play insofar as she, in the form of "an essential element in the progression", makes Hamlet, who had lost the pathway of his desire, move toward "his fatal rendezvous" (ibid., p. 307). According to Lacan, fantasy is "the final term" and "prop" of desire (ibid., p. 309), and as such, desire finds its support in fantasy, "fantasy being the imaginary prop or substrate of desire" (ibid., p. 310). And Hamlet's desire is captured in the form of its reflection on the screen of his fantasy involving his relationship with Ophelia. Here, Lacan's formula for fantasy, ($\barred{S} \lozenge a$) or barred subject lozenge object a, stands for Hamlet's changing relationship with object Ophelia as the phallus:

> [I]n the articulation of fantasy, the object takes the place of what the subject is deprived of—namely, the phallus. It is owing to this that the object assumes

the function it has in fantasy, and that desire is constituted with fantasy as its prop.

(Ibid., p. 312)

Above all, in neurotic fantasy, the very basis of the subject's relations to his object is his relationship to time, which is the reason that the signification of the object must be sought out in neurosis not at the level of truth but at "the moment [*heure*] of truth" (ibid., pp. 314–315). Accordingly, the last stage of Hamlet's relationship with Ophelia will enable him to rush toward his final fatal rendezvous and his own time.

In order to explain the first stage of Hamlet's changing relationship with object Ophelia in his fantasy, Lacan takes us to the scene in which Hamlet meets Ophelia soon after his unsettling encounter with the Ghost. We learn about Hamlet's looks and state of mind from Ophelia's subsequent report to her father and brother. For Lacan, the terms in which she describes his behaviour are noteworthy:

> My lord, as I was sewing in my closet,
> Lord Hamlet, with his doublet all unbraced;
> No hat upon his head; his stockings foul'd,
> Ungarter'd, and down-gyved to his ankle;
> Pale as his shirt; his knees knocking each other;
> And with a look so piteous in purport
> As if he had been loosed out of hell
> To speak of horrors, he comes before me.
> . . .
> He took me by the wrist and held me hard.
> Then goes he to the length of all his arm,
> And, with his other hand thus o'er his brow,
> He falls to such perusal of my face
> As he would draw it.
> Long stay'd he so;
> At last, a little shaking of mine arm
> And thrice his head thus waving up and down,
> He raised a sigh so piteous and profound
> As it did seem to shatter all his bulk
> And end his being: that done, he lets me go,
> And, with his head over his shoulder turn'd,
> He seem'd to find his way without his eyes;
> For out o' doors he went without their helps,
> And, to the last, bended their light on me.
> (Shakespeare, 1603/1997, pp. 234–235)

Lacan describes Hamlet's experience as one of "depersonalization". Hamlet is "so sartorially disheveled" at this moment of pathological "subjective disorganization" due to his "experience of depersonalization" (Lacan, 2013/2019, p. 320). More specifically, Lacan finds the description, "[t]hen goes he to the length of all his arm" crucial and states:

> Hamlet's obvious scrutiny of Ophelia shows us Hamlet questioning the object, taking some distance with respect to the object as if to endeavor to identify it, something that has now become difficult for him, and vacillating in the presence of what had hitherto been a supremely exalted object to him. This gives us the first stage [*temps*] of the relation to the object, which involves, as it were, estrangement.
> (Ibid., p. 319)

We know that Ophelia was indeed a "supremely exalted object" to Hamlet prior to this moment, for Ophelia had earlier said to her father about Hamlet:

> He hath, my lord, of late made many tenders
> Of his affection to me.
> . . . he hath importuned me with love
> In honourable fashion.
> (Shakespeare, 1603/1997,
> pp. 204–205)

More pertinently, Hamlet had stated in one of his love-letters to Ophelia, read out for Gertrude and Claudius by Polonius:

> To the celestial and my soul's idol, the most
> beautified Ophelia—. . .
> these; in her excellent white bosom, these, &c. . . .
> Doubt thou the stars are fire;
> Doubt that the sun doth move;
> Doubt truth to be a liar;
> But never doubt I love.
> O dear Ophelia, I am ill at these numbers.
> I have not art to reckon my groans.
> But that I love thee best, O most best, believe it.
> Adieu.
> Thine evermore most dear lady, whilst this
> machine is to him, Hamlet.
> (Ibid., pp. 242–243)

After this episode, however, Ophelia "completely ceased to exist for him as a love object" (Lacan, 2013/2019, p. 320). Hamlet himself says to her a little later, "I did love you once" and then restates it as "I loved you not" (Shakespeare, 1603/1997, p. 282). This constitutes the first stage of the relation between the $barred{S}$ and the object *a* in Hamlet's fantasy, which is one of estrangement and distanciation of Ophelia as the object.

In the second stage of his changing relationship with object Ophelia in his fantasy, Hamlet's attitude toward Ophelia is sarcastic and full of "cruel aggression": "His cruel aggression, along with his highly sarcastic remarks, make these scenes with Ophelia among the strangest in classical literature" (Lacan, 2013/2019, p. 320). In the second stage, Hamlet treats Ophelia as a phallic object and rejects her because femininity degrades into maternity:

> [W]e see in the play . . . a horror of femininity as such, whose terms are articulated . . . by Hamlet himself. For he throws in Ophelia's face all the degrading, fickle, and corrupting possibilities linked to the unfolding of women's lives when they allow themselves to be dragged into all the acts that little by little make them into mothers—in the name of which Hamlet pushes Ophelia away in what seems to be a most sarcastic and cruel way.
>
> (Ibid., pp. 244–245)

Precisely put, Hamlet treats Ophelia as a debased phallic object in this stage:

> To Hamlet, Ophelia becomes a bearer of children and of sins of all ilks. She is doomed to engender sinners and to then have to succumb to all sorts of calumny. She becomes the pure and simple medium for a form of life that is, in its essence, now condemned. In short, what happens at this moment is the destruction or loss of the object, which is reintegrated into its narcissistic frame.
>
> To the subject, the object appears outside, as it were. . . . this object is equivalent to, what it takes the place of, and what cannot be given to the subject except at the moment at which he literally sacrifices himself, at which he is no longer it himself, at which he rejects it with his whole being. This object is clearly no other than the phallus.
>
> (Ibid., p. 321)

In this stage, therefore, insofar as Hamlet "externalizes and rejects" Ophelia for being a "signifying symbol of life", she is the phallus (ibid., p. 321). In this context, Lacan points to various words and expressions in the play that bring out the phallic status of Ophelia. Thus, Lacan cites Hamlet's words to Polonius: "Conception is a blessing, but, as your daughter may conceive—Friend, look to 't", and states that "[t]he entire dialogue with Ophelia shows that woman is conceptualized here only as carrying the vital turgescence that must be cursed and stopped up" (ibid., p. 321). That apart, Hamlet asks Ophelia to go to a nunnery four times:

> Get thee to a nunnery: why wouldst thou be a
> breeder of sinners? . . .
> Go thy ways to a nunnery. . . .
> Get thee to a nunnery, . . .
> To a nunnery, go . . .
> (Shakespeare, 1603/1997,
> pp. 282–283)

Lacan reminds us that "[a]s semantic usage shows, 'nunnery' could also at that time designate a brothel" (Lacan, 2013/2019, p. 321). Let us also recall in this context that Ophelia's prototype in Belleforest's version of "Hamlet" is a prostitute who loved him. Not only that, as Lacan points out, during the play scene, Hamlet says of Ophelia in her presence to his mother, "Here's metal more attractive" and asks her, "Lady, shall I lie in your lap?" (ibid., p. 321). Furthermore, Lacan draws our attention to the phallic connection of "dead men's fingers":

> [A]mong the flowers surrounding Ophelia as she drowns, there are "dead men's fingers" [IV, vii, 170], and explicit mention is made of the fact that they are called by a cruder name by common folk. The plant in question is *orchis mascula*, and it bears some relation to mandragora [or mandrake] and thus to the phallic element.
>
> (Ibid., p. 321–322)

Finally, with a bit of surprise that the psychoanalytically inspired readers of the play had never mentioned this, Lacan points out that Ophelia's name evokes the ancient Greek word "*omphalos*", meaning "navel" and related to "umbilical" (ibid., p. 318). In Gallagher's English translation of the seminar, the expression used in the place of *omphalos* is "*ho phallos*" (Lacan, 2002, p. 276). Thus, in the second stage, Hamlet rejects Ophelia as a phallic object.

In the third stage of the fantasy, Hamlet incorporates or reintegrates Ophelia in terms of mourning her death: "The object is reconquered here only at the price of mourning and death" (Lacan, 2013/2019, p. 322). Explaining this in detail, Lacan says that since no one ever experiences his own death, "[t]he truly intolerable dimension of human experience that comes with mourning" is the experience of the death of "another person" who is "essential to you", for such a loss constitutes a "*Verwerfung* [repudiation, foreclosure], a hole, [not in the symbolic] but in reality"; a hole that provides the place for the projection of the missing signifier. This missing signifier that is "essential to the structure of the Other" and whose absence "renders the Other unable to give you your answer", is essentially the veiled phallus that "[y]ou can only redeem . . . with your flesh and blood". Lacan thinks that in the final analysis, funeral rites are designed "[t]o propitiate [*satisfaire à*] . . . the memory of the departed" in terms of "the total, massive intervention, from hell to heaven, of the entire symbolic system [*jeu symbolique*]". Funeral rites thus have "a macrocosmic nature" since nothing other than "the totality of the signifier itself" is capable of filling "the hole in the real with signifiers". Therefore, mourning, first of all, presents itself as "a palliative for [*satisfaction donnée à*] the chaos that ensues owing to the inability of all signifying elements to deal with the hole in existence that has been created by someone's death". Mourning is able to act thus because "even the slightest case of mourning" invokes "[t]he entire signifying system" (ibid., pp. 336–337). Simply put, death creates a hole in the reality of the survivor, and this hole invites the invocation of the totality of the signifier, of the entire symbolic system, through the act of mourning so as to project the missing signifier, or the veiled phallus, at its place as a measure to cope with it.

Hamlet had acted "scornfully and cruelly" toward Ophelia and constantly subjected her to a "degrading, humiliating aggression" in the second stage, when she became for him "the very symbol of the rejection of his desire" (ibid., p. 335). Then, in the third stage, beginning in the graveyard scene in Act 5 Scene 1, when Hamlet saw Laertes mourning the death of Ophelia, whose body had just then been lowered into the grave, Hamlet leapt into it and rushed for Laertes' throat. We are struck by the fact that all of a sudden, the object Ophelia, in Lacan's words, "reassumes its full value to him" (ibid., p. 335). Hamlet challenges Laertes, saying:

> I loved Ophelia. Forty thousand brothers
> Could not with all their quantity of love
> Make up my sum. What wilt thou do for her?
> (Shakespeare, 1603/1997,
> pp. 391–392)

Thus, following her death, Ophelia suddenly takes on for Hamlet her immediacy and worth once again, which Lacan explains in terms of the obsessional's requirement that his desired object signifies impossibility:

> In short, it is to the extent to which Ophelia has become an impossible object that she once again becomes the object of his desire.... We believe we find ourselves here on a familiar path, where we can recognize one of the characteristics of the obsessive's desire....
> What characterizes the obsessive is not so much that the object of his desire is impossible, for there is always a note of impossibility in the object of desire, which has to do with the very structure and foundations of desire.... What specifically characterizes the obsessive is that he emphasizes the encounter with this impossibility. In other words, he orchestrates things in such a way that the object of his desire takes on the essential value of signifying this impossibility.
> (Lacan, 2013/2019, p. 335)

On the question of Hamlet's incorporation of Ophelia through mourning, Lacan reminds us that Freud, in *Mourning and Melancholia*, tried to define "the [kind of] identification involved in mourning, . . . most precisely by designating it as an incorporation" (ibid., p. 335). Thus, in the third stage, the subject identifies with the missing object through mourning and thereby reintegrates it. One sign of Hamlet's reintegration of the rejected object *a* is that he once again says here that he "loved Ophelia" after having said to her earlier, "I loved you not".

But what about the number "forty thousand" mentioned by Hamlet? Freud said in *The Psychopathology of Everyday Life* that arbitrarily made-up numbers are, in fact, strictly determined by some psychical logic:

> I have known for some time that one cannot make a number occur to one at one's own free choice any more than a name. Investigation of a number

made up in an apparently arbitrary manner—one, let us say, of several digits uttered by someone as a joke or in a moment of high spirits—reveals that it is strictly determined in a way that would really never have been thought possible.

(Freud, 1901/2001, p. 240)

Freud goes on to establish the validity of his view in terms of the analysis of the arbitrarily concocted figure of "2467" from one of his own letters, followed by the analysis of the number "1734" that Adler had heard from an informant and had passed on to him, (ibid., pp. 242–246) as well as a number of other examples in the twelfth chapter of the book (ibid., pp. 247–250). Randomly uttered numbers indeed seem to be psychically determined in a precise way in this case, too, for, on the question of honesty, Hamlet could be "one man picked out of" not ten thousand but forty thousand men (Shakespeare, 1603/1997, p. 246). More pertinently, Hamlet's "forty thousand" is exactly twice the number comprising Fortinbras' troop against Poland, "twenty thousand men" (ibid., p. 346), that had strongly aroused Hamlet's sense of honour.

The changing relation between the $barred{S}$ and the object a that is projected on the veil of Hamlet's fantasy in these three stages at once masks and reveals the lack in the Other. It moreover offers a precise reflection of the three "times" of Hamlet's Oedipus complex, insofar as the Oedipus complex is about the changing relation between the barred subject and the phallic object in terms of the three times chronologically marked by the following questions and resolution: To be or not to be the maternal phallus? To have or not to have the phallus? To have the phallus by not having it (Lacan, 1998/2017, pp. 163–196). We find the support of Hamlet's Oedipal desire for Gertrude in his fantasy involving Ophelia.

Above all, Hamlet's genuine scuffle with Laertes inside Ophelia's grave is structurally related to their supposedly sham fencing contest that takes place toward the end of the play. Although the "first manifestation of Hamlet's rivalry with Laertes is far more authentic than the second" (Lacan, 2013/2019, p. 334), they are interrelated. As a matter of fact, Shakespeare's invention of this "furious battle at the bottom of a grave", which is not present in any of the earlier versions of the legend, is designed not only to depict Hamlet's re-conquest of Ophelia as the object by mourning her death but also to make "something occur": "We should highlight here a connection between what presents itself as a reintegration of a and Hamlet's possibility of finishing things off [or: coming full circle, *boucler la boucle*]—in other words, of finally running headlong toward his destiny" (ibid., p. 322). Simply put, his scuffle with Laertes at the cemetery enabled Hamlet, who had lost the way to his desire, to rediscover his desire and to rush toward his final rendezvous and his own hour at last as a result of the rediscovery.

Shedding further light on this, Lacan specifies that in the course of Hamlet's mourning and physical tussle with Laertes, something all of a sudden grabs Hamlet, which ultimately enables him to fight and to kill—acts that he had been unable to perform until that point despite wanting to:

> Why did Hamlet decide to jump in? Because he could not bear to see someone other than himself showing everyone what? Overflowing grief. . . .
>
> > The bravery of his grief did put me
> > Into a tow'ring passion.
> >   [V, ii, 78–9]
>
> . . . The backdrop is this scene in which Hamlet suddenly sees the passionate relationship of a subject with an object, this relationship being manifested by someone else [Laertes]. This scene grabs him and offers him a prop by which his own relationship as a subject, $ with Ophelia—little object a, which had been rejected owing to the confusion or compounding of objects—is suddenly re-established.
>
> And it is this suddenly re-established level that is momentarily going to make a man of him. It is, in other words, going to make him into someone capable—for only a brief moment, no doubt, but a moment that suffices for the play to end—of fighting and killing.
>
>   (Ibid., pp. 288–289)

The Three Identifications of Hamlet

Hamlet makes three crucial identifications around his two fights with Laertes. These identifications respectively enable Hamlet to renew his desire, whose track he had lost, to discover his desire in its totality for the first time, and to possess the phallus that he did not have. These identifications, in turn, empower him to accomplish his mission by avenging his father. He makes the first two identifications at the time of his first fight with Laertes.

Hamlet's first identification is his imaginary identification with Laertes as his ideal ego. In his paper, "The Mirror Stage as Formative of the *I* Function as Revealed in Psychoanalytic Experience", whose first version was presented in 1936 and which constitutes the first of Lacan's many major original contributions to psychoanalysis, Lacan offers the psychoanalytic theory of the genesis of the ego and explains why the "*I* function" in psychoanalysis is at odds with the Cartesian *cogito*. According to Lacan, the self or the ego comes into being, and the human being thereby enters the imaginary order when a human baby, who is roughly between 6 and 18 months old, recognises its mirror image as its own and identifies with it by assuming, as in putting on, the image. The ego is thus the other of the mirror image that is often referred to as a "semblable" by Lacan. However, since the baby is unable to stand upright or to control its bodily movements at this stage owing to its vital insufficiency or real physical deficiency, the image of the body that the baby identifies with is one that is more complete, competent, and in control over its movements than what its real body lacking in motor functions truly is at this time. This, in turn, makes the identification itself anticipatory and, therefore, anachronistic, which has extraordinary consequences. Lacan names the more perfect mirror image with which the baby identifies in order to make the birth of the ego possible, the ideal ego. He further indicates that the ego strongly loves and hates the ideal ego, for the baby at once adores its mirror image and hates it to the point of wanting to kill it or wishing it was dead (Lacan, 1949/2006). Thus, the ideal ego is at once an admirable and a detestable other, which is the basis of the psychoanalytic notion of aggressiveness (Lacan, 1948/2006). In the seminar on *Hamlet,* as well as elsewhere, Lacan compares the aggressive tension between the ego and the ideal ego in the imaginary order to the fight between the two self-consciousness in Hegel's master-slave dialectic, which is a fight unto death for power, mastery, and pure prestige (Lacan, 2013/2019, p. 329). In this context, Lacan equates Hamlet's identification with Laertes in the present seminar with the ego's identification with the ideal ego for the reasons that Hamlet admires Laertes as a superior swordsman; he considers him an admirable rival he must kill or be killed by, and aggressively engages him in a fight unto death for the sake of honour that, unlike Hegel's master and slave who are both alive at the end of the contest, leaves both of them dead. Thus, Lacan explains Hamlet's mourning and physical tussle with Laertes in terms of the narcissistic relation between the ego and the ideal ego in the mirror stage.

> Hamlet sees Laertes jump into the grave in order to embrace his sister, and he jumps in after him to do the same. . . . Stated otherwise, Hamlet proceeds by the pathway of mourning, but it is a type of mourning that is adopted in the narcissistic relationship that obtains between . . . the ego, and the image of the other.
>
> (Ibid., p. 288)

Shakespeare's depiction of Hamlet's identification with Laertes is, therefore, already remarkable for its similarities with the ego's imaginary identification with the ideal ego discussed by Lacan. However, Hamlet's identification with Laertes is rendered particularly stunning owing to the two words employed by Shakespeare to describe it, albeit within a parody, over and above all the other details—"semblable" and "mirror"—words that directly align this identification with Lacan's teaching and diction on the imaginary:

> We cannot fail to dwell for a moment on the sureness of the connection established by Shakespeare, for you recognize in it an element that has long been part of our discourse and dialogue here—namely, the mirror stage. It is expressly stated in the text that Laertes is, at this level, a semblable for Hamlet. He is indirectly Hamlet's semblable—at least within a parody.
>
> I am referring to the response he makes to Osric, the . . . courtesan. Coming to Hamlet to propose that he participate in a duel, Osric highlights the outstanding

skill of the adversary to whom Hamlet will have to prove his mettle. Hamlet cuts him off and ups the ante. . . .

And he gives an extremely precious, complicated speech that in some sense parodies the style of his interlocutor, before concluding,

> I take him to be a soul of
> great article, and his infusion of
> such dearth and rareness, as, to make true diction of him,
> his semblable is his mirror, and who else would trace
> him, his umbrage, nothing more.
> [V, ii, 115–119]

In short, regarding Laertes' qualities, Hamlet refers to the other's image as something that cannot fail to be completely absorbing to he who contemplates it. All of this is puffed up in a highly Gongoresque manner, in the fullest sense of the word *concetto*, and it is with this same attitude and on the same ground that Hamlet meets Laertes prior to the duel. It is quite significant that the playwright situates the manifest point of aggressiveness at the height of imaginary absorption, formally articulated as a specular, mirror relationship.

The person we most admire is the one we are battling. He who is my ideal ego is also he who must be killed, according to Hegel's formulation regarding the impossibility of our coexisting.

(Ibid., pp. 329–330)

Above all, in Laertes as the other, Lacan adds, Hamlet found a rival who was equivalent, or more than equivalent, to him, and thus allowed him to uphold his end of the human wager and be a man:

> Hamlet, for whom men and women are no longer anything but insubstantial and putrid shadows, finds a worthy rival in this remodeled semblable, whose presence allows him, at least for a moment, to uphold the human wager [*soutenir la gageure humaine*] that he, too, is a man.

(Ibid., p. 333)

At almost the same time, Hamlet makes a second identification, a symbolic identification with a symbolic aspect of himself, in answer to his own question: Who is mourning the death of Ophelia?

> What is he whose grief
> Bears such an emphasis? whose phrase of sorrow
> Conjures the wandering stars, and makes them stand
> Like wonder-wounded hearers? This is I,
> Hamlet the Dane.
> (Shakespeare, 1603/1997, pp. 390–391)

Lacan states that Hamlet emerges as a different man following his embrace with Laertes—who is Hamlet's support and example—inside Ophelia's grave, in the sense that he is able to lay hold of his desire once again:

> Shakespeare . . . included, in the play's articulation, an odd character like Laertes in order to have him serve—at the crucial moment of the play, at its climax—the role of an example and prop. Hamlet furiously wrestles him to the ground, and gets him into a hold from which he literally leaves other than before, with the cry . . . : "This is I, Hamlet the Dane" [V, i, 245] . . . [T]his is the moment at which something happens that allows Hamlet to take hold of his desire anew.
> (Lacan, 2013/2019, p. 289)

Stating it in more precise terms, Lacan says that Hamlet, in the course of mourning the death of Ophelia—that is, $, in a relationship with a—quite unexpectedly identifies with his Danish identity for the first time in the play, and thereby discovers his desire in its totality, too, for the first time in the play:

> Hamlet, who has just returned unexpectedly, thanks to the pirates who allowed him to foil the plot to assassinate him, happens upon Ophelia's burial. He has not yet heard about her death; he did not know what had happened during his brief absence. We see Laertes clawing at his own chest, and jumping into the grave in order to embrace his sister's cadaver one last time, loudly proclaiming his despair.
>
> Not only can Hamlet not stand this display of grief over the loss of a girl whom he had clearly mistreated up until then, but he throws himself into the grave with Laertes after having truly bellowed, having given a war cry in which he says the most unexpected thing: who is grieving the death of this young girl? And he concludes, "This is I, Hamlet the Danc" [V, i, 244–5].
>
> No one has ever heard him claim that he was Danish. He abhors the Danish! Suddenly, a revolution takes place in him owing to something that is highly significant . . . It is insofar as $ is there in a certain relationship with little a that he suddenly identifies with something that for the very first time makes him find his desire in its totality.
> (Ibid., p. 267)

Hamlet's symbolic identification with his Danish identity is, in fact, an identification with a signifier that, from the moment of the identification on, enters into a special relationship with the subject. Above all, Hamlet is able to take hold of his desire, whose path he had lost, as well as to discover his desire in its totality for the first time, following this identification at the height of his scuffle with Laertes inside Ophelia's grave.

Hamlet's third and most crucial identification, one which takes place in the course of the tournament, is with the signifier of lack in the Other, or the phallus.

Lacan says that the distinguishing sign of Hamlet as the barred subject is that he did not have the phallus when he set out for the tournament: "he does not enter the game with his phallus" (ibid., p. 330). Lacan further clarifies that the phallus that Hamlet did not have could appear only with the subject's disappearance, which means Hamlet must first be mortally wounded by the phallic object, by the mortal phallus, before he could have access to it as the weapon that will help him complete his act: "The phallus cannot assume its formal function except with the disappearance of the subject himself. What makes it possible for the subject to succumb even before taking in hand the foil with which he himself becomes a killer?" (ibid., p. 333). Why is the subject's disappearance a necessary precondition for the phallus to become operative? Well, this is so because the phallus gets its value from the subject's narcissistic demand, as correctly explained by Freud: "Freud... presents the subject's narcissistic demand [*exigence*] as one of its fundamental mainsprings, insofar as this demand is what gives the phallus its value, which is precisely what we are seeking" (ibid., p. 346). Since the phallus gets its value from the narcissistic demand of the subject, Hamlet will have access to the phallus, or the instrument with which he would be able to complete his act, only after he has overcome all his narcissistic demands and attachments in terms of the awareness of his imminent death. Hamlet will be able to possess the phallus and act with it only after he knows he is mortally wounded and is as good as dead, which is an awareness that lies beyond all narcissistic ties with oneself:

> It is the phallus that is at stake here. Which is why Hamlet can never reach it until the moment at which he has sacrificed—in spite of himself, moreover—his entire narcissistic attachment. It is only when he is fatally wounded, and knows that he is, that he can perform the action that lays Claudius low.
>
> (Ibid., p. 353)

In "The Seminar on 'The Purloined Letter'", where the letter symbolises the phallus, Lacan has already illustrated that the letter/phallus "will be *and* will not be where it is wherever it goes". Similarly, he shows in the present seminar how, in Act 5 Scene 2 of the play, the phallus is there in spite of not being there. Lacan gives due credit to the combination of "the scriptwriter's gall" and "the playwright's formidable intuition" for the depiction of the absence of the phallus and states:

> During the fight, the poisoned weapon changes hands, God only knows how. This must be one of the difficulties of the staging, and the scriptwriter does not work terribly hard to explain it to us. After Laertes has dealt Hamlet the blow from which he cannot recover, from which he must perish, there is a sort of scuffle in which they are grappling with each other, and a few moments later the poisoned rapier is in Hamlet's hand. No one gives much thought to explaining how such an astonishing switch can occur.
>
> No one need, moreover, give it any thought, for what is at stake is to show that the instrument of death, the instrument that kills—which is in this case the

most veiled instrument of the drama, one which Hamlet can only receive from the other—lies elsewhere than in what can be represented materially here. For the accomplishment of Hamlet's desire does not take place at the level of the skill displayed [or: parrying, *parade*] in the contest, at the level of the rivalry with he who is his semblable, albeit more handsome than him, the rivalry with the *himself* [*moi-même*] that he can love. The drama is played out beyond that. And the phallus is what lies beyond that.

(Ibid., pp. 330–331)

However, Lacan explains how, despite thus being absent, the phallus is not only present in this very scene, but Hamlet identifies with it in the course of the same encounter with Laertes. It is present here as the "fatal signifier" in the pun on the word "foil":

The King mentions foils when they are handed out: "Give them the foils, young Osric" [V, ii, 248]. Before that, Hamlet had said, "Give us the foils." But, in between these two occurrences of the word, Hamlet makes a pun:

I'll be your foil, Laertes. In mine ignorance
Your skill shall, like a star i' th' darkest night,
Stick fiery off indeed.
[V, ii, 244–246]

. . . "Foil" cannot mean rapier [alone] here. It had another perfectly well-known meaning at the time, which was even rather frequently used: "foil" . . . is used preciously to designate the foil leaf in which something precious is carried—that is, a case or setting [*écrin*].

In short, Hamlet says, in fighting with you, Laertes, I will be your setting, I will merely highlight "your star-like brightness in the dark sky". These are, moreover, the very conditions on which the duel was accepted. Hamlet, who is thought to have no chance of winning, will be proclaimed the winner if, in the course of twelve passes, his opponent does not hit him three times more than he hits his opponent. . . . Hamlet is thus given a handicap.

. . . The pun involving "foil" is not included here by accident, and it is justifiable to explore what is included in its depths. When he says to Laertes "I'll be your foil," Hamlet uses a word that also means rapier. The subject thus identifies with the mortal phallus itself here. "I'll be your foil," he says to Laertes, "to showcase your skill," but a moment later Laertes' sword strikes, the sword that fatally wounds Hamlet before he himself has it in hand and completes his trajectory by killing both his opponent and he who is the final object of his mission—namely, the king.

(Ibid., pp. 331–332)

In short, the phallus is there in the text in spite of not being there because, while the stage direction of the scene indicates that the phallus lies beyond the stage, beyond representation, and therefore, it is missing from the action on the stage and is not present there, the phallus is nevertheless very much present in this very scene at the level of language, of wit, in the form of the pun on the word "foil".

Thus, Hamlet's pun on the word "foil" in his remark to Laertes, "I'll be your foil", where the word "foil" at once stands for backdrop and fencing foil, indicates his third and most crucial identification, which is his identification with the signifier that he did not so far have, in the form of his identification with the mortal phallus, or the poisoned foil with which he will accomplish his act. All in all, Hamlet's encounter with Laertes enables him to identify himself with the phallus as the mortal signifier that would eventually help him complete his task.

Hamlet is ultimately able to complete his act by killing Claudius after securing access to the mortal phallus at the cost of his life. Hamlet came to know that he held a poisoned foil in his hand exactly when he came to know that he had already been mortally wounded by it, which forcefully took him beyond all narcissistic attachments that had held him back from completing his act of revenge. Thus, Hamlet had to purchase his phallus with his life. It could appear in his hand, but not before he was about to disappear. However, as soon as he had access to the phallus, it was his hour, albeit a very brief hour. This brief hour of Hamlet is his time. He, at last, entered the time that was exclusively his and no one else's. And Hamlet, like the three prisoners in Lacan's essay on logical time, at once rushes to conclude (Lacan, 1945/2006, pp. 164, 168). It is noteworthy that Hamlet wasted absolutely no time in accomplishing his act when it was his time immediately following his possession of the phallus toward the end of the play.

The Dissolution of the Oedipus Complex in *Hamlet*

The Oedipus complex has its moment of inception, its period of blossoming, and its time of decline or dissolution. The Oedipus complex is never perfectly dissolved, however. Bits and pieces of its unresolved remnants stay on and stage a return in terms of neurotic symptoms at puberty. The third and final stage of the Oedipus complex, namely, the stage of its dissolution, makes human sexuality civilised in terms of the subject's renunciation of instinctual—as in phallic—gratification from the mother's body and its accession to the laws of the family and of the society. The subject does not renounce such instinctual gratification until it confronts the threat of castration from both the father and the mother, albeit in different ways, and is well and truly not left with any avenue of escape. Freud discusses the stage of the decline of the Oedipus complex in his essay titled "The Dissolution of the Oedipus Complex" (Freud, 1924/2001). Freud further explains in *Totem and Taboo* that the subject accedes to the locus of the law in terms of the murder of the father of the primal horde (Freud, 1912/2001). In Lacanian parlance, the third time of the Oedipus complex is about having the phallus in terms of the essential prior recognition that it cannot be had. It is a question of the structuring of the subject's desire in terms of the significant substitution of the Name-of-the-Father for the desire of the mother in the paternal metaphor. Lacan discusses the resonances of these two aspects of the dissolution of the Oedipus complex—the sacrifice of the phallus and accession to the law in terms of parricide—in *Hamlet* in the present seminar.

Lacan raises the question of the talk about lack of mourning throughout the play: "[P]eople talk about nothing but mourning from one end of *Hamlet* to the other" (Lacan, 2013/2019, p. 339). To be precise, Lacan means "inadequate mourning", for the play is indeed full of that. Hamlet's father's death was not mourned adequately because of Gertrude's over-hasty remarriage. Hamlet's father himself thinks that he died in the blossoms of his sin and carried an inexpiable grievance for being deprived of the opportunity to repent or say his last prayers: "Before his death, the father did not have time to prepare himself to appear at the Last Judgment" (ibid., p. 340). Polonius' death could not be mourned properly because his body was hidden away by Hamlet. His body "is buried secretly, quickly, and unceremoniously for political reasons" (ibid., p. 340). And Ophelia's burial rituals were truncated by the priests because of her death by suicide. Lacan says: "Thus we cannot fail to be struck by the fact that, in all the major instances of mourning that are called into question in *Hamlet*, what we always find is that the rituals have been abbreviated or carried out clandestinely" (ibid., p. 340).

Lacan states that all these indications of the lack of mourning in the play imply that the play is stuck in the final stage of the Oedipus complex that Freud called the stage of its "dissolution", giving the phallus the status of something that is rotting: "The 'something rotten' [I, iv, 90] that poor Hamlet needs to set right is closely related to his position as a subject with respect to the phallus" (ibid., p. 351). The Oedipus complex does not properly go into its decline, and the phallus continues to rot until the loss of the phallus is mourned: "[t]he Oedipus complex begins to dissolve when the subject . . . mourn[s] the loss of the phallus" (ibid., p. 345).

The dissolution of the Oedipus complex is moreover related to the renewal or rebirth of the order of the law whose primordial foundation takes place in terms of the primal murder of the father as an essential prerequisite. Lacan first points to the importance of the relation between the primal murder and the inauguration of the primal law in Freud:

> Freud's myth . . . *Totem and Taboo* . . . indicates to us the early, essential, and altogether necessary link that is such that we cannot conceptualize the law, as an order, except on the basis of a still earlier fact that presents itself as a crime. This is the meaning of Freud's myth. The crime is the primal killing of the father. In Freud's view, it forms, let us note, the horizon or endpoint of the problem of origins in all psychoanalytic matters, for Freud finds it everywhere and no topic seems to him to have been exhausted if it has not yet been connected up with it. It is all too obvious that this primal killing of the father has a mythical necessity for him, whether he situates it at the origin of the primal horde or at the origin of the Judaic tradition.
>
> (Ibid., pp. 341–342)

Lacan then explains how the order of the primal law, thus founded in terms of a crime, is renewed by every individual. He states that every individual accomplishes the rebirth of the law by reproducing the elements of incest and parricide of the Oedipal drama as desires, adding that this rebirth takes place at a tragic level because the reproduction of the Oedipal drama ends in "castration" as an essential element, one that is not adequately illuminated by the myth of the primal murder and the primal law:

> The relationship between the primal law and the primal crime is one thing; the drama that shapes the Oedipus complex is another. By this, I mean what happens when the tragic hero—who is Oedipus, but who is also, virtually, each of us at some point of our being when we reproduce the Oedipal drama—kills his father and sleeps with his mother, accomplishing at the tragic level, in a sort of lustral bath, the rebirth of the law.
>
> Oedipus corresponds perfectly to the definition I just gave of ritual reproduction of the myth. Oedipus is, in short, completely innocent and unconscious. He repeats—unbeknownst to himself, in the sort of dream his life consists of, "Life is a dream"—actions that run from the crime to the restoring of order and the punishment he administers to himself, which makes him seem castrated to us at the end.
>
> This castration is the essential element to take into account, and it remains veiled when one confines oneself to the level at which we see the genesis of the primal murder. In the final analysis, the meaning that shines through is that this punishment, sanction, or castration contains its result—namely, the humanization of man's sexuality—within itself, under lock and key. It is a key that we, owing to our practice, are in the habit of using in order to account for all the incidents that arise in the course of the unfolding of desire.
>
> (Ibid., pp. 342)

Castration, which brings about the dissolution of the Oedipus complex, encloses within itself the humanisation of sexuality produced by it. Such locked-up, humanised sexuality accounts not only for the civilised sexual morality of human beings and all the psychopathology that comes with it but for all the incidents arising during the unfolding of their desires as they grow up.

In order to pinpoint the specificity of the crime described in *Hamlet*, Lacan goes on to differentiate it from the crime described in *Oedipus Rex*. Let us conclude the chapter by examining Lacan's discussion on the differences between these two tragedies.

Differences between *Oedipus Rex* and *Hamlet*

The differences between *Oedipus Rex* and *Hamlet* are important because, as Freud said, they have their roots in the same soil. *Hamlet* is an Oedipal play. Lacan rightly states that Freud compared "the homologous threads" in *Oedipus Rex* and *Hamlet* in order to identify the "correlated modifications" in the second play around these threads (Lacan, 2013/2019, p. 242). In "Dostoevsky and Parricide", Freud points to three such differential relations between the two plays. To begin with, whereas in *Oedipus Rex*, Oedipus himself commits the crimes of killing his father and marrying his mother, in *Hamlet*, these crimes are not committed by Hamlet. Moreover, for Claudius, who committed the crimes of killing Hamlet's father and marrying his mother, they are not acts of incest or parricide. Second, whereas in *Oedipus Rex*, the sexual rivalry between Oedipus and Laius is completely disguised, the sexual rivalry between Hamlet and Claudius for Gertrude in *Hamlet* is completely undisguised. And third, whereas Oedipus' Oedipal wishes are depicted directly in *Oedipus Rex*, in *Hamlet*, Hamlet's Oedipal wishes are depicted indirectly, in terms of the effect of Claudius' crime on him; that is, in terms of Hamlet's reaction to Claudius' fulfilment of Hamlet's Oedipal wishes (Freud, 1928/2001, pp. 188–189).

Taking Freud's project further ahead, Lacan points to a number of other differential relations between the two plays. In the first place, "[i]n *Oedipus*, the crime occurs during the hero's generation. In *Hamlet*, it occurs in the prior generation" (Lacan, 2013/2019, p. 342). That apart,

> In *Oedipus*, the crime is committed when the hero does not know what he is doing and is in some sense guided by *fatum* [fate]. In *Hamlet*, the crime is committed in a deliberate manner, since it is committed through treachery. In *Hamlet*, the crime catches its victim, Hamlet's father, while he is sleeping.
>
> (Ibid., p. 342).

Differently put, whereas the crime of killing the old man in the Greek tragedy is somewhat unintended, governed by fate and not treachery, the crime in *Hamlet* is the result of treachery, as Hamlet's father is poisoned in his sleep by his brother. In addition, in *Oedipus Rex*, the Oedipal crime is initially unknown to the perpetrator, Oedipus, as well as to the other citizens, all of whom came to know about it later. However, in that play, the Oedipal crime remained unknown to the victim, Laius, forever because he never came to know that he was killed by his son. In *Hamlet*, by contrast, the Oedipal crime is known not only to the perpetrator, Claudius, but also to the victim, King Hamlet, who moreover informs his son, Prince Hamlet. Thus, the Oedipal crime may be said to have been committed unconsciously by Oedipus in *Oedipus Rex*, while the Oedipal crime is committed consciously by Claudius in *Hamlet*:

> [I]n *Hamlet* . . . the father quite clearly knows that he is dead as his brother Claudius wished, Claudius having wanted to take his place. The crime is not hidden from him, but from the world, a world that is represented on the stage. . . . It is significant that the fable is designed in such a way that the father does know. This is an absolutely essential element, and it constitutes a major difference in thread with respect to the first major tale, the tragedy of *Oedipus*. Oedipus

does not know. But once he does, once he has discovered everything, the drama moves into high gear, and continues right up to his self-punishment . . . But the Oedipal crime is committed by Oedipus unwittingly [or unconsciously] [*dans l'inconscience*]. In *Hamlet*, the Oedipal crime is known, and it is known to its victim, a victim who emerges in order to bring it to the subject's awareness [*connaissance*].

(Ibid., pp. 241–242)

In other words, whereas Oedipus did not know who killed Laius and Laius did not know that his aggressor was his son, both Senior Hamlet and the Prince knew it all. This means that whereas Oedipus had a question without an answer—who killed Laius?—until the end of the play, Hamlet had the answer to the question as to who killed his father right at the start of the play: "In *Hamlet*, the question is resolved—the father knew. And because he knew, Hamlet also knows. In other words, he has the answer" (ibid., p. 297). In this context, Lacan further clarifies that unlike in *Oedipus Rex*, in *Hamlet*, the father reveals the truth of his death, even though his knowledge of it is arbitrarily attributed to him:

For if the father, who had fallen asleep in the garden, was laid low by having this delicate juice, hebenon, poured into his ear . . . he should not have been aware of it. We are never told that he woke up from his sleep to observe what was happening, and the scurf patches that covered his body were never seen by any but those who discovered his corpse. We must then assume that people in the hereafter are very well informed about how they got there. Although this might, in theory, be possible, it is nevertheless not something that we must immediately consider to be true. I am saying all of this to underscore the arbitrary nature of the father's initial revelation, the revelation that gives the entire plot of *Hamlet* its impetus.

(Ibid., p. 296)

Not only that but since Oedipus did not know, his castration, in the form of his self-blinding, is direct and prompt. By contrast, since both Hamlet and his father were in the know, castration comes about slowly and in zigzagging or roundabout ways in Shakespeare's play:

It is precisely because something—namely, castration—is missing in the original, initial situation of the drama of *Hamlet*, insofar as it is distinct from that of Oedipus, that things present themselves in the play in the form of a slow zigzagging progression, following many a detour, a slow birthing of the necessary castration.

It is precisely because something finally becomes equivalent to what was missing, because something finally is realized, that Hamlet takes the final action to which he succumbs [and completes his act].

(Ibid., p. 248)

Also, as Lacan says, unlike Oedipus, who carried out the murder without thinking about it, Hamlet is required to listen and talk before he can act:

> I have already drawn your attention to an essential element that is constitutive of the structure of the Oedipus myth: Oedipus did not have to go back and forth dozens of times before taking action; he did so even before thinking about it and without even knowing he was doing it.
>
> (Ibid., p. 296)

Besides, unlike in the usual Oedipal situation—not in *Oedipus Rex* as such—where the father functions as an authority of sanction from the locus of the Other, the father in *Hamlet* reveals himself from the very beginning as the barred Other:

> In the father's message, with which the drama begins, we see the Other present himself in the most signifying form as a barred A. He has been wiped away not only from the surface of the living, but from the recompense that should have been his. The crime sent him into the bowels of hell—in other words, he has a debt that he has been unable to pay, an unatonable debt, as he puts it. To his son, this is the most horrible and anxiety-provoking meaning of the father's revelation.
>
> (Ibid., p. 343)

Moreover, whereas Oedipus had settled his family debt, Hamlet's father must complain forever that he has been irredeemably denied the opportunity to settle his debt:

> Returning to the case of Oedipus, we see that he himself paid. He presents himself as someone who shoulders the burden of the discharged debt in his destiny as a hero. What Hamlet's father shall complain of for all eternity is that the thread of his destiny was interrupted and broken, such that he will never be able to answer for it.
>
> (Ibid., p. 343)

Furthermore, while Oedipus' act sustains his life, Hamlet is guilty of being from the very beginning. Therefore, whereas the Oedipal drama is opened at the end of *Oedipus Rex*, the Oedipal drama is open right from the beginning of *Hamlet*, offering Hamlet the choice between being and not being. And it is precisely because there is established this either/or in terms of this being/not being that he is taken up into the chain of the signifier, making him a victim of his choice no matter what he chose:

> Hamlet's action is not the same as that of Oedipus. Oedipus' action sustained Oedipus' life. It made him into the hero he was prior to his fall, while he knew nothing. It gave the story's conclusion its dramatic character. Hamlet, on the

other hand, knows that he is guilty for being. It is unbearable to him to be. Well before the beginning of the drama, Hamlet knows what it means to have committed the crime of existing. It is on the basis of this beginning that he finds himself faced with a choice, a choice in which the problem of existence arises in his own terms—namely, "To be, or not to be," which irremediably involves him in being, as he quite clearly articulates.

It is precisely because, in *Hamlet*, the Oedipal drama is there at the beginning and not at the end that a choice is offered to the hero between *being* and *not being*. The very fact that there is this *either/or* proves that he is caught up in the signifying chain, in what makes it such that he is in any case a victim of this choice.

(Ibid., pp. 245–246)

Finally, unlike in *Oedipus Rex*, where the phallus is gone following the father's murder, in *Hamlet*, the phallus is still there, embodied by Claudius, even after the murder of the father:

We cannot fail to connect this up with an obvious fact in the tragedy of *Hamlet*, and one that distinguishes it from the Oedipal tragedy: after the father has been killed, the phallus is still there.

It is quite plainly there, for it is Claudius who is given the task of embodying it. What is constantly at stake is Claudius' real phallus. In short, Hamlet has nothing else to reproach his mother for than to have gotten herself filled up by it the minute his father disappeared. And he ends up sending her back, with discouraged arm and speech, to this fatal and fateful object which is quite real here. The whole drama seems to revolve around this.

. . . It seems that Hamlet's action revolves and hesitates around this point. Here his "daunted genius" trembles, as it were, before something completely unexpected.

For the phallus is in an entirely ectopic position here with respect to the Oedipal position as it is articulated by psychoanalysis. The phallus is clearly real here; it is in this respect that it is important to strike it, and Hamlet always balks at doing so. His uncertainty and hesitation before the object that must be struck is manifest at the moment at which he finds our Claudius praying and says to himself that he could obviously kill him: "Now might I do it pat" [III, iii, 73]. The precise mainspring of what constantly deflects Hamlet's arm is the very narcissistic link that Freud tells us about in "The Dissolution of the Oedipus Complex." One cannot strike the phallus because, even if it is clearly real, it is but a shadow [*ombre*].

(Ibid., p. 352)

The real phallus is a shadow or a ghost—the French word "*ombre*" stands for both—in the sense that "erection" is akin to a shadow or a ghost. In the play, however, this means that the real phallus is a thing of nothing. In fact, it is because the phallus is a shadow that "what he [Hamlet] must strike is something other than what is there" (ibid., p. 353). This would explain why Hamlet did not strike Claudius when the latter was praying, although he had the reason and the opportunity to do so, and why he did strike the invisible object moving behind the arras only a few moments later, although he had neither the reason nor the opportunity to kill Polonius. Lacan identifies this shadow-like phallus in Hamlet's riddles and in the style of his speech. For an example of this, he points out that Hamlet is least affected by the assassination of Polonius, whom he considered "a 'calf,' a 'capital . . . calf' [III, ii, 101–2] . . . offered up as a sacrifice to his father's manes". He casually shoves Polonius' corpse in a "closet under the stairs", and when others ask him what is going on, he comes up with one such riddle or joke that his enemies always find highly disconcerting (ibid., p. 353):

> Hamlet thus says the following things, which have remained up until now quite perplexing to commentators. "The body is with the king"—please note that he does not use the word "corpse," he says "body"—"but the king is not with the body" [IV, ii, 26–7]. I would ask you to simply replace the word "king" with the word "phallus" to realize that it is the phallus that is involved here. For the body is tightly bound up in this business of the phallus, but on the other hand the phallus is bound to nothing and always slips between your fingers.
>
> Immediately thereafter, he adds, "The king is a thing—" "A thing, my lord?" his interlocutors ask [IV, ii, 27–8], completely shocked as they are whenever he comes out with one of his aphorisms, and Hamlet replies, "Of nothing" [29].
>
> (Ibid., pp. 353–354)

With reference to the "thing" and "nothing" with which Hamlet refers to the phallus, Lacan points out that in one of his sonnets, Shakespeare had, in fact, dared to point to the phallus in relation to his desire for the Earl of Essex with the help these very words:

> An attentive reading of the *Sonnets* inclines me to believe that, in his own life, Shakespeare was imbued with a rather extreme and peculiar desire. Somewhere, in one of the sonnets, whose audacity we can hardly imagine . . . he speaks to his love object who, as everyone knows, was of the same sex as him, quite a charming young man, it seems, who appears to have been the Earl of Essex. Your looks leave nothing to be desired, he says to this young man; you look like a woman in every regard; there is but "one thing" that nature wanted to give you, God only knows why, and I unfortunately could not care less about this little thing: it is "to my purpose nothing." Too bad it delights women. And Shakespeare adds, oh well, as long as "Mine be thy love, and thy love's use their treasure."
>
> (Ibid., p. 354)

Lacan is referring to Sonnet XX, whose first line is: "A woman's face with nature's own hand painted". The operative lines are:

> Till nature as she wrought thee fell a-doting,
> And by addition me of thee defeated
> By adding one thing to my purpose nothing.
> But since she pricked thee out for women's pleasure,
> Mine be thy love and thy love's use their treasure.
> (Shakespeare, 1609/1978, p. 1073)

Hamlet anticipatorily offers the phallus its precise psychoanalytic definition—thing of nothing—which is exactly how Shakespeare happened to define it himself. In terms of making this point, however, Lacan effectively contradicts himself by reading Shakespeare's sonnet, and through it some of Hamlet's riddles, psycho-biographically.

Notes

1 Freud's six relatively long discussions on *Hamlet* may be found in *The Origins of Psychoanalysis* (1897), *The Interpretation of Dreams* (1899), the 1905–1906 book *Psychopathic Characters on Stage* published posthumously in 1942, *An Autobiographical Study* (1924), "Dostoevsky and Parricide" (1927), and *An Outline of Psychoanalysis* (1938).
2 In *All's Well that Ends Well*, written a few years later, the First Lord describes sexual desire as a "rebellion" (IV, iii, 13–18) (Shakespeare, 1623/1978, p. 289).
3 Speaking on the traits of neurosis displayed by the character of Hamlet, Lacan says that Hamlet's desire gives us a complete picture of the neurotic's desire, for it gives us "the neurotic's desire at every moment of its impact [*incidence*]" (Lacan, 2013/2019, p. 289). This means Hamlet's desire is both obsessional, because it rests on an impossible desire, and hysterical, because it creates an unsatisfied desire. To that, Lacan adds:

> People have said that Hamlet's desire is an hysteric's desire. This is perhaps quite true. Other people have said that it is an obsessive's desire. That, too, might be argued, for it is a fact that he is full of psychasthenic symptoms, even severe ones. But that is not the point. In truth, Hamlet is both. He is purely and simply the place of desire.
> (Ibid., p. 289)

In the final analysis, however, Hamlet as a character is closer to an obsessional than to a hysteric because "the major function of desire consists here in keeping at bay and awaiting the hour of the desired encounter" (ibid., p. 295) and more important because the central structural question that animates his discourse is not about his gender, as is the case in hysteria, but rather about his existence: "To be, or not to be?"
4 Freud states, "first in a sudden outburst of temper, when he runs his sword through the eavesdropper behind the arras, and secondly in a premeditated and even crafty fashion . . . he sends the two courtiers to the death that had been planned for himself" (Freud, 1899/2001, p. 265).

References

Freud, Sigmund (2001). Dostoevsky and Parricide. In James Strachey (Ed.) *The Standard Edition of the Complete Psychological Works of Sigmund Freud*, Vol. XXI. Vintage, Hogarth Press and the Institute of Psychoanalysis, 173–196 (Original work published 1928).

Freud, Sigmund (2001). The Dissolution of the Oedipus Complex. In James Strachey (Ed.), *The Standard Edition of the Complete Psychological Works of Sigmund Freud*, Vol. XIX. Vintage, Hogarth Press and the Institute of Psychoanalysis, 171–180 (Original work published 1924).

Freud, Sigmund (2001). The Interpretation of Dreams. In James Strachey (Ed.), *The Standard Edition of the Complete Psychological Works of Sigmund Freud*, Vol. IV. Vintage, Hogarth Press and the Institute of Psychoanalysis (Original work published 1899).

Freud, Sigmund (2001). The Psychopathology of Everyday Life. In James Strachey (Ed.), *The Standard Edition of the Complete Psychological Works of Sigmund Freud*, Vol. VI. Vintage, Hogarth Press and the Institute of Psychoanalysis (Original work published 1901).

Freud, Sigmund (2001). Totem and Taboo. In James Strachey (Ed.), *The Standard Edition of the Complete Psychological Works of Sigmund Freud*, Vol. XIII. Vintage, Hogarth Press and the Institute of Psychoanalysis, 1–162 (Original work published 1912).

Lacan, Jacques (2002). The Seminar of Jacques Lacan. Book VI. Desire and its Interpretation, 1958–1959. Unofficially translated by Cormac Gallagher from the unedited French typescripts of the seminar Le Séminaire de Jacques Lacan. *Livre VI. Le désir et son interprétation*, 1958–1959. Karnac Books.

Lacan, Jacques (2006). Aggressiveness in Psychoanalysis. In Bruce Fink Trans., in collaboration with Héloïse Fink and Russell Grigg, *Écrits: The First Complete Edition in English*. W.W. Norton, 82–101 (Original work published 1948)

Lacan, Jacques (2006). Logical Time and the Assertion of Anticipated Certainty: A New Sophism. In Bruce Fink Trans., in collaboration with Héloïse Fink and Russell Grigg, *Écrits: The First Complete Edition in English*. W.W. Norton, 161–175 (Original work published 1945).

Lacan, Jacques (2006). The Mirror Stage as Formative of the *I* Function as Revealed in Psychoanalytic Experience. In Bruce Fink Trans., in collaboration with Héloïse Fink and Russell Grigg, *Écrits: The First Complete Edition in English*. W.W. Norton, 75–81 (Original work published 1949)

Lacan, Jacques (2017). *The Seminar of Jacques Lacan. Book V. Formations of the Unconscious, 1957–1958*. In Russell Grigg Trans. Polity Press (Original work published 1998).

Lacan, Jacques (2019). *The Seminar of Jacques Lacan. Book VI. Desire and Its Interpretation, 1958–1959*. In Bruce Fink Trans. Polity Press (Original work published 2013).

Shakespeare, William (1978). All's Well that Ends Well. In *The Complete Works of William Shakespeare*. Abbey Library, 270–298 (Original work published 1623).

Shakespeare, William (1978). Sonnets. In *The Complete Works of William Shakespeare*. Abbey Library, 1071–1090 (Original work published 1609).

Shakespeare, William (1997). *Hamlet*. In Harold Jenkins (Ed.). Thomas Nelson & Sons (Original work published 1603).

Chapter 3

Antigone

Lacan spoke on Sophocles' play *Antigone* from 25th May to 15th June, 1960, in sessions 19 through 21 and a "Supplementary Note" to session 21 of his 1959–1960 seminar on *The Ethics of Psychoanalysis* (*L'Éthique de la psychanalyse*). In this seminar, Lacan reads *Antigone* and the psychoanalytic question of the human being's access to the signifying chain in terms of each other so as to let each discourse illuminate and be illuminated by the other. In the course of doing so, Lacan corrects Hegel's famous and widely accepted reading of the play and explains the play's relation to Kant's moral imperative and Sade's notion of enjoyment around the question of limitlessness. Finally, Lacan illustrates the four paradoxically stated ethical propositions of Freudian psychoanalysis with the help of aspects of Sophocles' play.

Hegel's Reading of *Antigone*

The tragedies of Sophocles, especially *Antigone*, fascinated Hegel since he was a boy of eighteen and a student at Tübinger Stift. While he was there, Hegel met and started long-term friendships with two fellow students, Friedrich Hölderlin and Friedrich Schelling, both of whom happened to admire *Antigone* as much as Hegel did. Hegel and Hölderlin were, in fact, responsible for a good part of the fascination with *Antigone* in the 19th century. Leaving aside indirect references and allusions, Hegel is likely to have directly referred to the play eleven times in three of his works: *Phenomenology of Spirit* (1807), *The Philosophy of Right* (1821), and the posthumously published *Aesthetics: Lectures on Fine Art* (1835). In this section, we shall focus only on the most important component of Hegel's reading of *Antigone* because that alone is pertinent to our discussion.

   Hegel's interpretation of *Antigone* must be understood in the context of his notion of the conflict between the two halves of the ethical sphere and its representation in art. Hegel's ethical sphere consists of two opposing halves in the form of two opposing laws—the natural laws of kinship and the social laws of the state—that are both right. According to Hegel, great art deals with this very conflict between the two correct but opposite laws of the ethical sphere. Hegel states that although this conflict between the two laws is the theme of other plays as

DOI: 10.4324/9781003470984-4

well, such as those written by Aeschylus, Euripides, and Sophocles himself (Hegel, 1835/1975b, p. 1213), of all the literary masterpieces of all eras, *Antigone* is the most magnificent and most satisfying because the play perfectly illustrates Hegel's internally conflicted ethical sphere by showing us how both Antigone and Creon violated the other law exactly in course of abiding by one of the two opposing laws; and how, as a result of the violation, both of them suffered at the hands of the very opposite law they had violated. In *Aesthetics: Lectures on Fine Art*, Hegel says that the "absolutely Divine" has two sons—the divine and the human. They are the two ideals. Both of them are equally rational, valid, and ethical in spite of the differences between them. Although man is therefore required to actualise both of them, Creon and Antigone choose to do otherwise in Sophocles' play on the question of the burial of Polyneices' dead body:

> Of this kind, for example, are the interests and aims which fight in the *Antigone* of Sophocles. Creon, the King, had issued, as head of the state, the strict command that the son of Oedipus, who had risen against Thebes as an enemy of his country, was to be refused the honour of burial. This command contains an essential justification, provision for the welfare of the entire city. But Antigone is animated by an equally ethical power, her holy love for her brother, whom she cannot leave unburied, a prey of the birds. Not to fulfill the duty of burial would be against family piety, and therefore she transgresses Creon's command.
>
> (Hegel, 1835/1975a, pp. 220–221)

In *Antigone*, the conflict is between the eternal law of the family and the temporal law of the state, variously described by Hegel as "the inner gods of feeling, love and kinship" and "the daylight gods of free, self-conscious natural and political life" (ibid., p. 464); the laws of the gods of the underworld and the laws of Zeus; the private law and the public law; the inner law and the outer law; the unconscious law and the conscious law; the subjective and the objective; and, the woman and the man in the main. Hegel argues that Antigone and Creon, the two protagonists, represent two different and conflicting orders of law and ethics that together constitute the ethical sphere in its totality. Whereas Creon represents the public law of the city and stresses the right of the state over the individuals in a political community, Antigone represents the private law of the family or the love between individuals that forms the basis of an ethical community. Therefore, the conflict in *Antigone* is at once between the human and the divine, the polis and the family, the state and the individual, man and woman, and conscious and the unconscious, which are both ethical and comprise the two interdependent halves of a sphere.

In *Antigone*, when Creon prohibits the burial of Polyneices on the grounds that he was an enemy of the state, the public law of the state comes into conflict with the familial and sacred duty of the individual to bury one's own dead. In choosing to go ahead and bury her brother, Antigone brings out the importance of the rights of the individual over the laws of the state for her. Antigone defends her brother's right to funeral rites as something more valid than any edict passed by the polis, justifying her action with an appeal to the universality of the divine law: "Death yearns for equal law for all the dead" (Sophocles, 441 BC/1954 at 519). Referring to his edict, Antigone says to Creon:

> For me it was not Zeus who made that order. Nor did that justice who lives with the gods below mark out such laws to hold among mankind. Nor did I think your orders were so strong that you, a mortal man, could over-run the gods' unwritten and unfailing laws. Not now, nor yesterday's, they always live, and no one knows their origin in time.
>
> (Ibid., at 450–457)

From Antigone's point of view, the divine law enjoys an absolute command, unlike the finite, relative, or conditional command of the human law. From Creon's point of view, however, any individual action undertaken against the state's decree is a transgression of the law of the state, where the absolute duty of the polis is to uphold its edicts and punish the traitors. As an upholder of the law of the state, Creon must, therefore, forbid the burial of Polyneices who had revolted against it. He says, "There is no greater wrong than disobedience. This ruins cities, this tears down our homes, this breaks the battle-front in panic rout. If men live decently it is because discipline saves their very lives for them" (ibid., at 672–676). Thus, Creon must deny the rebel who fought against the state the burial-rites that were otherwise due to him as a citizen. Since each side considered its own law to trump or prevail over the other law, no mediation was ever possible between them. Thus, insofar as both sides of the ethical sphere are right, according to Hegel, the conflict is between one right and another right. In this conflict, neither side can emerge victorious, as each is incomplete without the other. Since these laws were fundamentally interdependent and bound up with each other, to deny the legitimacy of the other law was to deny the legitimacy of the law one represented. Hegel states that in tragedy, both sides of the conflict are justified, but in seeking the one-sided fulfilment of their own end only, the tragic characters negate and violate the other law that is intrinsic to them, that they are dependent on, and that they should be honouring for their own sake:

> [T]hey violate what, if they were true to their own nature, they should be honouring. For example, Antigone lives under the political authority of Creon; she is herself the daughter of a King and the fiancée of Haemon, so that she ought to pay obedience to the royal command. But Creon too, as father and husband, should have respected the sacred tie of blood and not ordered anything against its pious observance. So there is immanent in both Antigone and Creon something that in their own way they attack, so that they are gripped and shattered by something intrinsic to their own actual being. Antigone suffers death before enjoying the bridal dance, but Creon too is punished by the voluntary deaths of his son and his wife, incurred, the one on account of Antigone's fate, the other because of Haemon's death.
>
> (Hegel, 1835/1975b, pp. 1217–1218)

Thus, Antigone denied the validity of the state's edicts and alienated the polis and her community even though without these, her own identity was threatened. That she hangs herself in a place outside the city indicates that there is a relationship between the loss of community-life and the loss of life itself. Similarly, by one-sidedly upholding the law of the polis, Creon loses his entire family and his happiness at the end of the play. It is only after his son committed suicide following Antigone's death and his wife committed suicide following his son's death that Creon is able to realise the importance of the family as an essential domain of the ethical sphere to which he had all along denied legitimacy. He says:

> This is my guilt, all mine. I killed you [i.e., Haemon], I say it clear.
> Servants, take me away, out of the sight of men.
> I who am nothing more than nothing now.
> (Sophocles, 441 BC/1954, at 1319–1321)

Thus, both Antigone and Creon became martyrs while one-sidedly fighting for one of the two complementary laws and bringing down the entire ethical sphere with them as a result. Hegel indicates that the tragic conflict in the Greek world between the polis and the family ends in the destruction of that world itself insofar as it becomes a "soulless and dead" community in the end (Hegel, 1807/1977, p. 289). According to Hegel, Sophocles had thus exposed the one-sidedness of both Creon and Antigone in the play by making each of them personify only one side of the law—Antigone's exclusive pathos is her family's welfare, and Creon's exclusive pathos is his state's welfare. There is a conflict despite both the laws being ethical because both Creon and Antigone abided by only one of the two laws and deliberately violated the opposite law while doing so. Therefore, Hegel writes in *Aesthetics: Lectures on Fine Art*:

> [T]he same clash appears in the *Antigone*, one of the most sublime and in every respect most excellent works of art of all time. Everything in this tragedy is logical; the public law of the state is set in conflict over against inner family love and duty to a brother; the woman, Antigone, has the family interest as her 'pathos', Creon, the man, has the welfare of the community as his. Polyneices, at war with his native city, had fallen before the gates of Thebes, and Creon, the ruler, in a publicly proclaimed law threatened with death anyone who gave this enemy of the city the honour of burial. But this command, which concerned only the public weal, Antigone could not accept; as sister, in the piety of her love for her brother, she fulfills the holy duty of burial. In doing so she appeals to the law of the gods; but the gods whom she worships are the underworld gods of Hades . . . the inner gods of feeling, love and kinship, not the daylight gods of free self-conscious national and political life.
> (Hegel, 1835/1975a, p. 464)

Hegel considered this conflict "ethical" in the highest sense because it is a conflict between the two ethical laws comprising the ethical sphere itself. The conflict is also "tragic" in nature because it takes place between two irreconcilable positions that are both ethical (Hegel, 1820/2001, p. 144). Hegel draws our attention to the detail that Sophocles made both Antigone and Creon suffer in the play: "Sophocles in his *Antigone* does not make Antigone alone suffer and die; on the contrary, we also see Creon punished by the grievous loss of his wife and Haemon, who both likewise perish owing to the death of Antigone" (Hegel, 1835/1975a, p. 471). The tragic ending of the play in terms of the three suicides of Antigone, Haemon, and Eurydice indicates, according to Hegel, that both the conceptions of law or ethical duty involved in the play are, in fact, incomplete and one-sided by themselves, that each of them is the unconscious of the other, and that each of the two conceptions dialectically contains the other as the germ of its collapse. Thus, in the end, both sides are led "despite all their justification, to guilt and wrong" (Hegel, 1835/1975b, p. 1196) and to their own destruction from within. This is the reason that Hegel thinks that their deed is at once legitimate and blameworthy: "A truly tragic suffering is only inflicted on the individual agents as a consequence of their own deed which is both legitimate and, owing to the resulting collision, blameworthy, and for which their whole self is answerable" (ibid., p. 1198). Hegel moreover thinks that, by representing both the one-sided ethical positions at stake, the play suggests the terms for an ethical reconciliation of public and private interests and duties. Hegel concludes from this that the play *Antigone* represents an ethical reconciliation in terms of its complete representation of the ethical sphere. He states that, in a drama as opposed to an epic, the special powers enter a simple and fundamental conflict—as two pathos belonging to two individuals or as two one-sided independent powers represented by two characters who oppose one another—so that the play as a whole "dissolves" any notion of the one-sidedness of these powers, for "both powers are ultimately and truly seen to be complementary and not independent of one another" (ibid., p. 1163, fn. 1).

In the *Philosophy of Right*, Hegel calls the two laws comprising the ethical sphere the two "self-originated and self-referring laws and regulations" (Hegel, 1820/2001, p. 132) of which the universal spirit is objective, and the unconscious spirit to which it is united is subjective. Speaking on them in passage number 144, Hegel once again cites Antigone's remark on the law of the gods in the following "Addition" to the passage:

> In the ethical principle as a whole occur both the objective and the subjective elements; but of this principle each is only a form. Here the good is substance, or the filling of the objective with subjectivity. If we contemplate the social order from the objective standpoint, we can say that man, as ethical, is unconscious of himself. In this sense Antigone proclaims that no one knows whence the laws come; they are everlasting, that is, they exist absolutely, and flow from the nature of things. None the less has this substantive existence a consciousness also, which, however, is only one element of the whole.
>
> (Ibid., p. 132)

In other words, each of the two elements of the ethical principle—the objective and the subjective—is only one element of the whole. Regardless of Antigone's emphasis on it, the everlasting law is only one of the two laws in Hegel's ethical sphere where it is never higher than the other law. According to Hegel, the objective and subjective moments always coexist in ethical life, but they are only the forms of ethical life, not its substance. The substance of ethical life is the good or filling up the objective with subjectivity. At the broadest level, Antigone's law represents the unconscious of Creon's law, for her law is unwritten, not fully knowable, and its time or place of origin unknown, while Creon's law represents the conscious of Antigone's law, for it is the law of the daylight that has been written and announced, whose time and place of origin is known to everyone, and which deals with the welfare of the community in general. In this work, Hegel moreover differentiates between the state of the spirit in the two sexes in passage 166 by contending that the spirit divides itself in the man and unites itself in the woman to thus give rise to two ethical dispositions (ibid., p. 144). Following this, he refers to the element of piety in *Antigone* as the law of the woman, or the law of nature,

> which realizes itself subjectively and intuitively, the law of an inner life, . . . the law of the ancient gods, and of the under-world, the eternal law, of whose origin no one knows, in opposition to the public law of the state.
> (Ibid., p. 144)

It is noteworthy that despite being an ardent admirer of Shakespeare and Molière, the literary work that Hegel attributed the highest place to is Sophocles' *Antigone*— a work that he situated at the center of a number of his major philosophical treatises: "Of all the masterpieces of the classical and the modern world—and I know nearly all of them and you should and can—the *Antigone* seems to me to be the most magnificent and satisfying work of art of this kind" (Hegel, 1835/1975b, p. 1218).

Hegel's reading of *Antigone* is questionable on several counts. To begin with, contrary to his reading of Antigone and Creon as ethical equals, which suited his notion of the ethical sphere, Sophocles' play, which deals with the theme of the conflict between Antigone's just moral law and Creon's unjust political law, points to Antigone alone as the defender of the good. That apart, insofar as Antigone went beyond the family, crosses over into the sphere of the polis, and risked her life in terms of her deed there, as men do, she transcends the framework of womanhood outlined by Hegel himself. While it is true that she acted in the polis on behalf of her family, she nevertheless underwent a certain division that characterises man, according to Hegel. And yet, Hegel views her as exclusively representing the position of a woman. Moreover, a point not discussed by Hegel is that if his interpretation of the ancient Greek life as an irresolvable tragic conflict between the family and the polis is right, then Antigone's decision to commit suicide becomes extremely pertinent, for it would imply that, unlike man, who endured the duality of Greek life and lived the tragic conflict, the woman found it impossible to endure and died from it. The impact of Hegel's reading of *Antigone* is nevertheless very deep. Despite all his limitations, no philosopher since Hegel has been able to ignore his remarks while speaking on *Antigone*. This is true for Kierkegaard and Heidegger, as well as for Lacan. Besides, although other philosophers have written on *Antigone* both before and after Hegel, such as Aristotle, Kierkegaard, Heidegger, and more recently Nussbaum, who approached the play radically differently from Hegel, Hegel's reading continues to exercise a very strong influence on the way the play is viewed by students of ethics, philosophy, and literature to this day.

Lacan's Critique of Hegel's Reading

Hegel's *Aesthetics: Lectures on Fine Art* has been highly appreciated by philosophers right up to Foucault and Derrida. Heidegger, for example, states in the "Afterword" to *The Origin of the Work of Art*: "The most comprehensive reflections on the nature of art possessed by the West—comprehensive because thought out of metaphysics—are Hegel's *Lectures on Aesthetics*" (Heidegger, 1950/2002, p. 51). Lacan's reading of Hegel's *Aesthetics: Lectures on Fine Art* is therefore somewhat exceptional when he says in the seminar on *The Ethics of Psychoanalysis*: "It is in any case true that Hegel nowhere appears to me to be weaker than he is in the sphere of poetics, and this is especially true of what he has to say about *Antigone*" (Lacan, 1986/1992, p. 249). Thus, despite being a great admirer of Hegel's teachings in general, Lacan thinks Hegel was at his weakest in his lectures on art, especially so in his remarks on *Antigone*.

More specifically, Lacan strongly disagrees with Hegel's interpretation of *Antigone* on two important counts. First, Lacan dismisses Hegel's notion of an ethical reconciliation at the end of the play—like Goethe, Erwin Rhode, and others had done before him—and states that he found the play's conclusion, like the conclusion of *Oedipus at Colonus*, irreducibly devastating:

> I just wonder what the reconciliation of the end of *Antigone* might be . . . Let us not forget that in Sophocles's last play, *Oedipus at Colonus*, Oedipus's final malediction is addressed to his sons; it is the malediction that gives rise to the catastrophic series of dramas to which *Antigone* belongs. *Oedipus at Colonus* ends with Oedipus's last curse, "Never to have been born were best. . . ." How can one talk of reconciliation in connection with a tone like that?
> (Ibid., pp. 249–250)

Lacan explained this very tone of Oedipus in his seminar on the *Ego in Freud's Theory and in the Technique of Psychoanalysis*, in terms of Oedipus's remark in *Oedipus at Colonus*, "Am I made man in the hour when I cease to be?" (Lacan, 1978/1993, pp. 229–230) and in terms of the following lines sung by the Chorus:

> Say what you will, the greatest boon is not to be;
> But, life begun, soonest to end is best.
> (Ibid., p. 230)

At the end of *Antigone*, we are left with three dead bodies and a king who has lost all his dear ones and is on the verge of losing his sanity. It is hard to relate this final picture of complete devastation to any form of "reconciliation".

And second, Lacan thinks that the conflict in the play is not between one right and another right, as Hegel consistently considered it to be, but between one wrong and a passion, or, precisely put, between Creon's mistake and Antigone's passion (Lacan, 1986/1992, p. 254).

Creon's Mistake

Almost everyone in the play considers Creon wrong, as a glance at the play would reveal. To begin with, Antigone thought Creon had made a mistake in enforcing the edict that forbade Polyneices' burial because, despite being a mere human being, Creon had dared to enforce an edict that contradicted the unwritten laws of the god of the dead:

> Nor did I think your orders were so strong
> that you, a mortal man, could over-run
> the gods' unwritten and unfailing laws.
> (Sophocles, 441 BC/1954,
> at 453–455)

The Chorus, too, thought Creon had made a mistake. The Chorus expresses the first sign of doubt about Creon's decision when, after hearing the Guard describe the "burial all accomplished, thirsty dust/strewn on the flesh, the ritual complete" (ibid., at 246–247), it wonders: "Isn't this action possibly a god's?" (ibid., at 279). If god had acted against Creon's edict, then that would mean Creon and his edict were wrong. At the end of Scene 2, the Chorus says that due to his ambition, failure would ultimately trip Creon unawares as he is doomed to suffer. The passage goes as follows, in E.F. Watling's translation:

> Roving ambition helps many a man to good
> And many it falsely lures to light desires,
> Till failure trips them unawares, and they fall
> On the fire that consumes them. Well was it said,
> Evil seems good
> To him who is doomed to suffer;
> And short is the time before that suffering comes.
> (Sophocles, 441 BC/1947, p. 143)

Creon's son Haemon, too, considered Creon's edict wrong and Creon unjust. They have the following exchange in Scene 3:

Creon: Wicked to try conclusions with your father.
Haemon: When you conclude unjustly, so I must.

Creon: Am I unjust, when I respect my office?
Haemon: You tread down the gods' due. Respect is gone.
              (Sophocles, 441 BC/1954, at 742–745)

A few moments later, Haemon adds, "If you weren't father, I should call you mad" (ibid., at 755) and points to what he considered Creon's chief flaw: "You wish to speak but never wish to hear" (ibid., at 757).

Not only that, in Scene 5, Tiresias asks Creon to correct his mistake. He says to him:

> All men may err,
> but error once committed, he's no fool
> nor yet unfortunate, who gives up his stiffness
> and cures the trouble he has fallen in.
> Stubbornness and stupidity are twins.
> Yield to the dead. Why goad him where he lies?
> What use to kill the dead a second time?
>   (Ibid., at 1024–1030)

In Fitts and Fitzgerald's translation:

> Think: all men make mistakes,
> But a good man yields when he knows his course
> is wrong,
> And repairs the evil. The only crime is pride.
>   (Sophocles, 441 BC/1977, p. 232)

Creon is not only wrong but also stubborn or proud and stupid. When Tiresias says to Creon a few moments later, referring to his own advice, "How better than all wealth is sound good counsel" (Sophocles, 441 BC/1954, at 1050). Creon, who considered Tiresias to be wrong and motivated, retorts mockingly, "And so is folly worse than anything" (ibid., at 1051), to which Tiresias says, "And you're infected with that same disease" (ibid., at 1052). He then spells out not Creon's "folly" but his "great wrong" of confusing the upper and lower worlds by preventing the burial of a corpse and imprisoning a living person in a tomb:

> Know well, the sun will not have rolled its course
> Many more days, before you come to give
> Corpse for these corpses, child of your own loins.
> For you've confused the upper and lower worlds.
> You sent a life to settle in a tomb;
> You keep up here that which belongs below
> The corpse unburied, robbed of its release.
> Not you, nor any god that rules on high

Can claim him now.
You rob the nether gods of what is theirs.
So the pursuing horrors lie in wait
to track you down. The Furies sent by Hades
and by all gods will even you with your victims.
Now say that I am bribed! At no far time
shall men and women wail within your house.
And all the cities that you fought in war
whose sons had burial from wild beasts, or dogs,
or birds that brought the stench of your great wrong
back to each hearth, they move against you now.

(Ibid., at 1065–1083)

Even the Messenger speaks of Creon's mistake to the Chorus in terms of his hand in the death of Haemon:

Chorus: What is the grief of princes that you bring?
Messenger: They're dead. The living are responsible.
Chorus: Who dies? Who did the murder? Tell us now.
Messenger: Haemon is gone. One of his kin drew blood.
Chorus: But whose arm struck? His father's or his own?
Messenger: He killed himself. His blood is on his father.
Chorus: Seer, all too true the prophesy you told!

(Ibid., at 1171–1177)

Similarly, Creon's wife, Eurydice, considers Creon guilty of killing their son. Following the death of Eurydice, the Messenger reports to Creon: "she cursed you as the killer of her children" (ibid., at 1304). He also tells him, "she held you guilty in the death of him before you" (ibid., at 1311–1312).

Above all, Creon himself recognises and acknowledges his mistake, variously calling it his "fault", his "crime", his "unblest planning", his "wild strange ways", and "disaster" in his conversation with the Chorus following Haemon's death:

Chorus

But look, the king draws near.
His own hand brings
The witness of his crime,
The doom he brought on himself.

Creon

O crimes of my wicked heart,
harshness bringing death.

> You see the killer, you see the kin he killed.
> My planning was all unblest.
> Son, you have died too soon.
> Oh, you have gone away
> through my fault, not your own.

Chorus

> You have learned justice, though it comes too late.

Creon

> Yes, I have learned in sorrow. It was a god who struck,
> who has weighted my head with disaster; he drove me to
> wild strange ways,
> his heavy heel on my joy.
> Oh sorrows, sorrows of men.
>
> (Ibid., at 1257–1276)

When the death of Eurydice is reported to him, Creon further remarks:

> This is my guilt, all mine. I killed you, I say it clear.
> Servants, take me away, out of the sight of men.
> I who am nothing more than nothing now.
>
> (Ibid., at 1319–1321)

Creon's concluding lines in the play, in Watling's translation, is:

> Lead me away ...
> That have killed unwittingly
> My son, my wife.
> I know not where I should turn,
> Where look for help.
> My hands have done amiss, my head is bowed
> With fate too heavy for me.
>
> (Sophocles, 441 BC/1947, pp. 161–162)

Creon suffers from both flaws in character and errors of judgment. His flaws of character consist of his pride, arrogance, and unyielding nature, and his error of judgment consists of the edict that he stubbornly enforced. Not only Tiresias but Creon himself retrospectively considered his stubborn pride as his greatest flaw, and his self-assessment sounds correct if, among other things, we recall his conversation with the Chorus regarding Haemon:

Chorus

Lord, if your son has spoken to the point
you should take his lesson. He should do the same.
...

Creon

At my age I'm to school my mind by his?
This boy instructor is my master, then?
(Sophocles, 441 BC/1954,
at 723–727)

According to Lacan, the Chorus is quite straightforward in answering the question of Creon's mistake. Lacan points out that, following Antigone's condemnation, the Chorus separates its desire from the desire of Creon and sides with Antigone, saying that they did not want to be Creon's companion anymore because he had arranged the laws "wrongly", he had got them "all mixed up" (Lacan, 1986/1992, p. 276). Lacan specifies that the Greek expression for being a "companion" also means having the same desire, being in the same place, and having close relations (ibid., p. 276). And again, when Creon returns with the body of Haemon, the Chorus says: "It is not a misfortune that is external to him; it is his own mistake" (ibid., p. 277). Mistake or blunder is the word used by the Chorus to describe Creon's act in general. According to Lacan, the mortal fruit harvested by Creon through his obstinacy and insane orders is the dead son in his arms, which proves he had made a mistake. Lacan also indicates that Aristotle's understanding of Creon's mistake may be approximately translated as "error of judgment" (ibid., p. 258). Lacan clarifies in this context that when the Chorus says that Antigone has gone in search of her *Atè* and expresses its interest in her for that very reason, *Atè* does not stand for a mistake or an error but stands for something else (ibid., p. 277).

However, Creon's greatest mistake, according to Lacan, is not his pride. Lacan thinks that Creon illustrates the function of doing good. As king and leader, the good that he promotes is the good of all. This has textual support:

For I believe that who controls the state
and does not hold to the best plans of all
but locks his tongue up through some kind of fear,
that he is worst of all who are or were.
(Sophocles, 441 BC/1954,
at 178–181)

But out of his very concern for the best plan of all, Creon crosses over into another plane, failing to realise that doing the good of all involves a transgression of limit. Creon's mistake, in other words, was in his assumption that the good of all is a law without limits or that the sovereign law could easily exceed or go beyond the limit without causing any harm (Lacan, 1986/1992, p. 259). In this context, Lacan points out that before Plato had introduced the idea of the "Supreme Good", which is "to promote the good of all as the law without limits", or Kant had, in "the ethical progression . . . from Aristotle to Kant", made "clear the identity of law and reason" by regarding the concept of the good "as a rule of [practical] reason with a universal validity", Sophocles had anticipatorily raised the first objection to these ideas in tragedy (ibid., p. 259). The play shows us that good cannot reign over all without producing an excess that has fatal consequences of the kind best revealed in tragedy, where the sphere one must not cross into is that of the unwritten laws. The fact that Sophocles had stated this argument many years before the introduction of the earliest ethical formulations of Socrates, Plato, and Aristotle implies that most of the existing humanist formulations in ethics dealing with the universal good have resulted from the not-recognition or forgetting of, or disregard for, Sophocles' preemptive objection against it in *Antigone*.

Lacan explains that Goethe's remarks on *Antigone*, too, imply, albeit in a different sense, that Creon had gone beyond the limit, beyond what was right, when he struck Polyneices after his death. Driven by his desire to do good beyond the limit, Creon transgressed the limit imposed by death by inflicting a second death on Polyneices that he had no right to inflict on anyone (ibid., p. 254). Lacan thinks that most of Creon's speeches are aimed at that zone beyond death insofar as Creon either wanted to do good beyond the limit—and therefore, he wanted to punish the enemy of the state beyond the limit, beyond his death—or, he rushed toward his own destruction. Lacan also thinks that Goethe, who was otherwise astute enough to identify and correct Hegel's simplification in his own way, was struck by "some madness" on the question of Antigone's aim. Lacan points out that Goethe wanted Antigone's crucial justification of her act of burying Polyneices to be proved an interpolation and removed from the play (ibid., p. 255). Lacan thinks Goethe thought so because he did not understand the passion that bore Antigone along.

Antigone's Passion

The name of Antigone's passion, in short, is her desire for death. It ought to be understood in the play in terms of the concepts of *Atè* as the limit, the Choral ode on man, Antigone's invocation of the chthonic laws, the singular individual induced by language, Antigone's criminal desire, *Atè* as destiny, and cylindrical anamorphosis.

Antigone's Desire for Death

From the psychoanalytic point of view, Antigone's desire to embody the *Atè* is an expression of her desire for death in its purest form. Death-wish, pure and simple, is thus the psychoanalytic name for Antigone's passion, which is in perfect consonance with her own words and actions throughout the play. She has been insisting all along, "I am dead and I desire death" (ibid., p. 281). Moreover, she concentrates all her attention on her brother's dead body and its burial at any cost. For the offence of burying her brother's corpse in defiance of Creon's edict, Antigone is locked up in her sepulchre alive, which in turn brings about three suicides at the end of the play.

Antigone invokes the divine law in defense of burying her brother. But what does she say immediately following that? She tells Creon:

> I knew that I must die; how could I not?
> even without your warning. If I die,
> before my time, I say it is a gain.
> Who lives in sorrows many as are mine
> how shall he not be glad to gain his death?
> And so, for me to meet this fate, no grief.
> (Sophocles, 441 BC/1954,
> at 460–465)

Antigone, the daughter of Oedipus, with regard to whom the Chorus had declared, "the greatest boon is not to be", not surprisingly longs for death. The divine law becomes inseparable from death and from the reasoned activities surrounding death, such as purification, burial, and mourning.

For Antigone, the question of fulfilling her pure desire for death is also a matter of an absolute choice. "Absolute" because the choice is motivated by no good other than the desire for death as such. This is also the reason why even though Creon is moved by fear toward the end, Antigone feels neither pity nor fear in the course of the entire play, barring the brief period of her *kommos*. Her pure desire for death had rendered Antigone pitiless and fearless, for one can realise one's desire for death only after having overcome the inner constrains of pity and fear. Lacan thinks that she pushes to the limit the realisation of her pure desire for death; that she well and truly incarnates that desire (Lacan, 1986/1992, p. 282).

Atè as the Limit

According to Lacan, the heroes of all seven plays of Sophocles to have survived, barring Oedipus in *Oedipus Rex*, are characterised by the sense that for all of them, "the race is run" (ibid., pp. 271–272). They are at a limit. They right away find themselves in a limit zone, between life and death. Among them, Antigone is marked by the stance that the race is run "in the most obvious of ways", and her stance is clearly established right from the outset. At lines 559–560, Antigone says that her soul has died long ago and that she is destined to give help to the dead, and at lines 611–614 and 620–625, the Chorus speaks on the *Atè*. It is around this, Lacan thinks, that Antigone's desire is played out. Both passages end with the expression "beyond *Atè*", or going beyond the limit. "[S]omething beyond the limits of *Atè* has become Antigone's good, namely, a good that is different from everyone else's" good, which is why she dares to proceed toward the *Atè*, unlike anyone else in the world of the play (ibid., p. 270). Antigone's passion, in other words, is to embody the *Atè* if not to go beyond it.

Atè is a word repeated twenty times in this short play. It is the name of the ancient Greek goddess of criminal recklessness or fatal blindness and consequent punishment. The word "*Atè*", therefore, variously stands for the spirit of recklessness; divine punishment for recklessness, in the form of bewilderment caused by delusion or blindness; ruin brought about by criminal recklessness or fatal blindness; and destiny. Accordingly, it is often translated as the spirit of delusion, mental aberration, infatuation, blind folly, oblivion, rash action, or reckless impulse leading to ruin. In Lacan's reading, too, *Atè* broadly stands for criminal recklessness and self-destruction; but more precisely, it stands for the limit between life and death or destiny. Lacan says *Atè* is the limit between life and death, which human life can only briefly cross into; meaning, human life can spend a few moments only at the place of the *Atè*. That is the place Antigone wanted to go to, but after her arrival there, she finds it difficult to withstand being there for too long.

Lacan points out that Antigone, who will later say, "I am made for love rather than hate", is immediately introduced in the play with the word "enmity" in relation to Ismene. Later, she will act with cruelty and scorn toward her when she says to her, "Go back to your Creon, since you love him so". How do we resolve the enigma of Antigone? Lacan points to the answer of the Chorus in reply: she is "inhuman"; not as in monstrous, but as in "inflexible", "uncivilized", or "raw". If Antigone goes beyond the limit of the human, it means that her desire aims at the beyond of *Atè*, where *Atè* is akin to atrocious (ibid., p. 263). One does or does not approach *Atè*. When one does, Lacan adds, "it is because of something that is linked to a beginning and a chain of events, namely, that of the misfortune of the Labdacides family". In other words, Antigone was driven to the border of *Atè* owing to the misfortune or "resentment" of the Labdacus family, especially her memory of her father and the death of her two brothers, stemming from a long chain of curses. For her, it was a matter of protecting and defending her family *Atè* by embodying it (ibid., p. 264). The dust storm that took place when the burial was being carried out by Antigone for the first time signifies for Lacan that "what goes beyond a given limit must not be seen" (ibid., p. 264).

The Choral Ode on Man

After the messenger's departure from Creon's court following his first visit to report the lapse, the Chorus sings in praise of mankind:

> "There are a lot of wonders in the world, but there is nothing more wonderful than man".... man cultivates speech and the sublime sciences; he knows how to protect his dwelling place from winter frosts and from the blasts of a storm; he knows how to avoid getting wet . . . "he who knows all kinds of tricks" . . . "Nothing is impossible for man; what he can't do, he ignores". That's the tone of the text.
> (Ibid., p. 274)

After thus pointing to the deliberately ambiguous tone in which the ode is sung, Lacan adds:

> "He advances toward nothing that is likely to happen, he advances and he is . . . artful, but [in the end] he is . . . always [ruined]". He knows what he is doing. He always makes things come crashing down on his head. . . . [T]here is only one thing he can't come to terms with and that has to do with Hades. Dying is something he doesn't know how to come to terms with. . . . Having said that . . . the Chorus says that he has come up with an absolutely marvelous gimmick, namely, translated literally, "an escape *into* impossible sicknesses". . . . he invents marvelous gimmicks in the form of sicknesses he himself fabricates.
> (Ibid., p. 275)

Lacan specifies that the unstated preposition in the original text ought to be translated as "into" rather than as "from", as many translators have erroneously translated. Thus, Lacan thinks that the power laid upon man here is an ambiguous power. Antigone, by contrast, does not escape into an impossible illness while dealing with death; instead, she dares to embody the *Atè* alive. The dust storm recurs when Antigone tries to repeat the deed, but she is apprehended by the messenger, who is more vigilant on this occasion. Antigone is brought in by the messenger immediately after this ambiguous praise of mankind by the Chorus, and not too long after Antigone's arrival, the Chorus sings about mankind's relation to *Atè*.

Antigone's Invocation of the Chthonic Laws

Regarding the companion or collaborator of the gods below, both Creon and Antigone placed them on their own side up to a point, which makes the matter appear ambiguous in its totality, but there is no doubt that Antigone is, above all, concerned not with the companion of the gods below but with their laws, which, notably, are the chthonic laws, or the laws of the earth. When Antigone says that she resisted Creon's order for the sake of her brother, that is to say, for someone with whom she had a blood relation, she is stressing the most chthonic of all relations. Thus, Antigone fully distinguishes herself from the companion of the gods below by directly invoking an order of the law that is not developed in any signifying chain and hence is described as "unwritten" by her in the play. These laws indicate "a limit" beyond which mortal beings cannot go (ibid., p. 278). This limit or horizon is "determined by a structural relation; it only exists on the basis of the language of words" that has an "unsurpassable consequence", insofar as the language of words enables Antigone to speak about her brother in the manner in which she does:

> My brother is what he is, and it's because he is what he is and only he can be what he is, that I move toward the fatal limit. If it were anyone else with whom I might enter into a human relationship, my husband or my children for example, they are replaceable . . . But this brother . . . who has in common with me the fact of having been born in the same womb . . . and having been related to the same

father . . . this brother is something unique. And it is this alone which motivates me to oppose your edicts.

(Ibid., p. 278–279)

Goethe found the contents of these lines (904–912), in which Antigone explains why she would only have defied the edict to bury a brother and not a husband or a child, baffling, and an interpolation that the play could do without (ibid., p. 255). There have been others, such as the group of scholars headed by August Jacob which included the great Sophoclean scholar Richard Claverhouse Jebb, who viewed these very lines as forged. By contrast, Lacan thinks that the message contained in these lines is essential for us to grasp the meaning of Antigone's action in its specific relation to language. The lines in question are:

Had I had children or their father dead,
I'd let them moulder. I should not have chosen
In such a case to cross the state's decree.
What is the law that lies behind these words?
One husband gone, I might have found another,
Or a child from a new man in first child's place,
But with my parents hid away in death,
No brother, ever, could spring up for me.
Such is the law by which I honoured you.
(Sophocles, 441 BC/1954,
at 905–914)

In other words, according to Antigone, her brother alone was irreplaceable, not her husband or children, because her parents were dead. This means no one other than her dead brother could occupy the place of that brother. And for that reason, she moved toward the fatal limit. Lacan explains how, in Antigone's reasoning, two overlapping elements are implied. First, the question of the very existence of Polyneices, his existence as such independent of his qualities, or "the unique value of his being without reference to any content". And second, the uniqueness of Polyneices as the occupant of the place of her brother. He might have been a criminal, a murderer, and an anti-national, but he was her brother nonetheless, regardless of "whatever good or evil Polyneices may have done, or to whatever he may be subjected to". To that, Lacan adds the vital theoretical detail: "The unique value involved is essentially that of language" (Lacan, 1986/1992, p. 279). Antigone could not have pointed to the specific specialty of either Polyneices or of a brother without invoking the name of her parents, that is, first of all, a language. More important, she could not have separated the being of her brother from the events of his life or his individuality from the "characteristics of the historical drama he has lived through", from outside of language. This detachment or separation, Lacan thinks, is not merely made possible by language but is "the break that the very presence of language inaugurates in the life of man" (ibid., p. 279).

This is the reason that Lacan says, "the unique value involved is essentially that of language".[1]

Language and the Singular Individual

According to Lacan, individuality is singular because it is derived from language. Precisely put, the singularity of the individual results from a signifying cut on the surface of the being by language, whose most important final effect is the emergence of the subject of the unconscious as a fading subject and the corresponding loss of being due to the signifier's conquest of a part of the being that moreover has a profound relation to death.

In the classical teaching of Lacan, the unconscious is structured by, like, and in a language, which is precisely what makes the subject singular. Human instincts and human biology are more or less the same for all. But the words one grows up hearing, in their totality, that take the form of one's symbolic universe, are bound to be different for each individual. Thus, man derives his singularity from his unconscious, made up of the words heard that are unique for each individual. Moreover, the unconscious comprising words of the Other is also the basis of speech. Man speaks because he has an unconscious that speaks in him and through him. Each man is thus a unique speaking being because of this twofold effect of the unconscious on his speech. Apart from its role in introducing the subject of the unconscious that speaks, language is furthermore related to the marking of the being by a name, a family name, and the Name-of-the-Father that, once again, contribute toward making him different from others. In all these senses, language gives the individual his singularity and gives others a reason to regard him as unique.

Out of these, the effect of the Name-of-the-Father on the subject can be illustrated textually. It may be said that the Name-of-the-Father or the operative signifier, in this case, is "Oedipus", which is the Name-of-the-Father of both Polyneices and Antigone, as well as of Eteocles and Ismene, and as such it definitively groups the four siblings together in a relation of blood, which is precisely what Antigone is invoking here by saying that her brother alone is irreplaceable, now that her parents were dead. The Name-of-the-Father, as the master signifier, also situates the siblings within the symbolic network of the Labdacus family and all its good and bad fortunes. In this sense, Antigone's reasoning here is related to the very break that language, in the form of the Names "Oedipus" and "Labdacus" in this case, introduced to their lived lives. On her part, Antigone invokes no other right than what this implies. Therefore, at the most general level, Antigone is claiming that anyone who is identified by a name must be allowed the funeral rites, and at the most particular level, she is claiming that she must perform the burial of her brother precisely because he is irreplaceable. Therefore, these lines, in terms of which Antigone affirms a unique and absolute individuality with reference to the non-replaceability of her brother, far from being spurious or redundant, as Goethe and others thought, serve to demarcate the very threshold that Creon had crossed in his bid to do good without limit, where the threshold stands for the signifying chain that introduces the unconscious as a unique discourse that renders individuals unique.

Antigone's Criminal Desire

At the broadest level, the foundation of subjectivity is defined in psychoanalysis in terms of a crime, one that is related to man's Oedipal wishes—conscious in the infant and unconscious in the adult—involving incest and parricide that are both criminal in nature. However, Antigone's desire for death is criminal not only because it is radically destructive but also because it is related to the desire of Jocasta, which is a criminal desire. Let us recall that Jocasta's desire for a child made her conceive Oedipus after making Laius drunk and unconscious because Laius was strongly against having children due to the threat to his life from his child ordained by the curse. Since Jocasta's husband was also the king or the maker of the law of the land, Jocasta's desire and her act were transgressive and, hence, criminal in nature. Her transgressive desire led to all the tragic crimes that followed the birth of Oedipus, of which those described in *Antigone* form the last part. More pertinently, Jocasta's desire to protect Oedipus from the castrating truth was a criminal desire insofar as it subverted the law and helped sustain an incestuous relation.

Antigone's desire is criminal, according to Lacan, for three reasons. First, "Criminal" is one of the important meanings of the word *Atè* in ancient Greece. Second, Antigone desires to transgress the limit of life, which is a crime in most states. And third, Oedipus and Jocasta's incestuous union had produced the two brothers who had killed each other shortly before the beginning of the play. Of them, Eteocles represents power, and Polyneices represents crime. While the state headed by Creon assumed the validity of the power, no one, barring Antigone, was present to assume the validity of the crime. Since the community refused to be the guardian of the criminal, Antigone is required to do so by sacrificing her being for the sake of maintaining her family *Atè*. Lacan says Antigone perpetuates, eternalizes, and immortalises the *Atè*. But she had to do so by upholding the place of her criminal brother.

Atè as Destiny

After Antigone's speech, the Chorus sings a mythological song evoking three dramatic destinies that are all situated on the boundary between life and death, as the still living corpse. The three myths—involving Danae, Lycurgus, and Phineas—moreover concern the relationship of man to the gods.

Danae was the daughter of Acrisius—the King of Argos—and Euridyce. In reply to his question as to whether he would have a male heir, the oracle told him to go to the end of the Earth and be killed there by his daughter's child. Since Acrisius's daughter was childless at that time, he shut her up in a bronze tower or cave. But Zeus came to her in the form of golden rain and impregnated her. Soon after this, their child Perseus was born, who went on to kill Acrisius, as predicted. Regarding the myth of Danae, Lacan's focus was on the fact that she "was shut up in a bronze chamber" (ibid., p. 281).

Lycurgus is referred to by Herodotus, Xenophon, and Plutarch, among others. According to Plutarch and the others, before visiting the oracle of Delphi following the success of the legal reforms he had introduced, Lycurgus convened a meeting of all the people of Sparta, including the kings and the senate, and made everyone take an oath to observe his laws until his return. After the oracle approved of his laws and appreciated him for introducing them, Lycurgus disappeared and never returned to Sparta, thus forcing Sparta to observe his laws forever. Lacan, however, had a different aspect of the myth in mind. He states that Lycurgus badly "persecute[d] the servants of Dionysos", for which Dionysos transformed him "into a madman". He was thus imprisoned in a state of madness by the punishment of god (ibid., pp. 281–282).

The Phineas in question seems to be the son of Poseidon, who had the gift of prophecy. Angry with Phineas for revealing too much of the plans of the gods to others, Zeus punished him by isolating him on an island with a stock of food. As he tried to eat, the food was stolen out of his hand by the Harpies or monstrous winged women. This continued until Jason and the Argonauts arrived and drove away the Harpies with the help of the Boreads, or the winged heroes named Calaïs and Zetes, the two sons of Boreas, the Greek god of the North wind. Lacan says Phineas "is found on a cup as the object of a conflict between the Harpies, who torment him, and the Boreads, the two sons of Boreas who protect him, and on the horizon there passes, strangely enough, the wedding procession of Dionysos and Ariadne" (ibid., p. 282). Phineas thus remained isolated on an island due to god's punishment, even though he was saved from the Harpies.

From this point of view, Antigone's misfortune is equal to all those caught up in the cruel sport of the gods. She is a victim situated by circumstances at the very centre of the story of her accursed family. In other words, Antigone's desire to embody the *Atè* by entering and staying in her tomb alive was a misfortune assigned by the gods; it was her destiny. Lacan directly relates the *Atè* to Antigone's "destiny" in two remarks made on 3rd May, 1961 in his seminar on *Transference* that he gave the next year: "Antiquity's heroine is identical to her destiny, *Atè*", (Lacan, 1991/2015, p. 276) and "The other's *Atè* has a meaning in which Antigone's fate is inscribed" (ibid., p. 278). According to Lacan, this was Sophocles' way of stating that Antigone had set her sights on her death-wish right from the start. In a word, the name of Antigone's passion is her death-wish, or precisely put, her death drive, which Lacan defined as the insistence of the signifier.

Antigone's Passion and Cylindrical Anamorphosis

In order to highlight the place and appeal of Antigone's passion in the play, Lacan compares the representation of Antigone to anamorphic art in the context of her radiant beauty and the litter of dead bodies surrounding it that it illuminates. Anamorphosis, according to Lacan, is "any kind of construction that is made in such a way that by means of an optical transposition a certain form that wasn't visible at first sight transforms itself into a readable image. The pleasure is found in seeing its emergence from an indecipherable form" (Lacan, 1986/1992, p. 135). Lacan dates the phenomenon to the 16th and 17th centuries, which is incorrect, as the first example of proper anamorphic art is Leonardo da Vinci's 1485 painting called "Eye".

There are several brief illustrations of the phenomenon offered by Lacan. In the present seminar, he mentions the scene represented on an eighteen-metre long wall in a chapel built by the order of the Jesuits in Descartes' time, which could not be read from any point in the room except very briefly from a point while entering by a certain corridor (ibid., p. 135). In the seminar on *The Four Fundamental Concepts of Psychoanalysis*, Lacan moreover mentions the hypothetical tattoo inscribed on the penis that is not fully visible without the anamorphic expansion offered to the surface bearing the inscription by an erection (Lacan, 1973/1998, pp. 87–88).[2] In the same seminar, Lacan offers the most sustained example of anamorphic art in the form of Hans Holbein's painting *The Ambassadors*. He points to the "enigmatic form" situated partly on the ground and partly above the ground, at the feet of one of the two men depicted in the painting, and says that although from the usual angles this "form" that resembles "fried eggs" looked enigmatic, "if you place yourself at a certain angle from which the painting itself disappears in all its relief by reason of the converging lines of its perspective, you will see a death's head appear" (ibid., p. 135). This enigmatic form, in other words, is the anamorphic painting of a skull visible only from an angle from which the rest of the painting is invisible.

However, unlike Holbein's painting, which is an example of non-cylindrical anamorphosis, the example that Lacan gives us in the present seminar is of a cylindrical anamorphosis. In a cylindrical anamorphosis, a series of distorted circular smears on a flat surface is reflected as a clear, undistorted image on the surface of an upright cylindrical mirror situated at the centre of the flat surface when viewed from an appropriate perspective. See Figure 3.1 for an example of cylindrical anamorphosis. The figure, named "Eye", was drawn by the Hungarian painter István Orosz with Indian ink and a cylindrical mirror (Orosz, 1999).

Speaking of a piece of cylindrical anamorphic art belonging to a collector who has been already mentioned by Lacan in this seminar, he states:

> It is formed of a polished cylinder that has the function of a mirror, and around it you put a kind of bib or flat surface on which there are also indecipherable lines. When you stand at a certain angle, you see the image concerned emerge in the cylindrical mirror; in this case it is a beautiful anamorphosis of a painting of the crucifixion copied from Rubens.
>
> (Lacan, 1986/1992, p. 135)

Explaining the phenomenon further, Lacan says:

> [O]ne can say that it is because an infinitesimal fragment of image is produced on each surface of the cylinder that we see a series of screens superimposed;

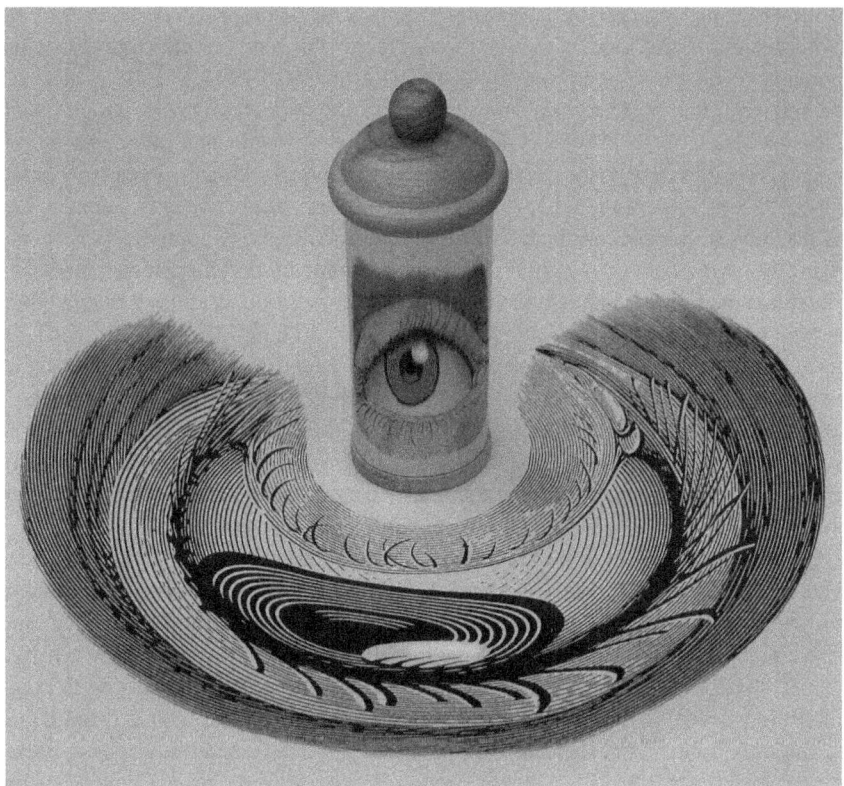

Figure 3.1 "Eye" (1999). Courtesy István Orosz

and it is as a result of these that a marvelous illusion in the form of a beautiful image of passion appears beyond the mirror, whereas something decomposed and disgusting spreads out around it.

(Ibid., p. 273)

This is what is involved in *Antigone,* according to Lacan, where the surface of tragedy at once "allows the image of Antigone to rise up as an image of passion" on it and invests the image with a radiant beauty that would illuminate all the decomposed and disgusting things spread all around it: "Seen from the outside, she appears as the victim at the centre of the anamorphic cylinder of the tragedy. She is there in spite of herself as victim and holocaust" (ibid., p. 282). This is how Antigone's passion is captured at the centre of the play.

The Limit of Life

According to Lacan, human beings undergo their first death at the hands of the signifier at the time of their entry into the symbolic order. In other words, man accedes to the order of language by paying for it with a bit of his life. The letter kills by symbolising the real, as well as by introducing the dimension of meaning to life, for meaning points to "life conjoined to death" (Lacan, 1978/1993, p. 232). Following this moment, the signifier insists throughout his life on its realisation, which Lacan terms the death drive. From this point of view, the physical death of the human being is his second death: "the death that simply involves kicking the bucket" (Lacan, 1986/1992, p. 306). Human life is thus situated at the limit between two deaths. For an instance of the second death, we may regard Antigone's apprehension by the guard following her act of burying her brother's body by defying Creon's edict that prohibited the same as the moment of her first death because, according to that edict, anyone caught violating it shall be buried alive, while her actual death that took place a little later inside the tomb as a result of the punishment was the moment of her second death. For another instance of a second death, we may turn to Lacan's seminar on *Hamlet*, given the previous year. In that play, when Hamlet is struck by the poisoned foil in the course of his fencing contest with Laertes and comes to realise that he has been mortally wounded, he entered the moment of his first death, while his actual death a little later was the time of his second death.

Lacan explains the notion of the second death in terms of three literary instances where, unlike the examples given above, the real physical death is the first death, not the second. This is so because the point Lacan wished to demonstrate over and above everything else through these is the human being's situation between two deaths thanks to the effect of the signifier, for the being is entirely reduced to a signifier after death. To begin with, the simplest metaphor for the second death could be the condition of Polyneices in Sophocles' play as a dead-body whose burial is prohibited. Already killed by his brother, his corpse bearing his name and his Name-of-the-Father has to moreover endure the ignominy of a second death due to Creon's transgressive edict. As we have seen, Tiresias asks Creon: "What use to kill the dead a second time?" This is precisely what Antigone tries to prevent by embodying the line of death as the limit of life. She tried to stall Creon's influence on Polyneices' life beyond his first death by "embodying" the line or the limit, in the sense of positing her own body as a barrier before Creon at the limit so as to protect both the limit and its beyond from the latter's transgression.

The second death may similarly be understood in terms of the notion of "hell" in *Hamlet,* where Hamlet wants to send Claudius. Accordingly, Hamlet spared Claudius's life when he found him down on his knees, praying, because Hamlet reasoned that if he killed Claudius when he was praying, he could be inadvertently saving him from going straight to hell after his death. In other words, like Creon, who wanted to kill the dead Polyneices, Hamlet, too, wanted to strike Claudius beyond the limit of his death by wishing to send him off to hell after his murder. Hamlet, however, was following the lead of Claudius and not of Creon because, for Hamlet, it was also a question of revenge, which in Elizabethan literature is often depicted in terms of paying back in the same coin, or talion punishment. Claudius had struck Senior Hamlet beyond his death by cutting him off in the blossoms of his sin and thereby depriving him of the opportunity to confess or repent before his death and thus be saved after it, and we do know that his ghost hovers over Denmark instead of resting in peace. Therefore, Hamlet wanted to make sure that Claudius suffered in the same way after his death (ibid., p. 251).

Finally, Sade's works, too, approach the same notion of the second death, albeit from a slightly different perspective. Sade depicts the transgression of the limit through the infliction of a second death in terms of the notion of the type of crime that defies the natural order. Sade thinks that it is only through crime that nature can be liberated from its own laws that imprison it. So, for Sade, it was a question of destroying the natural laws as thoroughly as possible to be able to begin once again from zero, *ex nihilo*. Hence, the second death imagined by Sade's heroes is the point at which the very cycle of transformation of nature, in the form of the cycle of death and rebirth, is annihilated. Lacan adds that this very place is articulated throughout *Antigone* as the limit. Sade directly claims in a passage in volume IV of *Juliette*, duly cited by Lacan, that in order to destroy the cycles of nature and thereby liberate both nature and man from the imprisoning laws of nature, it is necessary to inflict the second death on the individual that nature itself desires:

> Nature wants atrocities and magnitude in crimes; the more our destruction is of this type, the more they will be agreeable to it. To be of even greater service to nature, one should seek to prevent the regeneration of the body that we bury. Murder only takes the first life of the individual whom we strike down; we should also seek to take his second life, if we are to be even more useful to nature. For nature wants annihilation; it is beyond our capacity to achieve the scale of destruction it desires.
>
> (Ibid., p. 211)

Lacan further clarifies that in those cases where the second death constitutes the real physical death, the limit of the second death, or the zone between two deaths where life and death overlap, is marked by the phenomenon of the beautiful, adding that this radiant beauty at the limit splits desire. Lacan begins by pointing out that the central third of *Antigone* deals with life and death. It defines a zone where life and death overlap. In that zone, Lacan says, the effect of beauty on desire becomes manifest. In the zone between life and death, beauty is characterised by an overwhelming radiance, profundity, and magnificence. The French word used by Lacan for "splendour" is "*éclat*". The word has a wide range of meanings if we take its etymological, lexical, and idiomatic usages into account. The word variously means brilliance, flash, splinter, fragment, burst, to break violently, to split, brilliant performance or achievement, dazzling success, great acclamation or applause, and, in archaic usage, notoriety and scandal. Owing to Lacan's stress on the visual quality of Antigone's beauty, it is more appropriate to translate the word as "radiance" than as "splendour", as Dennis Porter has done. In this sense, Antigone's beauty derives from the intermediary place between the two fields. The glow of her beauty becomes most violently radiant following her moment of transgression and entry into the place of the limit between life and death alive.

Lacan moreover specifies that the radiance emitted by her beauty from the place of the limit, her tomb, splits and thus tempers the desires of the onlookers. Simply put, when desire arrives at the place of the *Atè*, it emits a radiant beauty that dazzles, petrifies, and overwhelms the onlookers to the point of splitting their desires into an old desire and a new, tempered desire that has recognised symbolisation by the signifier in some form. In the session immediately preceding those devoted to *Antigone* in the seminar *The Ethics of Psychoanalysis*, Lacan describes it as follows:

> [T]here is a certain relationship between beauty and desire. This relationship is strange and ambiguous. On the one hand, it seems that the horizon of desire may be eliminated from the register of the beautiful. Yet, on the other hand, it has been no less apparent—from the thought of antiquity down to Saint Thomas who has some valuable things to say on the question—that the beautiful has the effect, I would say, of suspending, lowering, disarming desire. The appearance of beauty intimidates and stops desire.
>
> (Ibid., p. 238)

In this passage, Lacan explains how desire is lowered by the beautiful. While speaking on *Antigone* a little later, Lacan states that desire is, in fact, "split" by the beautiful. Precisely put, the beautiful has effects on the imaginary order as well as on the aim of desire: On the one hand, the radiant image of Antigone at the limit generates a dissipatory power—it purges us of our imaginary excesses with which we construct consistent and aggrandised self-images. The imaginary dissolves at the sight of the radiance of Antigone as the embodiment of the *Atè*. On the other hand, the spectacle splits desire and produces a new desire, and thus the beautiful fulfils its function in relation to the aim of desire, for the function of the beautiful is to reveal a new aim of desire. Lacan adds that it is the power of her image of disturbing attraction situated at the centre of the tragedy that forces us to close our eyes at the very moment we look at it. In other words, we are prevented from seeing the true nature of the place of the *Atè* because of the dazzling quality of the beauty of its occupant that illuminates it. In the world of the play, this radiant beauty of Antigone plunges everyone into confusion, even blindness. Her beauty effect is a blinding effect, says Lacan. It affects the characters and the readers, including the wise ones like Goethe.

Lacan then relates the beauty of the hero at the limit to the Aristotelian notion of "catharsis", initially explaining Aristotle's concept with the help of three interrelated terms, namely, purgation, purification, and calming effect. "Purgation", or the medical term abreaction, means the discharge of unresolved emotion. It is the sense in which Hippocrates had used the term to denote the removal of morbid humours by evacuation. In addition to pointing out that in Hippocrates, "it is linked to forms of elimination, to discharge, to a return to normality", Lacan explains catharsis as purgation by quoting Molière: "which involves the elimination of 'peccant humors'" (ibid., pp. 244–245).

Lacan views "Purification" as "ritual purification" following Denis Lambin's reinterpretation of Aristotle (ibid., p. 245). The idea of catharsis as purification has several sources. The notable ones among them are the word "*cathars*", which means purification; Plato's use of the term "catharsis" in *Phaedo* where he says that the soul must be purified by philosophy; Empedocles's poem "Katharmoi" dealing with religious purification; and above all, Aristotle's discussions on "catharsis". Aristotle's most widely known reference to "catharsis" duly mentioned by Lacan figures in Book *VI* 49b27–28 of *The Poetics*, where it denotes purification: "A tragedy, then, . . . [deals] with incidents arousing pity and fear, wherewith to accomplish its *catharsis* of such emotions" (Aristotle, 335 BC/1920, p. 35). Commenting on the term "katharsis" in his Preface to Ingram Bywater's translation of *The Poetics*, Gilbert Murray sheds light on the nature of the purification involved with the help of two details. These are that "the Dionysus ritual itself was a *katharmos* or *katharsis*—a purification of the community from the taints and poisons of the past year, the old contagion of sin and death" (ibid., p. 16) and that "[i]t is worth remembering that in the year 361 B.C., during Aristotle's lifetime, Greek tragedies were introduced into Rome, not on artistic but on superstitious grounds, as a *katharmos* against a pestilence (Livy vii. 2)" (ibid., p. 16).

Speaking on catharsis as a "calming effect", Lacan points out that in Book VIII of *The Politics*, Aristotle associates it with "a certain kind of music" (Lacan, 1986/1992, p. 245). At 7.1341b37–40 of Book VIII of *The Politics*, Aristotle briefly speaks of catharsis in the context of the use of music and poetry in education. Then, at 7.1342a4–16 of the same book, he explains tragic catharsis in terms of the healing of people suffering from outbreaks of emotion (*enthousiasmos*) with the help of "cathartic songs". The sufferers were relieved of their emotional excesses by paradoxically having those very emotional excesses strongly aroused at first:

[T]he pipes are not an instrument of ethical but rather of orgiastic effect, so their use should be confined to those occasions on which the effect produced by the show is not so much instruction as a way of working off the emotions (*katharsis*).

(Aristotle, 350 BC/1992, p. 469)

[M]usic ought to be used to confer not one benefit only but many: (i) to assist education, (ii) for cathartic purposes . . . and (iii) to promote civilized pursuits, by way of relaxation and relief after tension. . . . Any feeling which comes strongly to some souls exists in all others to a greater or less degree—pity and fear, for example, but also excitement. This is a kind of agitation by which some people are liable to be possessed; it may arise out of religious melodies, and in this case it is observable that when they have been listening to melodies that have an orgiastic effect on the soul they are restored as if they had undergone a curative and purifying (*katharsis*) treatment. Those who are given to feeling pity or fear or any other emotion must be affected in precisely this way, and so must other people too, to the extent that some such emotion comes upon each. To them all inevitably comes a sort of pleasant purgation (*katharsis*) and relief.

(Ibid., pp. 473–474)

Later in the present seminar, Lacan specifies that catharsis is the "beauty effect". He explains that it derives from the relationship of the hero to the limit, or *Atè*; (Lacan, 1986/1992, pp. 281, 286) and that it is related to the "dissipatory power" of the hero's beauty there (ibid., p. 248) that serves to liquefy the imaginary of the audience, as well as to help both the hero and the audience overcome pity and fear on the way to identifying with their desire at its purest.

Lacan, moreover, describes the limit of life as intolerable. He states that the closer Antigone went to her tomb representing the limit, the more maddening it became for everyone, including Antigone herself. Thus, when Creon decrees the punishment on Antigone, the Chorus at first sings, "invincible love of combat", and then it says, this story is driving us mad. With that, Lacan thinks, we encounter "desire made visible" (ibid., p. 268), where the desire concerned is a transgressive desire present in all human beings that Antigone, by embodying it, makes manifest in the play. The image of Antigone at the place of the limit causes the Chorus to lose its head. As a result, the just appears unjust to the Chorus, and it transgresses all limits, including those imposed by Creon's edicts. Lacan thinks nothing is more moving than the desire that visibly emanates from the eyes of Antigone situated at the limit, and the Chorus is duly dazzled by it.

The impact of the limit on Creon and Haemon is even stronger. Creon and Haemon initially depict the relation of man to his good. In his conversation with Haemon, Creon does not lose his nerve; rather, he threatens his son. Then, when he is conversing with Tiresias, Creon gives the impression that, for him, everything is political, or everything is a question of interest. But soon after his conversation with Tiresias, Creon is characterised by doubt and hesitation. He gives in and countermands his orders, which proves ethically catastrophic. Lacan thinks that Creon is not a hero. He is a secondary hero in one sense and a common man in another. In tragedy, Lacan explains, the hero is situated in relation to the goal of desire, and what occurs in the play with Creon concerns subsidence or a collapse back into its premises instead of reaching out to the goal of desire. Therefore, the different layers of the secondary hero that are piled up in the course of the unfolding of a tragedy subside after a point. In the play, although he has announced that he will never yield an inch, Creon, after speaking to Tiresias, loses his nerve and asks the Chorus whether he should not yield, using the word *Atè* for the purpose. He rolls back his orders because he is a secondary hero. At the bottom, Creon is an ordinary human character. He is not a martyr who knows neither pity nor fear (ibid., pp. 265–266). In its penultimate appearance, the Chorus sings a hymn to the most hidden and supreme god, Dionysus. The limit has been breached, as Antigone has been walled in at the limit. One cannot witness the scene inside the tomb because it is beyond the reach of onlookers. Lacan mentions that Haemon emerges from there as a possessed man, someone who has lost his reason. He attacks his father and misses, and then kills himself. Creon returns to the palace to discover that his wife is dead. He, too, goes out of his mind and demands that he be dragged out by his feet.

Antigone's *kommos*, meaning complaint or lamentation, begins when she crosses the entrance to the zone between life and death and is kept in suspension there. As soon as she reaches the place of the limit, she is eliminated from the world of the living but not yet dead. At this moment, her perennial longing to be in the kingdom of death is finally consecrated, and yet, instead of being contented, she laments. Antigone is not pleased when she is rushed to the tomb by Creon, and then, after crossing the entrance, she begins her *kommos* by uncharacteristically complaining that she has been denied the marital bed, marital song, children, as well as that no one wept for her.[3] She even compares her fate to that of the ever-weeping Niobe imprisoned in a cavity in the rocks and thus forever exposed to the assault of rain and weather.[4] Lacan calls Antigone's invocation of Niobe the "image of the limit" around which "the whole play turns" (ibid., p. 268). By depicting herself as Niobe situated inside a cavity in the "rocks", Antigone identifies herself with the desire to return to the original inanimate condition in terms of which Freud sought to explain the death drive. In *Beyond the Pleasure Principle*, Freud reminds us that the inanimate state is the most natural state, as well as the aim and origin, of all living matter:

> If we are to take it as a truth that knows no exception that everything living dies for *internal* reasons—becomes inorganic once again—then we shall be compelled to say that '*the aim of all life is death*' and, looking backwards, that '*inanimate things existed before living ones.*'
> (Freud, 1920/2001, p. 38)

Notably, Freud's explanation of the death drive is thus biological or neurological in essence, which Lacan sought to rectify by offering a linguistic explanation for it or, better still, by explaining it in terms of the insistence of the symbolic order.

According to Lacan, Antigone's *kommos* can therefore be understood in two ways. The secondary meaning of Antigone's *kommos* is that one cannot embody the limit for too long. The burden is just too heavy for anyone. This is the reason that even a supremely brave and defiant character like Antigone, who alone had the courage to embody the limit in the world of the play, flinches after the act. Though Antigone's lamentation is perfectly natural from this point of view, as well as a faithful depiction of the extraordinary difficulty of embodying the limit, many commentators have been disturbed by this passage as well and failed to comprehend how it should be read in the context of the play. However, the primary meaning of Antigone's *kommos* is that, for Antigone, life can only be lived or thought of from the place of the limit where her life is already lost. Only from that place beyond life can she live life and see life necessarily as something already lost. In this sense, *kommos* is the only means available to Antigone to relate to and thus live her lost life as her lost life.

Finally, Lacan explains that the limit of life is marked by eternal suffering. Lacan thinks that Sadean thought is situated at the limit that is depicted by his fundamental fantasy of eternal suffering. This explains why Sade's victim is an indestructible support to the suffering. Although he is made to suffer endlessly, he is never destroyed by his suffering. In other words, the suffering in Sade is endless, and the victim is fixed in his state of suffering. Therefore, Lacan thinks that the limit erected by Christianity in terms of the image of crucifixion is the apotheosis of Sadism. The limit at which Christ remains fixed is his state of suffering. Which means Christ is not only fixed to his suffering, to the moment of his crucifixion, but he will remain in that state forever—he will neither be rescued and thus relieved from his state of suffering nor fully destroyed and thus liberated from suffering by death. Lacan thinks this image of desire, the desire for deathless suffering, absorbs all other images of desire. In this context, Lacan draws our attention to the significant detail that Sade, who adds the threat of unlimited suffering falling short of destruction in his depiction of his victims at the limit, also adorns his victims with beauty and grace. Thus, in *Philosophy in the Bedroom*, for instance, the victim, Eugenie, is introduced in terms of the following hyperbolic description of her beauty: "I am going to hand over to your passions a young virgin, a girl, more beautiful than Love itself" (Sade, 1795/2002, p. 7). At the Sadean limit, too, beauty is thus related to pain, though necessarily in a different way.

Kant, Sade, and *Antigone*

Lacan regarded the appearance of Immanuel Kant's *The Critique of Practical Reason* in 1788 as a turning point in the field of Western ethics. He upholds that Kant's perspective on the field of ethics has "proved to be pivotal" (Lacan, 1986/1992, p. 108). Kant, Lacan tells us, defined moral action in terms of the formula: "Act in such a way that the maxim of your action may be accepted as a universal maxim", or "act so that the maxim of your will may always be taken as the principle of laws that are valid for all" (ibid., pp. 76–77). According to this formula, which represents the moral law or the "categorical imperative" of Kant, an action is worthy of being regarded as morally sound only if it has been carried out for the sake of the moral law itself. A moral action motivated by any criterion other than pure respect for the moral law itself, no matter how good or useful it is or proves to be, is, therefore, not a morally good action. A purely moral action can be carried out only by a rational being, and it depends on, as Lacan explains, a purposeful detachment from reference to any object of passion or sentiment (ibid., p. 76). Kant's formula also points to the need for the maxim of the action to be always acceptable and universally valid.

This somewhat straightforward thesis is problematised by something in the third chapter of *The Critique* to which Lacan draws our attention: "Kant acknowledges after all the existence of *one* sentient correlative of the moral law in its purity, and strangely enough . . . it is nothing other than pain itself" (ibid., p. 80). In Kant's own words, cited by Lacan: "Consequently, we can see *a priori* that the moral law as the determining principle of will, by reason of the fact that it sets itself against our inclination, must produce a feeling one could call pain" (ibid., p. 80). The complete passage in Abbott's translation goes as follows:

> The essential point in every determination of the will by the moral law is that being a free will it is determined simply by the moral law, not only without the co-operation of sensible impulses, but even to the rejection of all such, and to the checking of all inclinations so far as they might be opposed to that law. So far, then, the effect of the moral law as a motive is only negative, and this motive can be known *a priori* to be such. For all inclination and every sensible impulse is founded on feeling, and the negative effect produced on feeling (by the check on the inclinations) is itself feeling; consequently, we can see *a priori* that the moral law, as a determining principle of the will, must by thwarting all our inclinations produce a feeling which may be called pain; and in this we have the first, perhaps the only, instance in which we are able from *a priori* considerations to determine the relation of a cognition (in this case of pure practical reason) to the feeling of pleasure or displeasure.
>
> (Kant, 1788/1889, p. 165)

In other words, since a morally good action carried out for the sake of nothing but the moral law itself sets itself against our inclination, it produces the feeling of pain. Kant sought to legitimise the pain by variously relating it to positive pride, practical advantages, moral elevation, signs of a morally good heart, et cetera. At this point, Lacan brings in the works of the Marquis de Sade. Focussing on Sade's *Philosophy in the Bedroom,* published six years after *The Critique of Practical Reason*, and especially in the chapter in the book entitled "Frenchmen, one more effort to become republicans", Lacan explains Sade's argument as follows:

> [G]iven the ruin of those authorities on which . . . the creation of a true republic depends, we should adopt the opposite of what was considered up to that point as the essential minimum of a viable and coherent morality.
>
> (Lacan, 1986/1992, p. 78)

Accordingly, Sade praises calumny, incest, adultery, theft, and so on in order to justify "the reversal of the fundamental imperatives of the moral law" (ibid., p. 78). Thus, Sade invites everyone to pursue and realise the demands of his lust to the limit, which enables Lacan to articulate the Sadean definition of moral action as follows: "Let us take as the universal maxim of our conduct the right to enjoy any other person whatsoever as the instrument of our pleasure" (ibid., p. 79).

There is no dearth of Kantian echoes in that, says Lacan. And he is dead right. In the first place, the words "universal" and "always" in Kant's definition of a morally good action, which implies doing good without limit, and the words "universal" and "any other person" in Sade's, which implies enjoyment without limit, point to the utter irrelevance of the limit for either of them. In addition, this disregard for limit is related to the elimination of every element of sentiment or passion in both Kant and Sade (ibid., p. 79). Moreover, on the question of reaching the Thing (*das Ding*), Lacan ratifies that Kant is, in fact, "of the same opinion as Sade" owing to the dimension of pain that is opened up by both:

> For in order to reach *das Ding* absolutely, to open the flood gates of desire, what does Sade show us on the horizon? In essence, pain. The other's pain as well as the pain of the subject himself, for on occasions they are simply one and the same thing.
>
> (Ibid., p. 80)

Lacan is right. The character of the Madame in *Philosophy in the Bedroom* tells us on two occasions that pleasure itself—which is the avowed goal of Sade's ethics—is attained by way of pain: "It has pleased Nature so to make us that we attain happiness only by way of pain" (Sade, 1795/2002, p. 15). And "bear in mind that it is always by way of pain one arrives at pleasure" (ibid., p. 77). Eugenie, too, describes her feelings as: "imperceptibly the pain metamorphoses into pleasure" (ibid., p. 47). But it is Dolmance who best explains why pain is necessary to produce the precondition for pleasure:

> [T]he reverberations that result in us when the sensation of pain is produced in others will essentially be of a more vigorous character, more incisive, will more energetically resound in us, will put the animal spirits more violently into circulation and these, directing themselves toward the nether regions by the retrograde motion essential to them, instantly will ignite the organs of voluptuousness and dispose them to pleasure . . . hence, pain must be preferred, for pain's telling effects cannot deceive, and its vibrations are more powerful . . . What . . . do these pains occasioned in others do to us? Hurt us? No: on the contrary, we have just demonstrated that from their production there results a sensational delight to us.
>
> (Ibid., pp. 54–55)

Dolmance repeats these views once again a little later in the text (ibid., p. 126). Therefore, Lacan contends that the Kantian turning point in ethics is by itself incomplete. Rather, it is the Other as the superego in the Sadean bedroom as an insatiable monster, coupled with the pathetic figure of the subject reduced to an instrument of this monster's limitless enjoyment, that completes the ethics of Kant. At the beginning of the essay "Kant with Sade", which illuminates Lacan's original argument better than the text of the seminar, Lacan explains that the goal of the piece is to show how *The Philosophy in the Bedroom* gives us the truth of the *Critique of Practical Reason*:

> Sade represents here the first step of a subversion of which Kant, as piquant as this may seem in light of the coldness of the man himself, represents the turning

point—something that has never been pointed out as such, to the best of my knowledge.

Philosophy in the Bedroom came eight years after the *Critique of Practical Reason*. If, after showing that the former is consistent with the latter, I can demonstrate that the former completes the latter, I shall be able to claim that it yields the truth of the *Critique*.

(Lacan, 1963/2006, pp. 645–646)

In *Antigone*, Creon represents the monstrous excess of Kant with Sade in terms of his wish to do good without limit and his strong opposition to the passion represented by Antigone, which Antigone, in turn, opposes in terms of her passion to embody the limit itself. Thus, Antigone at once directed her innermost criminal passion for death to the welfare of a singular individual, her brother, who is confronted by his second death, and opposed Creon's obsession with the welfare of "all" in his state. It is an instance of a contest between singular and all. This is what the play reveals in the context of Kant with Sade.

Antigone and the Ethics of Psychoanalysis

The ethics of psychoanalysis concerns a new relationship between action and desire that informs action. Moreover, it is an ethics, Lacan tells us, that is always related to the tragic sense of life, for it is related to the question of overcoming the limits of pity and fear. That is, psychoanalytic ethics is a path that one can take only by paying a price (Lacan, 1986/1992, p. 323). In the final section of the seminar, Lacan offers an outline of the ethics of Freudian psychoanalysis in terms of what he calls the four paradoxical propositions.

Lacan describes the first paradox as follows: "First, the only thing one can be guilty of is giving ground relative to one's desire" (ibid., p. 321). In other words, regardless of its nature and intensity, guilt, as witnessed in psychoanalysis, invariably issues from only one source:

[F]rom an analytical point of view, the only thing of which one can be guilty is of having given ground relative to one's desire. . . . In the last analysis, what a subject really feels guilty about when he manifests guilt at bottom always has to do with . . . the extent to which he has given ground relative to his desire.

(Ibid., p. 319)

Lacan clarifies that one often gives ground relative to one's desire for a good motive. However, since the question this opens up—for whose good?—does not have an "obvious" answer, such acts often end up producing guilt. Doing things in the name of the good, especially the good of the other, does not protect us from guilt because desire is concerned with "an unconscious theme" and with "a particular destiny" that insistently calls for the settling of the debt, (ibid., p. 319) rather than with the good of the other. From the point of view of psychoanalysis, therefore, the question is not whether one has acted in conformity with the good of the other but somewhat of the nature of its opposite: "Have you acted in conformity with the desire that is in you?" (ibid., p. 314). The question implies that one will tend to feel guilty if one has not done so owing to desire's tendency to remind one of one's unpaid debt unrelentingly. In other words, it is one's most important duty to pay heed to and try to fulfil one's own desires. As we have seen, Antigone took this duty seriously, for the only thing that forced her to speak and act was her own desire. All of Antigone's words and actions in the play are in conformity with her own desire, in its purest form, moreover, which is why there is no guilt in Antigone.

According to Lacan, giving ground relative to one's desire is not only related to acting in conformity with the good of the other but also related to betraying oneself or tolerating betrayal by another:

> What I call "giving ground relative to one's desire" is always accompanied in the destiny of the subject by some betrayal—you will observe it in every case and should note its importance. Either the subject betrays his own way, betrays himself, and the result is significant for him, or, more simply, he tolerates the fact that someone with whom he has more or less vowed to do something betrays his hope and doesn't do for him what their pact entailed—whatever that pact may be, fated or ill-fated, risky, short-sighted, or indeed a matter of rebellion or flight, it doesn't matter.
>
> (Ibid., p. 321)

Lacan adds that in such cases of betrayal, one gives ground relative to one's desire by promptly giving up one's claim by demeaning one's worth, as well as by condoning the betrayer by regarding him or her as superior to oneself:

> [O]ne gives ground to the point of giving up one's own claims and says to oneself, "Well, if that's how things are, we should abandon our position; neither of us is worth that much, and especially me, so we should just return to the common path." You can be sure that what you find there is the structure of giving ground relative to one's desire.
>
> (Ibid., p. 321)

In the final analysis, Lacan's first ethical proposition constitutes a paradoxical command insofar as traditional ethics, beginning with Aristotle, as well as politics, religion, and society, in general, demand the contrary of an individual: "As far as desires are concerned, come back later. Make them wait" (ibid., p. 315). However, as Lacan rightly maintains, "this is not an easy question to sustain" (ibid., p. 314). The instance of Antigone sufficiently indicates how difficult the aim to not give ground relative to one's desire can prove to be. Even a more or less pitiless, fearless, reckless, and adamant character like Antigone did not find the position easy to sustain.

Lacan's first proposition on ethics can well be read awry. It may be argued that this first proposition is paradoxical because the expression "giving ground relative to" in it may be read in contradictory ways, as "yielding to" and as "not fulfilling". We have already seen how giving ground relative to one's desire means giving up on, not fulfilling, or not paying heed to one's desire, where the guilt results from abandoning one's desire. However, giving ground relative to one's desire can also mean the exact opposite of this, in the sense that the only thing one can be guilty of is giving way to, yielding to, one's desire, as is evident in all instances of guilt, especially those that are unconsciously expressed, that ensue when one has acted upon a transgressive desire, where the guilt results from having fulfilled one's desire. Read thus, Lacan's first proposition may be seen as suggesting two ways of avoiding guilt in one go, owing to the paradox in terms of which it is expressed. Simply put, whereas certain excessively indulgent neurotics need to learn to turn deaf to and not yield to their desire all the time, certain extremely ascetic neurotics need to learn to yield to and fulfil the desire that is present in them. From this point of view, the beauty of Lacan's paradoxical proposition is that it offers solutions to the two contradictory problems of desire in terms of a single directive.

Lacan's second proposition is as follows: "Second, the definition of a hero: someone who may be betrayed with impunity" (ibid., p. 321). The hero, as opposed to the ordinary man, may be betrayed with complete disregard for consequences. Despite having the same relationship of womb and blood with Polyneices as Antigone, Ismene, for example, could easily refuse to assist Antigone in her hour of need without inciting any retaliation by doing so. Antigone, who was determined to carry out the act, decided to go ahead and do so on her own. It implies that the hero does not desert his desire under any circumstance, and he backs it against all odds, including loss of life.

Not only that, whereas the ordinary man responds to betrayal with contempt or with thoughts of revenge, the hero, paradoxically, shows us that there can be a completely different response to betrayal, in the form of indifference to the betrayal as may be seen in Antigone's response to Ismene's betrayal. However, Lacan carries the argument a step further by explaining how the act of betraying the hero might paradoxically lead to the betrayer's liberation. Thus, in *Antigone*, Antigone is the hero, and Creon is the ordinary man who betrays her without evoking any retaliation from her. In fact, "the hero bears his partner into that [liberated] zone along with him", which is the reason that:

> At the end of *Antigone* Creon henceforth speaks loudly and clearly of himself as someone who is dead among the living, and this is because he has literally lost all other goods as a result of the affair. As a consequence of the tragic act, the hero frees his adversary too.
>
> (Ibid., p. 320)

Lacan moreover gives the example of Philoctetes, who went to the shores of Troy, full of enthusiasm, to die for his country. However, he was bitten on the foot by a snake while walking on the sacred ground of Chryse with bare feet, which caused him great anguish and also emitted a horrible smell, owing to which he was dumped by Odysseus and the Atreidai on the desert island of Lemnos where he was compelled to spend ten years consumed with hatred. While he was there, Neoptelemes tried to deceive him and take Heracles's bow, which was needed for victory in the war, away from him. Lacan states that Philoctetes is a hero because he could be betrayed with impunity:

> What makes Philoctetes a hero? Nothing more than the fact that he remains fiercely committed to his hate right to the end. . . . This reveals to us not only that he has been betrayed and he is aware that he has been betrayed, but also that he has been betrayed with impunity. This is emphasized in the play by the fact that Neoptelemes, who is full of remorse because he betrayed the hero and thereby demonstrates his noble soul, comes to make proper amends and gives him back the bow that plays such an essential role in the tragic space of the play.
>
> (Ibid., p. 320)

Notably, instead of defining the hero in terms of his valour, courage, or intellect, Lacan, following Antigone, defines the hero in terms of his ability to tolerate or disregard betrayal. It is a paradox because instead of punishing the betrayer for his act of betrayal, the hero helps him to be liberated for the same.

Lacan's third proposition goes as follows:

> Third, . . . the [mysterious] difference between the ordinary man and the hero . . . For the ordinary man the betrayal that almost always occurs sends him back to the service of goods, but with the proviso that he will never again find that factor which restores a sense of direction to that service.
>
> (Ibid., p. 321)

The ordinary man is always pushed back to square one by a betrayal where he finds himself in a worse situation than before. The ordinary man is invariably betrayed, following which he collapses and falls back on the original premise, as Creon does in the play by revoking his edict, which, in fact, makes matters worse. The ordinary man thus makes the betrayal effective. The hero, by contrast, persistently embodies his deepest desire and constantly pays the price for doing so without too much complaint, as Antigone does in the play, instead of being swayed by betrayal. Even when betrayed, the hero does not allow the betrayal to be effective, as the betrayal is never allowed to make him change his position. In spite of the betrayal, the hero never loses focus of his goal and continues to make progress along the path of his desire.

Shedding further light on the difference between the ordinary man and the hero, Lacan states, "In each of us the path of the hero is traced, and it is precisely as an ordinary man that one follows it to the end" (ibid., p. 319). Differently put, the hero and the ordinary man are the same in terms of their inherent qualities. Their difference lies in the way they allow the quality to express itself. One chooses to be an ordinary man, paradoxically defying one's destiny to be a hero, primarily due to one's inability to overcome pity and fear. Lacan said, "the voice of the hero trembles before nothing" (ibid., p. 323), unlike the ordinary man who can change his position radically and undo his actions out of pity and fear. Moreover, the hero experiences the same passions as the ordinary man, with the difference that while the hero guides himself correctly, the ordinary man does not; while the passions experienced by the hero are "pure", those experienced by the ordinary man are diluted or contaminated; and while the hero is able to support himself fully in his passions, the ordinary man flinches and backtracks (ibid., p. 320). Thus, even though both Antigone and Creon find themselves in the same liberated space at the end, and they both experience similar passions at the place of the limit, they behave in quite opposite ways: Antigone embraces her death, while Creon loses his sanity. This is somewhat inevitable, given that in the world of the play, Antigone seems to be the only character, with the exception of Tiresias, who has a clear understanding of her desire. Although it is not known why, despite inheriting the same quality, some actualise it while others squander it, which makes Lacan consider their difference "mysterious", there is no doubt that the neurotic converts a hero's destiny into the life of an ordinary man. As always, he paradoxically converts his gift into shit.

Lacan's fourth proposition is, "There is no good other than that which may serve to pay the price for access to desire" (ibid., p. 321). Here, paying the price is related to five things: First, to the notion of catharsis, that is, to the overcoming of the barriers of pity and fear on the way to identifying with one's desire, something that Antigone perfectly accomplishes in the play (ibid., p. 323). Second, one is always required to pay a price for following one's desire. In Antigone's case, her life is the price she pays on the way to fulfilling her desire. It is the only price that is worth paying in life. Third, as Kant says, "the value of prudence", as in "the wholly relative value of beneficial reasons, attachments or pathological interests ... that might keep him on that risky path" (ibid., p. 323). Fourth, as Lacan explains following Freud, "to pay the price for access to desire" means that the operation of sublimation invariably exacts a price in the form of jouissance (ibid., p. 322). And fifth, the only good is that which helps us pay the price for access to our desire. At a practical level, this also means that one should work to produce the goods necessary to pay for the objects one needs to satisfy one's desire. In other words, there should neither be any surplus labour, or effort whose fruit one does not enjoy, nor any surplus enjoyment, or enjoyment that is not duly earned. In this sense, this ethical option is also the most economical option. Here, the paradox lies in regarding the act of paying the price, or the act of overcoming pity and fear, which people in general tend to avoid out of fear, as the only good that one can do.

Notes

1 While Antigone argues that a husband or a child is replaceable, and Lacan does not question her reasoning while commenting on it, I am thankful to Russell Grigg for helping me

realise that, strictly speaking, no one is replaceable. I agree with him because everyone is singular, and therefore, the sense of loss created by the death of a person cannot be eradicated by the introduction of another. In this context, Grigg drew my attention to an excerpt from one of Freud's letters to Ludwig Binswanger. In the second part of a single letter in two parts dated 11th and 12th April, 1929, respectively, the latter date being the birthday of his fifth child and second daughter Sophie, whom he had lost when she was 27, Freud consoled Binswanger who had lost his 20-year-old eldest son Robert, stating:

> We know that the acute sorrow we feel after such a loss will run its course, but also that we will remain inconsolable, and will never find a substitute. No matter what may come to take its place, even should it fill that place completely, it remains something else. And that is how it should be. It is the only way of perpetuating a love that we do not want to abandon.
>
> (Freud & Binswanger, 1992/2003, p. 196)

2 Lacan wonders, "How is it that nobody has ever thought of connecting this with . . . the effect of an erection?" (Lacan, 1973/1998, pp. 87–88). The connection between anamorphism and erection must have occurred to the Indian comedian who performed in the early 1980s at an informal gathering in our college canteen, of course, without any knowledge of Lacan's teaching. For he spoke of the word "Voss" tattooed on the penis of an individual whose meaning became clear to his friends one day when he had an erection in his sleep: "Victoria Cross"!
3 Antigone is not right on the last count, as Haemon's account to Creon suggests. People did sympathise with her, and they did so genuinely, although they did not have the courage to embody the limit themselves.
4 Niobe was the daughter of Tantalus, the ruler of Sipylus, and the wife of Amphion of Thebes. In Greek mythology, Niobe—who had fourteen children, seven male and seven female—boasted of her superiority to the goddess Leto for having seven times more children than her. For doing so, Artemis and Apollo slayed the children of Niobe, the sight of whose dead bodies led Amphion to kill himself in grief in one version, and be killed by Apollo for vowing to take revenge in another version. A devastated Niobe fled to Mount Sipylus and was turned into a stone waterfall in the course of her incessant weeping. Owing to the dramatic nature of her life, Niobe has been the subject of writing by Homer, Aeschylus and Sophocles.

References

Aristotle (1920). *Poetics*. In Ingram Bywater Trans. Clarendon Press (Original work published 335 BC).
Aristotle (1992). *The Politics*. In T.A. Sinclair Trans. Penguin Books (Original work published 350 BC).
Freud, Sigmund (2001). Beyond the Pleasure Principle. In James Strachey (Ed.), *The Standard Edition of the Complete Psychological Works of Sigmund Freud*, Vol. XVIII. Vintage, Hogarth Press and the Institute of Psychoanalysis, 7–64 (Original work published 1920).
Freud, Sigmund and Binswanger, Ludwig (2003). *The Sigmund Freud—Ludwig Binswanger Correspondence, 1908–1938*. In Gerhard Fichtner (Ed.) and Arnold J. Pomerans Trans. Other Press (Original work published 1992).
Hegel, Georg Wilhelm Friedrich (1975a). *Aesthetics: Lectures on Fine Art*, Vol. I. In T.M. Knox Trans. Oxford University Press (Original work published 1835).
Hegel, Georg Wilhelm Friedrich (1975b). *Aesthetics: Lectures on Fine Art*, Vol. II. In T.M. Knox Trans. Oxford University Press (Original work published 1835).
Hegel, Georg Wilhelm Friedrich (1977). *Phenomenology of Spirit*. In A.V. Miller Trans. Oxford University Press (Original work published 1807).

Hegel, Georg Wilhelm Friedrich (2001). *Philosophy of Right*. In S.W. Dyde Trans. Batoche Books (Original work published 1820).
Heidegger, Martin (2002). The Origin of the Work of Art. In Julian Young and Kenneth Hayness (Eds.) and Trans. *Off the Beaten Track*. Cambridge University Press, 1–56 (Original work published 1950).
Kant, Immanuel (1889). *Critique of Practical Reason and Other Works on The Theory of Ethics*. In Thomas Kingsmill Abbott Trans. Longman's, Green & Co, 85–262. (Original work published 1788).
Lacan, Jacques (1992). *The Seminar of Jacques Lacan. Book VII. The Ethics of Psychoanalysis, 1959–1960*. In Dennis Porter Trans. Routledge (Original work published 1986).
Lacan, Jacques (1993). *The Seminar of Jacques Lacan. Book II. The Ego in Freud's Theory and in the Technique of Psychoanalysis, 1954–1955*. In Sylvana Tomaselli Trans. W.W. Norton. (Original work published 1978).
Lacan, Jacques (1998). *The Seminar of Jacques Lacan. Book XI. The Four Fundamental Concepts of Psychoanalysis, 1964*. In Alan Sheridan Trans. W.W. Norton (Original work published 1973).
Lacan, Jacques (2006). Kant with Sade. In Bruce Fink Trans., in collaboration with Héloïse Fink and Russell Grigg, *Écrits: The First Complete Edition in English*. W.W. Norton, 645–668 (Original work published 1963).
Lacan, Jacques (2015). *The Seminar of Jacques Lacan, Book VIII: 1960–1961: Transference*. In Bruce Fink Trans. Polity Press. (Original work published 1991).
Orosz, István (1999). *Eye*. Available at https://istvanorosz.com/ (Accessed on 4th December, 2023).
Sade, Marquis de (2002). *Philosophy in the Bedroom*. In Richard Seaver and Austryn Wainhouse Trans. Supervert 32C Inc. (Original work published 1795).
Sophocles (1947). Antigone. In E.F. Watling Trans. *The Theban Plays*. Penguin Books, 126–162 (Original work published 441 BC).
Sophocles (1954). Antigone. In Elizabeth Wyckoff Trans. *The Complete Greek Tragedies*. University of Chicago Press, 158–204 (Original work published 441 BC).
Sophocles (1977). Antigone. In Dudley Fitts and Robert Fitzgerald Trans. *The Oedipus Cycle*. Harcourt Brace, 186–245 (Original work published 441 BC).

Chapter 4

The Coûfontaine Trilogy

Lacan held Paul Claudel in high regard as a writer. He was familiar with the plays, poetry, essays, art criticism, and correspondence of Claudel and considered him "one of the greatest poets who ever lived" (Lacan, 1991/2015, p. 271). He invoked Claudel's *The Coûfontaine Trilogy* between 3rd May and 24th May, 1961 in sessions 19 through 22 of his 1960–1961 seminar on *Transference* (*Le Transfert*) with an aim to illuminate certain important psychoanalytical concepts, such as the psychoanalyst's position in the transference, "refusal" (*Versagung*), the father in the Oedipus complex, structural repetition of family myths across generations, the stages of desire, et cetera, and at the same time shed psychoanalytical light on a number of key elements in the trilogy, such as, Sygne's "No", Turelure's abjection, Pensée's desire, the peculiarity of the names of the characters, et cetera. In order to assist Anglophone readers not familiar with Claudel and *The Coûfontaine Trilogy* in comprehending Lacan's discourse on the latter, it would be appropriate to begin with a brief introduction to the French playwright and the three plays.

Paul Claudel

Paul Claudel (1868–1955) was a French diplomat by profession who served as the French consul in China and several countries in Europe and Brazil before serving as the French ambassador to Japan, U.S.A., and Belgium. Claudel was, moreover, a devout Roman Catholic. According to Rabaté, "it was a particular Catholicism, since he was converted at the age of eighteen after reading Rimbaud's poems" (Rabaté, 2001, p. 149). Claudel derived his mysticism and many of his literary qualities from his faith in Catholicism. George Steiner states in *The Death of Tragedy* that "Claudel was less a Christian than a special and somewhat terrifying kind of Roman Catholic" (Steiner, 1961/1980, p. 340). Claudel passionately loved *The Bible* all his life and strongly believed that it ought to be read with the assistance of the teachings and the liturgy of the Church. His works were greatly admired by Pope Pius XII, who, according to Paul Lesourd's report to Claudel in May 1949, considered him "the greatest writer of Christian France" (Claudel, 1969, p. 684). Claudel, who had attended the inauguration ceremony of Pope Pius XII as an invitee in 1939, was, in fact, honoured by the latter in April 1950 in an unprecedented public ceremony in which some of Claudel's poems were dramatically represented by French actors at Vatican's Consistory Hall in the presence of the Pope himself.

But Claudel is known throughout the world as a major figure in French literature of the first half of the 20th century. He was a poet, essayist and playwright who is especially remembered for his 1906 play *The Break of Noon* (*Le Partage de Midi*), the 1912 play *The Tidings Brought to Mary* (*L'Annonce faite à Marie*), the 1929 play *The Satin Slipper* (*Le Soulier de Satin*), and his 1910 confessional lyric poetry *Five Great Odes* (*Cinq Grandes Odes*), which was greatly influenced by the Scriptures. Claudel's plays were distinctive for their Catholic, lyrical, and epic qualities. Apart from the scriptures, he was influenced in varying degrees by Aeschylus, Lope de Vega, Shakespeare, Calderón, Corneille, and Wagner in particular as a playwright, and by Rimbaud, Dante, Virgil, Verlaine, and Mallarmé in particular as a poet. He was also influenced by Dostoevsky on psychological matters as a writer. Apart from these authors, Claudel read and admired the works of Homer, Pindar, Catullus, Horace, Seneca, Pascal, Bossuet, Baudelaire, Hugo, Balzac, and others.

Like many of his contemporaries, such as Paul Valéry, Marcel Proust, André Gide, and Charles Péguy, Claudel, too, revolted in his own way against 19th-century positivism and the extreme use of symbolism at the cost of realism. Like these contemporaries, Claudel, too, experimented in his own way with the French language in order to offer new views of the world and of the function of art. Claudel is known for introducing a special type of free verse consisting of long and usually unrhymed lines of irregular metre that came to be known as the Claudelian verse (*verset claudélien*), which is Claudel's contribution to French prosody. He was also an innovative playwright who sought to "break the bounds of the traditional stage" by using in an interlaced form "the orchestra, the film, and the mechanical enlargement of the human voice" (Steiner, 1961/1980, p. 334), more specifically, Wagnerian play, Japanese Noh theatre, cinema of the 1920s and 1930s, and magnification of voice with the help of sound equipment. However, Claudel's plays are often difficult to stage because they are far too long and bear complexities that are extremely difficult to negotiate on stage, such as "the instantaneous transition from the real, in a visual and normal sense, to the purely imaginary" in *Le Soulier de Satin* (ibid., p. 341). The one director who was able to do justice to Claudel's plays more than any other is Jean-Louis Barrault in the 1940s.

Claudel's forever strong religious faith, which always informed his writing, increasingly overshadowed his literary bent over the years. He initially believed, for instance, that the object of poetry is the sacred universe of invisible things created by God:

The object of poetry, thus, is not dreams, illusions, or ideas, as many believe. Instead, its object is this sacred reality, given once and for all, in the center of which we have been placed. It is the universe of things invisible. It is all this that beholds us and that we behold. All of this is God's work, which cannot be exhausted by any description or any song, whether from the greatest of poets or from the tiniest little bird.

(Claudel, 1920/1995, p. 359)

But towards the end of his life, he rejected literature altogether and embraced the Scriptures alone. He said, "[s]trictly speaking, I have no further need to engage with literature", adding, "I have renounced all fictional work now and kneel before the Sacred Books in ever-increasing awe" (Cited by Rousseaux, 1949, p. 42).[1]

Despite being an original user of language, a powerful, innovative playwright, and a revolutionary writer with respect to some of his contemporary literary trends, Claudel's religious and socio-political views were that of a conservative. He disliked the protestants for what he considered their blindness and strongly disliked Martin Luther's writing. He detested the Church of England even more. His attitude towards Judaism was somewhat ambivalent: He remained anti-Jewish despite developing some pro-Jewish sentiments over time; even though he actively defended Israel and had several good Jewish friends, he believed that the Jews would convert to Catholicism one day. Although he usually glorified Judaism in his plays, he appears somewhat anti-Semitic in his 1940 poem "Paroles ou Maréchal" and the 1944 essay "Adieu à Giraudoux", and even complained in a letter in 1936, "everywhere Jews are at the forefront in parties of social or religious subversion" (Claudel, 1937, p. vii). He hated Muslims and compared Islam to Nazism even though he did not know the religion well. Socio-politically, he was a misogynist, an intense nationalist at times, a strong supporter of French imperialism, and an upholder of the values and traditions that prevailed in France prior to the French Revolution. No wonder then that Claudel's views and opinions were not admired by the modern, post-revolution generations. In his 1993 book *L'affaire Claudel*, Gilles Cornec discusses the reasons why he continues to be despised by such a large number of people in France even today (Cornec, 1993). However, despite being disliked for his conservative, even reactionary, views, he is admired for his literary abilities by most readers. Wystan Hugh Auden best captured this paradoxical response evoked by Claudel in his 1939 poem "In Memory of W.B. Yeats" where he wrote:

> Time that with this strange excuse
> Pardoned Kipling and his views,
> And will pardon Paul Claudel,
> Pardons him for writing well.
> (Auden, 1945, p. 50)

In other words, Time will pardon Paul Claudel's conservative views precisely owing to his ability to write well. Somewhat similarly, Steiner thinks that despite all the problematic attributes of his plays, he is one of the two great lyric playwrights of the century:

> Claudel is a maddening writer: he is pompous, intolerant, rhetorical, amateurish, prolix—what you will. Many of his plays are fantastically turgid, and there

are in all of them patches of arid vehemence. He stomps through the theatre like an incensed bull, goring and tossing and finally running into the wall with a great crack of horns. But no matter. There is enough grandeur left, enough sheer power of invention, to make of Claudel one of the two great lyric playwrights of the century. With Claudel there returns to the theatre the fantasy, the spaciousness, the blaze of rhetoric which had lain dormant since Shakespeare and Calderón.

(Steiner, 1961/1980, p. 333)

Steiner also proclaims that the three "masters of drama in our century are Claudel, Montherlant and Brecht" (ibid., xii). Somewhat like Freud, who never won the Nobel Prize despite being nominated thirteen times, Claudel received eight nominations for the Nobel Prize, six times between 1926 and 1955, but never went on to win the prize.

Claudel's *The Coûfontaine Trilogy* (*La Trilogie des Coûfontaine*) comprises *The Hostage* (*L'Otage*), *Crusts* (*Le Pain dur*), and *The Humiliation of the Father* (*Le Père humilié*). The three plays deal with the three generations of the Coûfontaine family. Claudel began to write *The Hostage* in 1908 when he was posted in Beijing, and he completed the play two years later when he was posted in Prague. The play was first published in two consecutive issues of *La Nouvelle Revue Française* in December 1910 and January–February 1911, and it premiered at the Théâtre de L'Œuvre on 5th June, 1914, produced by Lugné-Poe. Claudel wrote *Crusts* or *Stale Bread* between 1913 and 1915 when he was posted in Hamburg. The play was published in *La Nouvelle Revue Française* in 1918, and it was staged in Geneva in 1941 by the Pitoëff company and in Canada in 1943 before being produced in Paris at the Théâtre de l'Atelier on 12th March, 1949 by André Barsacq. Claudel began to write *The Humiliation of the Father* in July 1914, when he was posted in Hamburg, and completed it before July 1916, when he was posted in Rome. The play was published in the *La Nouvelle Revue Française* in September and October 1919, and it was first performed possibly in Germany in 1926, and then at Dresden's Schauspielhaus on 26th November, 1928. The play was staged in Paris for the first time at the Théâtre des Champs-Élysées under Jean Valcourt's direction on 10th May, 1946. All three plays are richly laden with historical and religious symbolism.

The Trilogy

The Hostage covers the period that followed the French Revolution up to the spring of 1814 when Napoleon I was in power. One of the protagonists of the play, the aristocrat Sygne de Coûfontaine, whose parents had been guillotined during the Revolution and whose privileges and possessions had been taken away from her, has been patiently reconstructing the former Coûfontaine estate for ten years: "[Her] whole youth spent gathering together and patching up the scraps of this estate" (Claudel, 1910–1911/1945, p. 13). It is in this estate that the play is set.

The play begins sometime in 1812 when Napoleon was in Moscow; his army that had invaded Russia was on the verge of losing the campaign, and his political captive, Pope Pius VII, was languishing in one of his prisons. One night around this time, when Sygne was sitting in the library checking her accounts, her cousin George arrived at the Coûfontaine estate. George de Coûfontaine, too, had lost his parents at the scaffold. However, unlike Sygne, who had stayed on, George went into exile following the Revolution and was Lord Lieutenant of King Louis of France, exiled to England. He secretly showed up at the estate from time to time. George had a wife and two children. He loved his wife a lot, but it was only after her death that he came to know the truth about her that was always known to everyone else, namely that she was the Dauphin's mistress, though this is historically untrue because, as Lacan tells us, no French Prince had emigrated to England at that time. George had also lost his son and daughter to English fever in quick succession. He thus returned home from England, having lost almost everything that he valued as a person, barring his loyalty to the royal cause. As Lacan rightly points out, the two cousins are depicted as "being thoroughly disappointed and truly tragically isolated" (Lacan, 1991/2015, p. 275). After sharing these sad pieces of information with Sygne, George declares his love for her. As Sygne loved him too, they gave each other their hand and made a sacred commitment before God to never take it back (Claudel, 1910–1911/1945, p. 19). George also speaks to Sygne about restoring the King of France to the throne even if Coûfontaine were to perish in the process (ibid., p. 20). Most importantly, George had, in fact, daringly kidnapped the Pope while he was being transferred to one of Napoleon's prisons—which, too, is historically untrue—and brought him to the Coûfontaine estate and hidden him in the cellar, which Sygne too gets know a little later. The Pope was thus effectively his "prisoner" (ibid., p. 28) and hostage. George offers to take the Pope to England to free him from the clutches of Napoleon, but he refuses to go into exile.

In the second Act, the arch-villain Baron Toussaint Turelure arrives at the Coûfontaine estate. He used to be a servant of the Coûfontaine family. He was a "*sans-culotte*" during the French Revolution, meaning a lower-class and usually extremely militant partisan in the Revolution, and was responsible for the death of Sygne's parents. Claudel describes his physical appearance as "slightly lame. His nose is long and hooked and grows directly from his forehead, giving him somewhat the appearance of a ram" (ibid., p. 39). As the Prefect of the Empire, he was in charge of the police. He was aware of the Pope's abduction and knew that he was hidden in the Coûfontaine estate. Since he was in love with Sygne, he agreed to free the Pope, as well as to free George and not confiscate the noble estate in exchange for Sygne's hand in marriage—a marriage that would make him the father of the future Lord of Coûfontaine. The priest Badilon, despite being perfectly aware of the unjust nature of Turelure's demand and the horrendous sacrifice Sygne is required to make in order to fulfil it, takes to encouraging Sygne to accept the atrocious proposal in order to save the Pope. For him, the Pope's well-being was far more important than Sygne's hate, love, values, commitment, and happiness. Badilon appeals to her weakness by stating that, as Lacan summarises it, "she would become the agent of an act of sublime deliverance" (Lacan, 1991/2015, p. 275). After violently refusing to marry the murderer of her parents, whom she deeply hated, she eventually resigns herself to this ghastly sacrifice. She becomes the Baroness Turelure and later gives birth to a son.

The last Act is set in the spring of 1814 when the armies of the enemy surround Paris. As the Prefect of Paris, Turelure agrees to restore King Louis XVIII's throne to him on condition that Sygne shall hand over her rights and the name Coûfontaine to her son. George, who is in charge of the negotiation, decides to assassinate Turelure. Turelure, too, decides to kill George. At 3 a.m., the two men open fire at each other simultaneously from their revolvers. While Turelure's shot kills George, the latter's shot kills Sygne, who had thrown herself in front of her husband (Claudel, 1910–1911/1945, p. 77). Before her death, which Lacan regards as a suicide rather than a sacrifice, Sygne develops a facial tic, which is akin to the gesture of negation. When Sygne is on her deathbed, Badilon commends her for her sacrifice while she laments breaking her oath of loyalty to George. When Badilon asks whether she has forgiven her husband, she makes a "negative gesture" (ibid., p. 80). When he asks whether he should bring her child to her, she says, "No" (ibid., p. 80).[2] When he asks her to make with him "rites of hope and charity", she makes a "negative gesture" (ibid., p. 80). In the last scene of the play, the bodies of the two Coûfontaines are allowed to rest side by side on the same table, covered with a flag embroidered with the fleur-de-lys (ibid., p. 81). Thus, as Rabaté rightly points out,

> in spite of Claudel's Catholicism there is a scathing critique of the Pope (old, weak, ineffectual, too compromised by the realpolitik of the times) and the confessor [Badilon], a shady type who uses moral blackmail to force Sygne to renounce her love and life.
>
> (Rabaté, 2001, p. 149)

At the end, the King enters. His order is restored, and he justly rewards Turelure by naming him Count (Claudel, 1910–1911/1945, p. 85). In this play, therefore, the Pope is a hostage in the most obvious and literal sense of first being a "prisoner" of George at the Coûfontaine estate and later being a hostage at the hands of Turelure, who would exchange him for the hand of Sygne in marriage. In a slightly less obvious but equally literal sense, the Coûfontaine estate and the Coûfontaine cousins, especially Sygne, are held hostage by the same Turelure. But in a more profound sense, Sygne is the hostage in the play, not merely, as Rabaté suggests, at the hands of Badilon, who forces her "to betray her own desire" and "to renounce all her hopes for the continuation of her true family heritage" (ibid., p. 149) but rather at the hands of Christianity itself.

Crusts is set twenty years after *The Hostage*, when France was under the reign of Louis-Philippe. The play's action is dominated by four out of its six dramatis personae. Turelure is as unscrupulous as before but an older and more sinister man now. The second is his son Louis, who was baptised on the day of the death of his mother, Sygne, and named after the restored King. He has a huge debt to settle and gives next to no importance to morality. Sichel, Turelure's cunning, sensitive, and self-seeking Jewish mistress whom he tyrannises, but who is as unscrupulous as him, is the third. And finally, there is Lumir, Louis's young Polish mistress who sincerely loves Louis but is far more passionate about serving the Polish cause related to the splitting of Poland into Prussia, the Habsburg monarchy, and Russia. She can go to any extreme to get what she believes is hers, including yielding to the advances of Turelure if required. There is a fifth character, Sichel's father, Ali Habenichts, who is relatively less important than the other four. When Louis demands his inheritance from his father soon after attaining adulthood (Claudel, 1918/1945, p. 121), Turelure employs Habenichts to help him retrieve the possessions of the Coûfontaines from his own son.

Louis has incurred a huge debt of twenty thousand francs, of which ten thousand francs or more was borrowed from Lumir, and he cannot pay it back due to his insolvency. The money lent to Louis was not Lumir's own. It was the savings of the Polish immigrants and martyrs kept in her custody. Leaving Louis behind in Algeria, Lumir arrives at Turelure's house to demand from the latter the money that Louis owes to her, though her ulterior motive is to retrieve twenty thousand francs from him. Since Turelure refuses to pay, Sichel and Lumir hatch a plot to kill this avaricious man after extracting the dues from him. Louis suddenly arrives from Algeria at this point.

Lumir infuriates Louis against his father by pricking his male ego. She tells him that Turelure had made advances to her and was trying to buy back Louis's land cheaply because he wanted to dispossess him of his property and his mistress:

> You want a woman and you're not able to protect her. Are you a man or aren't you? Are you going to let people walk all over you forever? Without saying a word? How much longer are you going to let that old corpse sit on your shoulders and drive you as he pleases? Wasn't it enough when he took your property . . . ? Now he wants your wife. Yes, me! He comes along and takes me away from under your very nose!
>
> (Ibid., p. 118)

After driving him mad, Lumir informs him that his father had twenty thousand francs on him at that time and arms him with two pistols. Although she had loaded both with bullets, she tells him that only the bigger one was loaded with a bullet while the smaller one was loaded blank. She suggests that he should fire the smaller one first, for the fright produced by the sound of the shot should be enough to kill the frail old coward, adding that "Sichel put that idea into my head" and that the latter shall not come in his way (ibid., p. 120), which indicates that both the women were involved in the plot to kill Turelure. Louis first implores his father for the money, but when his father repeatedly refuses to give it, he fires both pistols at once. Even though both the pistols misfire, Turelure dies out of fright from the noise, as anticipated. While Lumir is searching his body for the money, Louis checks the pistols and comes to know that both of them were loaded.

Louis receives his inheritance following the act of parricide and settles his debt with Lumir. He becomes an ambassador to Algeria and urges Lumir to accompany him to the Mitidja Plain. Although she loves him, she turns down his offer and leaves for Poland instead with an aim to try to liberate her homeland from foreign domination with the help of her compatriots, even if she were to fail in that mission, which Lacan thinks is Claudel's way of describing her "desire for death" (Lacan, 1991/2015, p. 324). She invites Louis to leave for Poland with her, but he refuses to do so even though he loves her. Before leaving, she suggests that Louis should marry Sichel, for she loved him and he had killed her man: "Marry your father's mistress! . . . Haven't you deprived her of Turelure . . . ? . . . She's in love with you!" (Claudel, 1918/1945, p. 139). Louis does get engaged to Sichel at the end, who, it is revealed, had always loved him and who won him over by returning to him all of Turelure's wealth, which the latter had placed in the hands of her father.

In this exceptionally scathing play by Claudel, Christian values are unscrupulously replaced by despicable self-serving behaviour, sordid disingenuousness, awfully mean designs, and, as Lacan puts it, "extreme calculations" (Lacan, 1991/2015, p. 286). This is aptly symbolised by the bronze statue of Christ saved by Sygne lying "on the floor"—and which shall be sold to Habenichts for a very low price at the play's end—while a "hideous idol" in the form of the portrait of "an old man with pink cheeks and a wig" hung at the place on the wall where the statue of Christ used to be (Claudel, 1918/1945, pp. 134–135).

The Humiliation of the Father is set twenty years after *Crusts*, in Rome, from 1869 to 1871, just before the capture of Rome by the Garibaldians. Act I of the play opens on the Feast of St. Pius, dated 5th May, 1869, with a costume ball on a beautiful evening in the garden of the villa of the exiled Polish Prince Wronsky. The feast is also meant to be a farewell to the Prince from Rome. He always wears on his arm a cameo of the Countess Lumir, who "died under rather tragic circumstances" (Claudel, 1919/1945, p. 164). Sichel, costumed as Night, is in the arm of Prince Wronsky, costumed as River Tiber. Pensée de Coûfontaine, the blind but beautiful daughter of Louis and Sichel, is costumed as Autumn. Although the audience knows that she is blind, no one at the party can guess as she moves about as though she is sighted. She meets Orian and Orso de Homodarmes, nephews of the Pope. Pensée takes Orian on a walk through the gardens, where they confess their love for each other. Although Orian is a committed soldier who received his spiritual mentoring from the Pope and was quite ambivalent about love, he does return Pensée's love even though he denies it to his uncle later.

In Act II, the Pope has a tense conversation with the Minorite Brother regarding the threats to the States of the Holy See. Later, when Orian and Orso join the Pope following the exit of the Minorite Brother, the Pope advises Orian to renounce his passion, serve his religious vocation, and let his younger brother Orso marry Pensée.

Act III is set in September 1870, when the Papal States under Pope Pius IX had been defeated by the Italian troops led by General Raffaele Cadorna, and France was defeated by the Prussian and German forces in the ongoing Franco-Prussian War. The Act begins with the meeting of Orian and Pensée after an interval of one year. Since both of them still loved each other very much, they yielded to their passion. Later, Pensée's engagement with Orso is broken. In the final Act, set in 1871, Pensée is an expectant mother of Orian's child. Orso arrives to inform Pensée that Orian has been killed in the battle against the Germans, and he has sent a message to her along with his heart buried in a pot of lilies. In the message, Orian tells Pensée that she should continue to live no matter what and urges her to marry his more handsome brother Orso, who is in love with her. Pensée decides to live for her baby's sake and agrees to marry Orso in order to save the name of her child from shame, but not before Orso proclaims that she shall always remain a sister to him (ibid., p. 222). The play thus points to the symbolic reunion of the two brothers through the figure of Pensée. At the end of the play, Pensée inhales the fragrance of the lilies growing out of Orian's heart in the flowerpot in order to "breathe in his soul" (ibid., p. 221). Among other things, Pensée's unborn child signifies the hope of reconciliation between Rome and Israel, in which Claudel forever had an interest. Claudel wanted to write a fourth play around the character of an old Pensée but was unable to do so at the end.

The Symbolic Affects the Flesh through the Signifier in the Name

Claudel was often innovative with the names of the characters in his work in terms of spelling and pronunciation, and he was very particular about these. Lacan's attention was drawn to *The Hostage* partly due to Claudel's insistence on the use of a circumflex in the upper case Û in the spelling of the name "COÛFONTAINE"—as part of the Dramatis Personae that is always written in the upper case in French plays, and as part of the motto "*COÛFONTAINE ADSUM*"—that had never been used in the French language before and not permitted by French typefaces. "[T]he sign of this missing signifier", among other things, made Lacan want to read the play (Lacan, 1991/2015, p. 272). Others, too, have noticed and interpreted the specialty of the names of Claudel's characters. Steiner, for instance, thought that such names attributed an element of strangeness to these characters so as to indicate that they had been specifically singled out for special suffering: "Claudel always chose names which surround his personages with a penumbra of strangeness, which convey that they are beings set apart for the grace of exceptional suffering" (Steiner, 1961/1980, p. 335). As someone who took a special interest in the signifier, Lacan did not overlook the specialty of these names.

Lacan states that Claudel spells the "odd" name "Sygne", which is akin to the French word "signe", meaning "sign", by substituting the "y" for the "i" in order to indicate to the readers that it contains a sign. Lacan adds that one must begin with "what is signified by the passion undergone by [the sign] Sygne" in the first play in order to understand what is meant by the "Pensée" of desire in the last play, Pensée being an undistorted French name meaning "thought" or "idea" (Lacan, 1991/2015, p. 300). With regard to "Coûfontaine", Rabaté points out that "cou", without a circumflex, means "neck", which would remind the readers that "the whole family has fallen victim to the revolutionary guillotine", while "coû", with the circumflex, tilts the meaning towards "Coût" or "cost", and through it, towards jouissance, in terms of the price extracted from the members of the family by Fate (Rabaté, 2001, p. 148). It may be noted in this context that the upper case "U" resembles the shape of the human neck, and the circumflex accent on it, Û, resembles a guillotine descending on the neck.

Regarding "Lumir", Claudel's specific instruction that the name should be pronounced "Loumyir" (Claudel, 1918/1945, p. 88) makes Lacan think that Claudel was taking on the role of Turelure "who changes everyone's name in a derisory way, calling Rachel Sichel (Claudel, 1918/1945, pp. 91–92), which in German means, as the text tells us, sickle—and in particular, the sickle that portrays the crescent moon in the sky" (Lacan, 1991/2015, p. 305). Although "Lumir" is a Polish character, the name plays on the French word for light, "*lumière*". Lacan specifies that the nature of the light shall become clear in the course of the conversation between the Pope and the two brothers, Orso and Orian, in the last play: "cruel . . . light" (Claudel, 1919/1945, p. 195) (Lacan, 1991/2015, p. 305). Lacan adds that the character who will incarnate the light is Pensée: "Pensée is going to become the incarnate object of the desire for this light. And the poet cannot but imagine and portray this flesh-and-blood thought [*pensée*], this living Pensée, to us as blind" (ibid., p. 305). In the French text, there is a circumflex on the "i" in "Lumîr". Insofar as the "i" resembles a lamp, more precisely a burning candle, the circumflex on it has the appearance of a bent palm or an object in the act of putting out the flame.

Lacan rightly mentions that the name "Orian" is just one letter away from the constellation "Orion" into which Diana had transformed the hunter by that name (ibid., p. 307). As a constellation, Orion has a relation to light or Lumir. The last name of Orian and Orso is "Homodarmes", which is a distortion of "*Homme d'armes*", literally "man with weapons", referring to the armed warrior in the Middle Ages, and is reminiscent of "*gendarme*" or "armed people". Since the brothers are soldiers, Lacan states that the distortion "is truly Claudelian in inspiration, given its resonance owing to the same slightly deformed and accentuated construction as a signifier that we bizarrely encounter in so many characters in Claudel's plays" (ibid., p. 306).

Lacan points out that in the name of Sichel's father, Ali Habenichts, "Habenichts" means "he who has nothing" (ibid., p. 287). Elsewhere, Lacan states that it is not by chance that Louis' words to his father, "*Tu es le père* [You are my father], all the same", is doubled by, or superimposes on, "*tuer le père* [kill your father]" that Lumir had suggested to Louis, (ibid., pp. 322–323) both the expressions playing on the name "Turelure".

Going beyond Claudel's own play on names, Lacan, pointing to the history of the name "Louis", states, albeit in order to provide comic relief:

> The name Louis comes from Ludovicus, Ludovic, Lodovic, and Clodovic that we find among the Merovingians, and is nothing other than Clovis with the C removed. That's easier to see when it's written. This makes Clovis the first Louis. And we might wonder if everything wouldn't have been different if Louis XIV

had known that he was actually Louis XV. Perhaps the style of his reign would have been different and so on indefinitely.

(Ibid., p. 285)

Above all, Lacan thinks that the characters in Claudel's trilogy are symbols only insofar as they are operative "at the heart of the impact of the symbolic on a person". Differently put, the "ambiguity of the names" suggests that they can justly be interpreted as "instances of the impact of the symbolic on our very flesh" (ibid., p. 300). The most pertinent example of this is Sygne, who makes the sign "No" in terms of the signifier of a facial, i.e., bodily tic.

Sygne's Sacrifice and Sygne's "No"

The nature of Sygne's bond with her motherland, a bond that ties the bond of kinship to a local bond, induced her to reconstitute the former Coûfontaine estate painstakingly. Her bond brings out the importance of certain values that are organised around a particular form of speech, such as giving one's word. Sygne had moreover given her word, made a sacred commitment to George, and offered herself to him as his wife. Despite her bond with her country, her family, her estate, and George, she is compelled to make a sacrifice of unimaginable proportion when Badilon, the priest, persuades her to marry Turelure in order to help save the Pope. As Lacan points out, the old Turelure is cynical, ugly, mean, lame, somewhat twisted, and hideous. Not only that, he was the son of a sorcerer who was Sygne's wet nurse and, therefore, her servant. Moreover, he was openly instrumental in having almost all the members of the Coûfontaine family decapitated in 1793 (ibid., p. 273). Therefore, Sygne's sacrifice of what for her was more worthy than her life itself, something in which she recognised her very being, takes her beyond her being, beyond the limit of life, beyond beauty, to the limits of the second death:

> She must renounce her very being—the pact that has kept her forever faithful to her own family, since what is being proposed is that she marry the very man who exterminated her family—and renounce the sacred commitment she has just made to the man she loves, her cousin. This is something that carries her, not to the limits of her life . . . but to the sacrifice of what for her, as for every being, is worth more than life itself—not simply her reasons for living but something in which she recognizes her very being.
>
> We thus find ourselves carried . . . to the limits of the "second death." . . . this locus ["between two deaths"] is outstripped by going . . . beyond beauty, strictly speaking; [and] indicated that the limit of this domain, the limit of the second death, is designated and also veiled by what I called the phenomenon of beauty . . . [Sygne] goes against everything related to her being right down to its very roots. Life is left far behind here.

(Ibid., pp. 275–276)

Sygne's second death will take place when she deliberately places her body in the way of the bullet shot at her husband. Lacan clarifies that unlike Antigone, who willfully chose to go to the limit of the second death, Sygne was indirectly compelled to do so; that, unlike Antigone, who had provoked Creon's condemnation, Sygne had not provoked anyone; that, unlike Antigone, who identified with the gods of the underworld, Sygne must go against everything related to her being right down to its roots; and, unlike Antigone, who embodied the limit, Sygne was required to go beyond it (ibid., pp. 275–276). In addition, as François Regnault rightly deduces from Lacan, unlike Antigone, who had to renounce her desire, Sygne had to renounce "her very being" (Regnault, 2015/2015, p. 2). These elements serve to amplify the magnitude of the sacrifice of the contemporary heroine to a far greater extent compared to that of the heroine of antiquity. Moreover, shortly before her death, Sygne develops a facial tic that mimics the gesture "no" even as she verbally says no to most of the entreaties of Badilon: "Throughout the act Sygne has a nervous twitching of the head from side to side, as though saying 'No'" (Claudel, 1910–1911/1945, p. 63). In effect, she doubly negated the appeals of Badilon, including the most sacred ones. In this context, Lacan specifies that "the endpoint that is respected even by Sade [and holds good for Antigone to a large extent] . . . that endpoint being beauty that is unaffected by affronts—is gone beyond here" (Lacan, 1991/2015, p. 277).

Although Badilon exhorts Sygne, the only thing he gets from her is a "no". Lacan states:

> [B]ut right up until the end he is unable to obtain from her anything other than a "no," an absolute refusal of peace, an absolute refusal to abandon or offer herself up to God who will receive her soul. All of the exhortations of this saint—he, too, being torn apart by the final consequence of what he himself has been the agent of—fail before this final negation. Sygne can find nothing, by any avenue whatsoever, that can reconcile her with a fate . . . that . . . goes beyond anything one can find in ancient tragedy related to what Paul Ricoeur calls the function of the evil God [*Dieu méchant*].
>
> (Ibid., p. 278)

According to Rabaté, Sygne's anti-Christian refusal constitutes "an important ethical step in the retrieval of Sygne's own desire, but will result in the equivalent of Antigone's *Atè* for her descendants" (Rabaté, 2001, p. 149). While that is correct, Lacan points to a far more subversive aim of Sygne's "No" with regard to the function of the Pope:

> Here we have gone beyond all meaning. Sygne's sacrifice does nothing but deride her goals [of saving the Pope]. The old man . . . is represented to us right up until the end of the trilogy—despite being the supreme Father of the faithful, as he is—as an impotent Father who, compared to the ideals that are on the rise, has nothing to offer his flock except the empty repetition of traditional words

which no longer have any power. The so-called restored legitimacy is but a decoy, fiction, or caricature, and is in reality but a continuation of the order that subverted the old regime.

(Lacan, 1991/2015, p. 278)

Lacan thinks that this "extreme failure" and "this extreme derision of the signifier itself" takes us to an image of desire that has gone beyond all pity and terror in the Aristotelian sense (ibid., pp. 278–279). Above all, Lacan remarks that in this play, a woman's image is substituted for the Christian cross. But what he finds far more remarkable is that the erotic theme of the play is allowed to coincide with the theme of going beyond the limit, of breaching all values based on faith (ibid., p. 279). Thus, while Sygne's sacrifice in terms of her marriage takes her to the limit of her second death, her repetitive "No" at the time of her death derides the signifier to an extreme degree emphatically and endlessly.

Lacan states that we learn from psychoanalytic practise the exact price we are required to pay for the fact that God is dead, pointing to Sygne's sacrifice as the adverse flipside of God's death. In Claudel, God is dead, and the dead God is represented by the "proscribed priest" who is called the Hostage, which implies that "[t]he figure of Antiquity's faith is henceforth held Hostage by politics" (ibid., p. 302). But this has serious consequences for those who are faithful:

[T]he flipside of this elimination of the dead God is that it is the faithful soul that is held Hostage. . . . Naturally, only she who believes can be held hostage—namely, Sygne. And because she believes she must attest to what she believes. This is precisely why she is caught and captivated in a situation that it suffices to create for it to exist: to be called upon to sacrifice to the very negation of what she believes. She is held hostage by the very negation she is subjected to of what is best in herself.

(Ibid., p. 302)

To this, Lacan adds that, whereas Antiquity's *Até* no doubt made us guilty of the debt created by God's death, our ability to renounce that debt now has, in fact, burdened us with "a still greater misfortune owing to the fact that fate is no longer anything [for us]". Differently put, since "the very debt that gave us our place . . . can be stolen from us", we "feel totally alienated from ourselves" (ibid., p. 302).

Above all, Sygne, as a "sacrificed woman who shakes her head saying no", raises "the mark of the signifier" to the "highest degree", and raises "refusal" to the "position of a radical stance" (ibid., p. 300). To explain this, Lacan invokes the Freudian term "*Versagung*" (refusal). The term implies "not making good on a promise, on a promise for which one has already given up everything", and as such, it brings out "the exemplary value of Sygne's character and drama". Already burdened by sacrifices, she is asked to give up "what she has put all of her effort into, what she has hitched her entire life to" (ibid., p. 300). She is not forced or constrained. Rather, "[s]he is made to freely commit herself, according to the law of marriage, to someone whom she calls the son of her servant and of the sorcerer Quiriace", someone simply "accursed to her". Since she cannot free herself from the *Versagung* or refusal here, "not saying becomes saying no here" (ibid., p. 301). This goes beyond the "would that I were not", which means "not to have been born" that we come across in *Oedipus at Colonus* (verse 1224). "In the final analysis, man is simply guilty of the responsibility [*charge*] he receives for the debt stemming from the *Até* that precedes him" (ibid., p. 301).

Lacan clarifies that Freud had maintained right from his earliest writings that at the origin of every neurosis is a *Versagung*, as in "something that is much closer to refusal than to frustration" (ibid., p. 322). This position does not establish a sequential progression from normal to the possibility of *Versagung* and then on to neurosis. Rather, "it establishes a *Versagung* right at the origin, beyond which a path may lead to neurosis or to normality, neither being worth more than the other in relation to what is, at the outset, the possibility of *Versagung*" (ibid., p. 322). "It is obvious", according to Lacan,

> that this untranslatable *Versagung* is only possible in the register of *sagen*, insofar as *sagen* is not simply the operation of communicating, but of speaking— that is, the emergence as such of the signifier insofar as it allows the subject to deny himself (something) [*se refuser*].
>
> (Ibid., p. 322)

Lacan thinks,

> We cannot get past this earliest, primordial refusal [*refus*], this power of refusal in what it has that is prerequisite [*préjudicielle*] to all our experience. In other words, we analysts operate solely in the register of *Versagung*, and don't we know it!
>
> (Ibid., p. 322)

He concludes the segment by stating that

> We must go into what this specific *Versagung* is, for it implies a progressive direction, which is the very one that we bring into play in analytic practice. . . . [W]e must be the messengers or vehicles of *Versagung*.
>
> (Ibid., p. 322)

Shedding further light on this in a much later session following the ones devoted to Claudel, Lacan asks, "What must the analyst's *Versagung* be?" He says in reply that the analyst must not only refuse to give his own anxiety to the analysand but must also refuse to occupy the empty place that the analysand invites him to and urges him to send out the signal of anxiety from (ibid., p. 368).

The Psychoanalyst and the Transference

Lacan asks, "In what respect must we consider ourselves to be involved in the transference?" (ibid., p. 312). He says in reply that at the heart of the phenomenon of transference in the subject is the analyst and the analyst's involvement in the transference is situated at the level of his being (ibid., p. 313). Lacan clarifies that even though the analyst plays his transferential role not at the level of reality for his patient due to the fiction and deviation from reality produced by the latter with the help of transference, "the analyst enters the picture through something like his being", adding, "[e]verything that has been said since Freud's time concerning the import of transference thus brings the analyst into play as an actual being [*un existant*]" (ibid., p. 314).

Lacan then discusses the two "trends" or the "two . . . different ways of articulating transference" associated with Melanie Klein and Anna Freud, respectively, that constitute the two poles of the spectrum. Lacan states that "[t]he Kleinian trend emphasizes the analyst's function as an object in the transference relationship". That is, for Klein, the analyst functions as a good object or a bad object for the analysand. Klein thought so because she believed that the analytic relationship is dominated by unconscious fantasies right from the beginning, although she hadn't correctly understood the function of fantasy, except for the element of the primordial function of symbolisation in it that she had grasped satisfactorily. Therefore, her belief and recommendation concerning the role of unconscious fantasies resulted from "the shortcomings of Kleinian thought". Neither she nor any of her followers had properly worked out the function of fantasy. Lacan considers the inadequate explanation of the function of fantasy despite regarding it as extremely important to be "the major failing of her work" (ibid., pp. 314–315). The other trend, associated with Anna Freud and her followers, upholds "that the analyst is involved in the transference as a subject". Here, emphasis is placed on "the therapeutic alliance" and on its correlate, "the powers of the ego". Regarding the place of these powers in therapeutic practise, the practitioners of this trend believe that, at first, they must deal only with defense for quite some time and must not bring in the unconscious. They converted the ego "into a kind of inertial mass". Heinz Hartmann and his followers even considered the ego to include "irreducible and uninterpretable" elements. Practitioners of this trend suggested that the ego should be provided with additional defences to make it still more irreducible. In the final analysis, according to Lacan, compared to the perspective of the Anna Freudians, the perspective of the Kleinians "is the more Freudian" one (ibid., pp. 315–316).

On the crucial question, "what the analyst's position must be in order to respond to transference?" (ibid., p. 265), Lacan states that the analyst can neither operate in the way in which Freud used to, namely, by adopting the position of the father, nor operate in the way in which the modern-day Freudians tend to, namely, by adopting the position of the mother. What, then, should be the position of the analyst with regard to transference (ibid., p. 294)? Answering the question, Lacan says that he pointed to the Socratic practise as described in Plato's *The Symposium* at the start of his seminar on *Transference* in order to draw our attention to "something that is given right from the outset of the establishment of psychoanalytic practice", namely the supposition that the analyst is in the know, that he possesses the secret knowledge that will complete the knowledge of the analysand and thus establish the falsity of his problem (ibid., p. 265). This is akin to the understanding of the Oracle of Delphi that Socrates was the wisest man and the belief of the latter's friends and followers that he possessed special knowledge, even though Socrates himself believed, as he said at 177e of *The Symposium*, that the only thing he understood or knew was "the art of love" (Plato, 385 BC/1997, p. 462). Lacan would begin to describe transference with the help of the term and the concept of the "subject supposed to know" or the supposed subject of knowledge (*sujet suppose savoir*), most probably in 1964 (Lacan, 1973/1998, pp. 230–243), and he would consistently continue to do so thereafter (for instance, Lacan 1991/2007, p. 38) till the end, where both the knowledge and the subject are suppositions of the analysand, although the idea of this supposition is discussed for the first time in the present seminar.

Since desire, according to Lacan, is of the Other and tied to our relationship with language, the analyst must be able to represent the analysand's missing signifier, Φ, for a while by occupying the empty place where it can be summoned. The position of this special signifier, one that can exist only by cancelling out the rest of the signifiers, is central to analytic practise: "we must know how to occupy its place inasmuch as the subject must be able to detect the missing signifier there". This is the very place where the analyst is supposed to know. It's the place where the analysand "effaces himself [as a subject] and subordinates himself to all the signifiers of his own demand". The analyst is able to occupy this very place precisely by being the subject that "vanishes or is barred" (Lacan, 1991/2015, pp. 268–269).

In the session following the discussion on *The Coûfontaine Trilogy*, Lacan sums up this discussion. He asks, "How can we situate what the analyst's place must be in the transference?" And he answers it by stating, "I told you last time that we must locate this place in two ways: where does the analysand situate the analyst and where must the analyst be in order to suitably respond to him?" (ibid., p. 329). In other words, the analyst should be at the empty place meant for the missing signifier where the analysand effaces himself as a subject. This is the place where the analysand situates the analyst, and this is the very place where the analyst must situate himself as a subject that vanishes or is barred. Since, at the end of the analysis by way of the end of the analysis of transference, the locus of the analyst is emptied out, and the analyst is left behind as a waste product, a trash object, or as the useless residue that the catalyst becomes at the end of a chemical reaction, Lacan thinks that the analyst ought to truly situate himself at this place of lack throughout the course of the analysis:

> Isn't it at least probable and palpable that he must already place himself at the level of this truly, that he must truly be in the place where he must arrive at the end of the analysis, which is precisely the analysis of the transference?
>
> (Ibid., p. 329)

The Oedipal Father in European Tragedy

Lacan disagrees with Hegel's view expressed in *The Phenomenology of Spirit* that Christian tragedy is related to "reconciliation (*Versöhnung*)", to a "kind of redemption" that, by resolving "the fundamental impasse" does not allow it to establish itself as a tragedy, and turns it into a "divine comedy" instead with the invocation of God who holds all the strings. Lacan thinks that Shakespeare's *Hamlet* shows that the Christian era does not bring the dimension of tragedy to an end. He argues that in spite of the presence of the "dimension of dogma or of Christian faith" in the play in the form of the ghost who tells his son how he has been damned by his killer,[3]

> we don't find the slightest trace of reconciliation in *Hamlet*. Despite the presence at the horizon of Christian dogma, there is no resorting at any point in *Hamlet* to the mediation of some sort of redemption. In *Hamlet*, the sacrifice of the son remains purely tragic.
>
> (Ibid., p. 281)

Moving on to the figuration of the father in European tragedy, Lacan states that in *Oedipus Rex*, Oedipus did not know that the father was dead, let alone that he had killed him. In *Hamlet*, by contrast, the father is damned, which means that in the latter play, "the father begins to know ... He knows in any case who killed him and how he was killed" (ibid., p. 282). Why does Lacan compare Oedipus' ignorance of his father's death to Senior Hamlet's knowledge of his own death? Notably, Laius knew when, where, and how he was killed but did not know the real identity of his killer. Shouldn't Lacan have compared Laius's ignorance of the identity of the young man who dealt him the mortal blow at the crossroads, as well as Oedipus' ignorance of the real identity of the person he killed, to Senior Hamlet's complete knowledge of his death and the knowledge of the same that Prince Hamlet received from his damned father? Lacan then indicates that Hamlet regarded his father as an ideal man—one who strewed flowers on the ground beneath his wife's feet and did not allow the wind to strike her face too roughly, which Lacan calls "the ideal of the knight in courtly love"—and contrasted him with the jouissance of his mother (ibid., p. 282).

Examining the "father's function", Lacan states that "[t]he very figure of Antiquity's father ... is that of a king", and that

> throughout the Biblical texts, the figure of the divine father raises a question that underpins a whole line of research. Starting when did the God of the Jews become a father? Starting when in history? Starting when in the prophetic tradition?
>
> (Ibid., p. 283)

Lacan thinks that by the time Freud asked, "What is a father?", the topic of the father had "shrunk considerably" and could therefore take the form of the "murderous" father in the Oedipus complex. Since Freud had thus "profoundly changed" the question of the father, Lacan considers "it opportune and indeed necessary . . . to wonder what the thematics of the father can be in a tragedy", especially in one that appeared around Freud's time (ibid., p. 283).

Lacan then offers a summary of the depiction of the father from antiquity to the modern time in European tragedy. He begins by stating that, in *Oedipus Rex,* the father has already been killed. He adds that, in *Hamlet,* the father is damned at the time of his death. Moving on to *The Coûfontaine Trilogy,* Lacan points out that the Pope as the father is an impotent fugitive or a hostage in the first play and "a servant unto servants" (Claudel, 1919/1945, p. 186) in the last play—in Lacan's words, "he who makes himself into the smallest of the small" (Lacan, 1991/2015, pp. 283–284)—while Turelure as the father is a "scorned father", and more important, the "duped father", which is the "fundamental theme of classical comedy" (ibid., p. 288). Lacan does not think that the humiliated father is the Pope. Rather, he thinks that the humiliated father is Turelure, the obscene, "impudent", "impulsive", "devalued", "ape-like" father of Freud's myth of the primal horde, who "takes on the form of the most extreme derision" verging on the "abject" and whose "death by murder . . . constitute[s] the pivotal point" (ibid., p. 284). Lacan does not mention this specifically, though it is implied by him: the fact that Louis becomes an ambassador, or a representative of the law, following the act of parricide is in tune with the sons of the primal horde becoming social beings out of a deep sense of guilt following the act of primal parricide in the myth elaborated on by Freud in *Totem and Taboo,* (Freud, 1912/2001) which made Lacan write in 1964: "aggression toward the Father is at the very heart of the Law" (Lacan, 1964/2006, p. 723). In the present seminar, Lacan says that "Louis himself accedes to the father function" around the "artifice of the crime" (Lacan, 1991/2015, p. 288). He moreover explicitly mentions:

> [I]t is at this very moment [of parricide] and owing to it that the boy becomes a man. Louis de Coûfontaine is told that this parricide will weigh on him his whole life long, but also that from this moment on he is no longer a good-for-nothing who botches up everything and who allows his land to be stolen from him by a bunch of meanies and clever cheats. He is going to become a fine ambassador who is quite capable of performing all kinds of dastardly deeds. This brings a certain correlation to mind. He becomes the father. He not only becomes the father, but when he talks about Turelure later, in *The Humiliation of the Father*, in Rome, he says, "I was probably the only man who really knew and understood him; he never wanted to hear about it; he was not the man people think he was" [p. 325/167] . . . Louis de Coûfontaine becomes the father. Moreover, this is the only way he could become the father, for reasons that are tied to things that occurred before the dramatic action begins.
> (Ibid., p. 323)

Lacan thinks it is in this sense that *Crusts* offers us a variation of the Oedipal myth (ibid., p. 322); even though he does take note of the other major Oedipal themes in the play, such as Louis killing his father, he is castrated in the sense that he is unable to get Lumir whom he desired, and he marries his father's mistress[4] (ibid., p. 323–324). Lacan adds two details regarding Turelure as an Oedipal father. First, that exactly as described by Freud, "[t]he father sees in his son [as] . . . someone just like himself, a repetition of himself, a figure born of himself in whom he can see nothing but a rival" (ibid., p. 287). Turelure says to his son, "you're a Turelure. . . . There's no need of having two Turelures. What am I good for if there are two?" (Claudel, 1918/1945, p. 122). And second, that taking a sexual interest in the son's mistress is an attribute of the father added to the Oedipus complex by Claudel (Lacan, 1991/2015, p. 286). On the whole, Lacan finds in *Crusts* "the extreme, paradoxical, and caricatural edge of the Oedipus complex" insofar as "an obscene old man forces his sons to marry his wives, and he does so to the very extent that he wishes to steal theirs from them", creating thereby a "scoundrel" rather than "a better quality father" (ibid., p. 304).

Structural Repetition of Family Myths across Generations

In his 4th March, 1953 lecture at the *Collège philosophique*, Paris, entitled "The Neurotic's Individual Myth, Or Poetry and Truth in Neurosis" ("*Le mythe individuel du névrosé ou poésie et vérité dans la névrose*"), Lacan, partly following Lévi-Strauss' structural analysis of myths,[5] elaborates on the structural repetition of the family myth across two generations in Freud's famous 1909 case history of the "Rat man" entitled, "Notes Upon A Case of Obsessional Neurosis" (Freud, 1909/2001), invoking Claudel's *The Humiliation of the Father* at one place while doing so. In his analysis, Lévi-Strauss examined all the important versions of the Oedipus myth, including those of Homer, Sophocles, and Freud, and arrived at the following pairs of oppositions around which all the versions had been constructed: "Overrating of blood relations", "Underrating of blood relations", "Denial of autochthonous origin", and "Acceptance of autochthonous origin" (Lévi-Strauss, 1955/1977). In the present seminar, Lacan thinks that the rules underlying myths can be so well-structured and precise because they have "the same kind of fecundity we find in mathematics" (Lacan, 1991/2015, p. 318). Departing from Lévi-Strauss' analysis, Lacan argued in his 1953 lecture how, going by the two family myths that the Rat man had grown up hearing, the same constellation of signifiers—"rich woman"–"poor woman" and "friend"–"debt"—ruled over the lives of the father and the son and determined the symptoms of the latter (Lacan, 1978/1979). This is the precise sense in which Lacan uses the term "fate" [*destin*] in his discussions. He says, "[w]ere we to forget the relationship that exists between analysis and what we call fate, . . . we would simply forget the origins of psychoanalysis. For psychoanalysis could not have made the slightest step forward without this relationship" (Lacan, 1991/2015, p. 317). Lacan is quick to point out that psychoanalysis does not involve presenting the subject with his fate, for "[t]hat would be to situate ourselves in the position of a demiurge, which has never been that of psychoanalysis" (ibid., p. 319). Rather, psychoanalysis is interested in fate because a figure related to it may be seen in the symptoms (ibid., p. 320) in the sense that the important signifiers of the family myth may be discerned in the symptoms of an individual. This is something that was not known prior to the advent of psychoanalysis, and this is the reason that myths are taken seriously in this discipline: "In any case, right from psychoanalysis' very first steps, in the *Traumdeutung* [*The Interpretation of Dreams*] and the letters to Fliess, Freud relies on myth and specifically on the Oedipal myth" (ibid., p. 318).

The first family myth is about the marriage of the Rat man's parents, where his father could have chosen between a rich woman, the Rat man's mother, whom he decided to marry, and the poor but pretty girl he loved but decided not to marry. His father's socio-economic gains resulting from his marrying the rich woman were regarded as his father's unpaid debts to his in-laws by the Rat man. The second family myth concerns the Rat man's father's debt to a friend, an officer in the regiment, who had saved him from the very serious trouble he once got into when he gambled away the regiment's funds by lending him the money needed to resolve the problem. This debt remained unpaid forever because that friend in need could not be located later on. The same four signifiers revisit the son. He loved a poor woman but his parents wanted him to marry a rich woman who was related to his mother. Besides, he was at once attracted to the rich lady at the post office and the poor, pretty daughter of the landlord at the nearby inn. Moreover, he considered the young lady he met on the staircase of Freud's house to be the latter's daughter and a rich lady and thought that Freud wanted to offer her hand in marriage to him, even when he was in love with the poor woman. At around the same time, while he was serving his term in the army, he lost his pince-nez during a halt in the course of a manoeuvre. He soon received a new pair he had ordered from his optician in Vienna after losing his old pair, but he was not sure who in the army or at the post office had made the payment for it on his behalf at the time of receiving it. This incident invoked the signifiers of friend and debt and the problem of an unpayable debt to a friend related to the army. That apart, the Rat man had an old friend, and although his attitude towards Freud was ambivalent, he considered the latter a friend. More pertinent, the Rat man's neurosis was triggered whenever he found himself in situations similar to those of his father involving these same signifiers. For instance, when his father tried to force him to ignore his poor beloved and marry the rich woman related to his mother. He tried to overcome his problem by seeking to symptomatically fuse or unite the two sets of signifiers to one and by trying to resolve that single set thereafter (Lacan, 1978/1979, pp. 406–417). He perpetually failed to resolve his problem as the two pairs of signifiers refused to fuse. Therefore, Lacan thinks that importance ought to be given to the knowledge of the fate of the analysands with reference to their family myths—or to the almost mathematical "signifying coherence" across generations—even though modern Freudian psychoanalysis tends to overlook such knowledge (Lacan, 1991/2015, p. 318). Lacan states, "The fact of knowing or not knowing is thus essential to the figure of fate. This is the right doorway. And myth confirms it" (ibid., p. 320).

Regarding the structural repetition of the same elements across three generations in *The Coûfontaine Trilogy*, Lacan points to "the repetition of an expression by which love is articulated throughout the text of Claudel's trilogy" (ibid., p. 297). It concerns a declaration or gesture of merging or exchanging the souls by two lovers, a man and a woman, who are otherwise all alone, which Lacan considers love's supreme aspiration. In the final analysis, however, the declaration is not honoured by one of the two parties involved. Thus, in *The Hostage*, Sygne says to George:

> Coûfontaine, I am yours; take me, and do with me as you will! Your wife, if you so wish it, or, if you prefer, beyond the limits of this life, where earthly bodies are no more, our souls shall be joined together, and indissolubly made one.
> (Claudel, 1910–1911/1945, p. 24)

To this, George responds by describing Sygne's love as the only thing that's lasting, other than his will: "Oh, Sygne whom I have found at last, do not fail me as the world has failed me! Shall I, then, in the end, have something lasting, other than my own will?" (ibid., p. 24). However, "Sygne finds herself betraying the very person to whom she has committed herself with all her soul", which "lends gravitas to the tragedy" (Lacan, 1991/2015, p. 298).

The theme of the exchange or merger of souls recurs in the course of a conversation between Louis and Lumir following the parricide in *Crusts*. Lumir refuses to go to Algeria with Louis and invites him to come with her to Poland instead. In reply, Louis appeals to her, saying that he loved her just the way she was, i.e., a manly woman, and that she was the only woman in his life. To this, Lumir, who had committed herself to the cause of her homeland, replies:

> We're alone; wholly, completely alone in this desert. Two human souls knocking about in the void of life! Two souls which can belong to each other. Two souls which, in the space of a single second, like the thundering report of time that is annihilated, can, through each other and to each other, be all things! How sweet it is to live without looking ahead. If life were only longer! It might be worth while to be happy. But life is short; and there are ways of making it shorter yet! Yes, so short that all eternity can be contained therein! ... So short that this world, this life which we scorn and do not want, could be hidden away in it. This happiness on which people lay such stress! Ah, life could be so small and tight and narrow and brief that there would be no room in it for anything or any one—except you and me. Just we two! ... Come with me! Come and be my strength and my might! I will be your country close held in your arms. To you I will be happiness foregone, the land of Ur, the old, old power of Consolation. You and I only exist; only you and I live in this world, and there will, throughout all time, be only this moment when we stood face to face—and saw! And we shall be able to understand—then—even that mystery which lies hidden deep within us. Come! There are ways of drawing our souls out of ourselves, as one can draw a flashing sword—loyal, clean, and with honor unbesmirched. Yes,

there is a way to break the chain, to batter down the prison wall. And there's a way of pledging one's oath and of sacrificing oneself, heart and soul, to the other—the only other! We can do it like brave men! We can! In spite of the horrible night, and the rain, and the awful emptiness which surrounds us. Oh, it can be done! There is a way of giving all of oneself, and having faith, true faith, in the other. There's a way of so giving oneself that, believing implicitly in the flash of inspiration, each shall belong to the other and to him alone.

(Claudel, 1918/1945, pp. 137–138)

Nevertheless, Lumir and Louis take two different paths shortly following this. Finally, in *The Humiliation of the Father*, the pattern seems to have been reversed insofar as the breach precedes rather than follows the vow. In the latter play, along with a message to her, Orian had sent his heart to Pensée's in a flowerpot. Pensée inhales the fragrance of the lilies growing out of Orian's heart in the flowerpot in order to "breathe in his soul" (ibid., p. 221) and feels the movement of Orian's child inside her womb while doing so. Here the two souls are symbolically unified when there is no possibility of actual union of the two lovers concerned. Lacan points to the complexity or difference of the merger of the souls in the third play compared to the previous two because there seems to be a messenger or a conveyor of the merger involved in it:

[L]et us not forget what Claudel tells us, which is that the child comes alive and begins to move for the first time at the very moment at which Pensée takes, as she tells us, within herself the soul of he who is dead. How is this capturing of the soul portrayed to us? It is a true act of vampirism. With the flaps of her shawl, Pensée wraps herself, as it were, around the basket of flowers that the brother, Orso, had sent, flowers that grew in soil that—as we learn from the dialogue, constituting a macabre note—contains the eviscerated heart of her lover, Orian. When she stands up again, she is supposed to have brought its symbolic essence inside herself . . . . It is this soul that she presses, along with her own, she tells us, on the lips of the brother, Orso—who has just committed himself to her in order to provide the child with a father—while telling him that he will never be her husband. This transmission or odd realization of the fusion of souls is what the first two quotes I cited for you at the beginning of class today—from *The Hostage* on the one hand, and from *Crusts* on the other—indicate as love's supreme aspiration. Orso, who we know is going to join his brother in death, is the designated conveyor, vehicle, or messenger of this fusion of souls.

(Lacan, 1991/2015, p. 310)

For another example of such "signifying coherence" or structural repetition across generations, Lacan draws our attention to the fact that in the first play, Sygne is emotionally blackmailed by the priest Badilon to renounce her love for George and to marry the despicable Turelure in order to save the Pope. Similarly, in the second play, Lumir, Louis's mistress, refuses to marry Louis, who loves her, and directs him to marry his father's mistress, the wealthy Sichel. Likewise, in the third play, Pensée's marriage with her lover Orian is denied by the latter's death in a battle, who, in his last message to her, urges her to marry his brother Orso, who loved her. Thus, in each of the three plays, the subject's object of desire is taken away from him or her, and he or she is sold to the usually abhorrent highest bidder or to the social order, which is how Lacan defines castration in this seminar (ibid., p. 324). The pattern is broken in the last play, however, where Pensée, unlike her predecessors, agrees to marry Orso on condition that he shall be like a brother to her, and, while fusing her soul with that of Orian, feels the movement of the latter's child inside her womb, all of which signifies that she had aligned herself with the object of her own desire.

There is one more minor repetition comprising marriage or its possibility between a brother substitute and a sister substitute that Lacan does not comment on. In *The Hostage*, Sygne loved George, her cousin and therefore a kind of brother, to whom she offered herself as a wife towards the very beginning of the trilogy: "Coûfontaine, I am yours; take me, and do with me as you will! Your wife, if you so wish it" (Claudel, 1910–1911/1945, p. 24). Shortly after this, she is compelled to marry Turelure. However, the fact that Turelure's mother was Sygne's wet nurse made her a surrogate sister of Turelure. At a critical moment following the parricide in *Crusts*, Lumir says to Louis, her lover: "Something that makes you my brother!" (Claudel, 1918/1945, p. 137). Later, in *The Humiliation of the Father*, Sygne's granddaughter Pensée agrees to marry Orso, who was her informal brother-in-law as well as her brother-substitute insofar as he was the brother of her lover, largely because of Orso's promise to her towards the very end of the trilogy that she shall always remain a sister to him: "Do you believe that the woman who was once my brother's, could ever be anything except a sister to me?" (Claudel, 1919/1945, p. 222).

The Three Stages of Desire

Lacan sums up *The Coûfontaine Trilogy* as a narrative on the three stages of desire represented by the three generations. He states that three generations are enough to realise the configuration of desire:

> The explosion at the end of which desire's configuration is realized can be broken down into three stages, and you can see this marked in different generations. This is why there is no need, in order to situate the composition of desire in a subject, to go all the way back, in a perpetual recurrence, to Adam, the father. Three generations are enough.
>
> (Lacan, 1991/2015, p. 295)

Thus, in the first play devoted to the first generation, we find the first stage of desire in the form of "the mark of the signifier" illustrated by the image of Sygne de Coûfontaine, "who is carried to the very destruction of her being, because she is totally ripped away from all her attachments based on speech and faith" (ibid., pp. 295–296). The mark of the signifier is encountered in the "were I not" that is a refusal, a no, a tic, or a grimace, which is the "giving way of the body" (ibid., p. 303). Sygne thus raises the mark of the signifier to the highest degree. In the second play devoted to the second generation, we find the second stage of desire in the form of "the appearance of a child" named Louis de Coûfontaine. Those who speak and are marked by words engender, while the child Louis is at first, such as in the first play, "*infans*", meaning "someone who does not speak" (ibid., p. 296). In this stage, Louis is "an object that is totally rejected ... [and] undesired" (ibid., p. 296). He is undesired by his parents and his mistress. In the third play devoted to the third generation, we find the third stage of desire. The third generation "configured before our eyes" is "the only true generation", as the previous two generations are its "artificial decompositions" and "antecedents of the only one that is of concern". In this stage, desire is composed "between the mark of the signifier and passion for the partial object" with the help of the figure of Pensée de Coûfontaine (ibid., p. 296).

According to Lacan, the desire represented by Pensée has a relation to death. Pensée, flesh-and-blood thought, has only one passion. She wants "absolute justice" (ibid., p. 304), the opposite of what her grandmother received. As a soul with closed eyes, she is "the most desirable object in the world" (ibid., p. 307), which is the opposite of the status of her father. She is the "incarnate object of the desire for ... light" (ibid., p. 305). She is surely "the sublime object of desire" that can be best situated on an "anamorphic cylinder" in terms of a "formless drawing astutely placed at its base" (ibid., p. 309). Explaining how she is born as innocence on a cylindrical mirror out of the unworthy drawings at its base, Lacan states that she "is truly the rebirth of all that is ill-fated, which begins with debauchery, continues with gambling one's honor, with misalliance, and with abjuration ... in order to be reborn from it as though before sin, as innocence" (ibid., p. 308). Like Sygne, she is "the figure of a woman who is deified in order to be crucified. ... The posture of crucifixion is indicated in the text" (ibid., p. 309). She is "offered up to our desire" from the position of Orso, and she can be ours "by representing our downfall". This is so because, "[i]n desire there is always some delight in death, but in a death that we cannot inflict upon ourselves" (ibid., p. 310). The set of four elements consisting of the two brothers, we as subjects, and the Other as a woman, "allow for the possibility of all sorts of varieties of inflicted death, among which we can enumerate the most perverse forms of desire. ... Orian—the true, perfect man who asserts himself and maintains his virility—who pays the price by dying" (ibid., p. 310). Lacan concludes by stating that Pensée becomes the object of desire by becoming frozen:

> At the end of the tragedy of the subjects as pure victims of Logos or language, he [Claudel] shows us what becomes of desire. And regarding this desire, he makes it visible to us in the figure of this woman, this astounding [*terrible*] subject who goes by the name of Pensée de Coûfontaine. She deserves her name

Pensée, for she is thought about desire. It is through love—the love that she expresses—for the other that she becomes the object of desire by becoming frozen [*en se figeant*].

(Ibid., p. 311)

Notes

1 Unless otherwise mentioned, all translations are mine.
2 In the play, it is Badilon who mentions her child to Sygne (Claudel, 1910–1911/1945, p. 80) and utters the words inscribed on the coat of arms of the Coûfontaine family shortly before and after it: "*COÛFONTAINE ADSUM!*" (ibid., pp. 78, 80). Lacan mistakenly attributes both of these remarks to Turelure:

> [I]n having Sygne exhorted by Turelure using the same words as are found on her family coat of arms, the motto that for her is the signification of her life: "Coûfontaine adsum, Coûfontaine, I am present".
>
> Standing before his dying wife, who is incapable of speaking or is refusing to speak, he tries to at least obtain from her a sign—any sign whatsoever, were it only consent to have her child brought before her—of recognition of the fact that her action was designed to protect him, Turelure.
>
> (Lacan, 1991/2015, p. 278)

A part of Lacan's mistake is repeated by Rabaté when he writes: "Lacan admires Claudel's stroke of genius at having Turelure utter the proud motto of the family—*Coûfontaine, adsum!* (Coûfontaine, here I am)—in a last attempt to get Sygne to forgive and bless him as she dies" (Rabaté, 2001, p. 149). The same mistake is repeated by Ann Bugliani:

> Claudel also adds to the second ending a scene in which Turelure himself exhorts Sygne using the motto of her family coat of arms which has defined her life—*Coûfontaine adsum*. He tries to get from her a sign of her acceptance or consent, perhaps in gratitude for the fact that she saved his life. She only answers no.
>
> (Bugliani, 1999, p. 53)

3 Lacan does bring out the "contradiction" in the play's depiction of afterlife by pointing out that while it is "never doubted whether the father attests to the flames of hell and eternal damnation", Hamlet effectively wonders, in terms of his "To be, or not to be . . . To sleep: perchance to dream", "[d]oes the afterlife deliver us from this accursed life, from the ocean of humiliation and servitude that life is?" (Lacan, 1991/2015, pp. 281–282).
4 Bugliani points out that "Claudel himself is quite conscious of this Oedipal dimension. He cites as antecedents of his work Noah, David, Oedipus, and Lear" (Claudel, *Théâtre*, Vol. II, p. 1418) (Bugliani, 1999, p. 59 fn. 11).
5 Lacan had attended Lévi-Strauss's lecture on "The Structural Study of Myth", published in 1955, at L'École Pratique des Hautes Études in 1951–1952.

References

Auden, Wystan Hugh (1945). *The Collected Poetry of W.H. Auden*. Random House.
Bugliani, Ann (1999). *The Instruction of Philosophy and Psychoanalysis by Tragedy: Jacques Lacan and Gabriel Marcel read Paul Claudel*. International Scholars Publications.
Claudel, Paul (1937) *Les Juifs*. Plon.
Claudel, Paul (1945). Crusts. In John Heard Trans. *Three Plays*. John W. Luce Company Publishers, 87–151 (Original work published 1918).

Claudel, Paul (1945). The Hostage. In John Heard Trans. *Three Plays*. John W. Luce Company Publishers, 9–85 (Original work published 1910–1911).
Claudel, Paul (1945). The Humiliation of the Father. In John Heard Trans. *Three Plays*. John W. Luce Company Publishers, 153–223 (Original work published 1919).
Claudel, Paul (1969). *Journal II (1933–1955)*. Gallimard.
Claudel, Paul (1995). Religion and the Artist: Introduction to A Poem on Dante (Introduction à un poème sur Dante). In David Louis Schindler, Jr. Trans. *Communio: International Catholic Review*, Vol. 22.2, Summer, Association Communio, 357–367 (Originally published 1920).
Cornec, Gilles (1993). *L'affaire Claudel*. Gallimard.
Freud, Sigmund (2001). Notes upon a Case of Obsessional Neurosis. In James Strachey (Ed.), *The Standard Edition of the Complete Psychological Works of Sigmund Freud*, Vol. X. Vintage, 151–318 (Original work published 1909).
Freud, Sigmund (2001). Totem and Taboo. In James Strachey (Ed.), *The Standard Edition of the Complete Psychological Works of Sigmund Freud*, Vol. XIII. Vintage, Hogarth Press and the Institute of Psychoanalysis, 1–162 (Original work published 1912).
Lacan, Jacques (1979). The Neurotic's Individual Myth, Or Poetry and Truth in Neurosis. In Jacques Alain-Miller (Ed.) and Martha Noel Evans Trans. *The Psychoanalytic Quarterly*, Vol. 48 (3), The Psychoanalytic Quarterly Press, 405–425 (Original work published 1978).
Lacan, Jacques (1998). *The Seminar of Jacques Lacan. Book XI. The Four Fundamental Concepts of Psychoanalysis, 1964*. In Alan Sheridan Trans. W.W. Norton (Original work published 1973).
Lacan, Jacques (2006). On Freud's Trieb and the Psychoanalyst's Desire. In Bruce Fink Trans., in collaboration with Héloïse Fink and Russell Grigg, *Écrits: The First Complete Edition in English*. W.W. Norton, 722–725 (Original work published 1964).
Lacan, Jacques (2007). *The Seminar of Jacques Lacan. Book XVII. The Other Side of Psychoanalysis, 1969–1970*. In Russell Grigg Trans. W.W. Norton (Original work published 1991).
Lacan, Jacques (2015). *The Seminar of Jacques Lacan, Book VIII: 1960–1961: Transference*. In Bruce Fink Trans. Polity Press. (Original work published 1991).
Lévi-Strauss, Claude (1977). The Structural Study of Myth. In Claire Jacobson and Brooke Grundfest Schoepf Trans. *Structural Anthropology*, Vol. 1. Penguin Books, 206–231 (Original work published 1955).
Plato (1997). The Symposium. In John M. Cooper (Ed.) and Alexander Nehamas and Paul Woodruff Trans. *Plato: Complete Works*. Hackett Publishing Company, 457–505 (Original work published around 385 BC).
Rabaté, Jean-Michel (2001). *Jacques Lacan: Psychoanalysis and the Subject of Literature*. Palgrave.
Regnault, François (2015). The Drama of Desire: Paul Claudel's Hostage, According to Jacques Lacan. In Ilya Merlin & Raphaëlle Desvignes Trans. *Lacanian Ink*, July 6, Wooster Press. Available at www.facebook.com/lacanianink/posts/988749451176727/?paipv=0&eav=AfaYFm8369itcT7SjWDdSKhUafBmoE-U9BGW6GUVAaLT8u0vAV-BGcaJL2QzUHcbNTE&_rdr, 1–4. (Accessed on 22nd November, 2023) (Original work published 2015).
Rousseaux, André (1949). *Litteréature du Vingtième Siècle*, Vol. I. Albin Michel.
Steiner, George (1980). *The Death of Tragedy*. Oxford University Press. (Originally published 1961).

Chapter 5

"Lituraterre"

"Lituraterre" is the title of an essay written by Lacan between late April and early May 1971 that was published in October 1971 as the introductory essay of the third issue, devoted to the theme of literature and psychoanalysis, of the literary quarterly named *Littérature* (Literature) (Lacan, 1971).[1] Not too long after writing the essay and several months before its first publication in the quarterly, Lacan devoted the seventh session, dated 12th May, 1971, of his then ongoing annual public seminar, *On a Discourse that Might not be a Semblance* (*D'un discours qui ne serait pas du semblant*) to his "Lesson on Lituraterre" (Lacan, 2007). Lacan's essay was subsequently reprinted in the issue of April–June 1987 of the journal *Ornicar? Revue du champ freudien*, (Lacan, 1971/1987) before it was given its proper place at the beginning of the posthumously published second volume of Lacan's writings, *Autres écrits* (2001), by its editor Jacques-Alain Miller, following the precedent set by Lacan when he placed an essay relating to literature at the head of his first volume of writings titled *Écrits* (1966) (Lacan, 1971/2001). Thus, there are two texts on "Lituraterre", one of which was written by Lacan and the other established by Miller out of the transcriptions and recordings of the seminar and notes left behind by Lacan. These two roughly similar texts that are nevertheless not identical at the level of detail at several places tend to complement and clarify each other. In the fairly long interface between psychoanalysis and literature that was inaugurated by Freud in 1897, "Lituraterre" arguably constitutes the most significant turning point because it discusses a set of crucial questions never raised before.

Meaning of "Lituraterre"

Lacan wrote the word "Lituraterre" on the blackboard at the start of the session and said that this coinage of his has been legitimised by Ernout and Meillet in their 1932 etymological dictionary of Latin (*Dictionnaire Étymologique De La Langue Latine: Histoire Des Mots*), urging the audience to look up the words "*lino, litura*, and then *liturarius*" in order to understand how this has been done (Lacan, 2007, p. 113).[2] In all likelihood, Lacan referred to the fourth edition of the dictionary published in 1959, and he mentions it for the second time in his annual seminar after the 1961–1962 seminar on *Identification*. According to Ernout and Meillet, "*lino*", meaning coat, smear, erasure, is related to "*litura*", meaning "coated, hence deletion, correction and stain", and to "*liturarius*", meaning "that which shows erasure or deletion" (Ernout et Meillet, 1932/2001, p. 360). Dany Nobus rightly mentions that "*liturarius*" is, moreover, "homophonic with *litorarius* (from *litus* and *litoris*), which means shore, coast, littoral" (Nobus, 2002, p. 27). Since "*terra*" in Latin—and "*terre*" in French—means "earth", the expression "Lituraterre" stands for "erasure-earth" in Latin.

Lacan further states that according to Ernout and Meillet, "this has nothing to do with *littera*, the letter", adding that this dictionary is auspicious for him because it is founded on the same point of departure as the one adopted by him when he started from the equivocation in terms of which Joyce slides from a letter to a litter or trash (Lacan, 2007, p. 113). In the entry on the word "*Littera*" in their dictionary, which variously means a letter of the alphabet, writing character, literature, culture, et cetera, Ernout and Meillet mention the misspelling of the word as "*litera*" "due to a false connection (*faux rapprochement*) with *lino* and *litum*", where "*litum*", as well as "*linere*", are words related to "*lino*" (Ernout et Meillet, 1932/2001, p. 363). In other words, "*lino*" or "*litura*" have nothing to do with, no true connection with, "*littera*". Moreover, by mentioning the slippage from "*littera*" to "*litera*", that is to say, from the letter or literature to coating, deletion, or erasure, Ernout and Meillet, in a way, anticipated Joyce's slippage from the letter to the litter in *Finnegans Wake* in 1939, insofar as "*littera*" stands for the letter, while the meaningless word "*litera*", whose spelling is similar to that of "litter", is in fact a kind of rubbish or litter. Lacan started his teaching in the 1950s by commenting on the instance of the letter in the unconscious, the purloined letter, Gide's letters, and the letter as litter in the Joycean sense, while Ernout and Meillet's dictionary consists of letters and is a commentary on letters with the help of letters that also touches upon the meaningless word "*litera*" in connection with the Latin word for "letter". In this sense, their dictionary is founded on an equivocation that is similar to the equivocation proposed by Joyce on which Lacan founded his teaching.

However, even though the expression "Lituraterre" has thus been legitimised by Ernout and Meillet—and in a manner, moreover, that is analogous to Joyce's equivocation with letter and litter that Lacan had adopted as his point of departure—Lacan states that his coinage owes its origin to the form of wordplay known as a Spoonerism rather than to any misspelt word mentioned in this etymological dictionary of Latin (Lacan, 2007, p. 113). Named after the Reverend William Archibald Spooner (1844–1930), Warden of New College, Oxford, who was notoriously prone to this tendency, "Spoonerism" is a play on words in which the corresponding consonants, vowels, or morphemes are transposed. For example, Spooner's declaration that he was leaving Oxford by "the town drain", meaning "the down train", or that at a marriage, it was "kistomary to cuss the bride", meaning "customary to kiss the bride" (The Guardian, 1930). In other words, Lacan arrived at the expression "Lituraterre" by way of a spoonerismic inversion of the

French word "*Littérature*" in terms of the transposition of the order of the two vowels "u" and "e" in the two words. Lacan's claim is correct also because whereas etymology produces the word "Lituraterra" rather than "Lituraterre", spoonerism on the word "*Littérature*" perfectly generates the word "Lituraterre". In effect, apart from aligning his coinage with the French language rather than with Latin, Lacan rejects the authorisation of the most prestigious etymological dictionary of Latin in French or the authorisation of a formal written text of importance and upholds the authorisation of the clownish Spooner who suffered from a kind of speech disorder, or the authorisation derived from the distorted speech of a relatively unimportant person. Above all, by at once referring to the transformation of *littérature* into lituraterre, to the erroneous conjunction of literature ("*Litterá*") and erasure ("*literá*", "*lino*", "*litura*"), and to the littoral condition ("*litorarius*") of the letter caused by its production of an erasure ("*liturarius*"), the very title of Lacan's essay is the first indicator of how literature may be in the process of turning towards lituraterre.

Jean-Michel Rabaté has pointed to an analogous sense in which the Latin word "*literatura*", along with a set of words closely associated with it that denote writing, erasure, and a shore, bring out how literature appears to tend towards lituraterre:

> In Latin the plural *literae* signifies writing, epistle, literature, while *literatura* in the singular means writing, grammar, learning or literature. However the latter noun comes from the verb *lino*, whose meaning is contradictory since it calls up 'I smear', 'I cover' or 'I erase'. . . As Lacan pursues the image, *literatura* as a signifier leads us closer to the Latin word *litus*—a word that has different meanings: as a noun, the act of smearing or covering a surface; as a participle, the same meaning as *lino*; as another noun, (*litus, litoris*), the 'littoral', a shore or coastline. 'Literature', then, generates a double pun: it suggests both letters and their erasure (a pun that is more obvious in French since one can always hear *rature*—erasure or crossing out—in the very signifier) and the limit or border of a territory, be it the sea, a hole or even another territory.
>
> (Rabaté, 2001, pp. 33–34)

This is how Lacan's coinage, "lituraterre", brings out how both etymologically and phonetically literature tends towards becoming lituraterre, though Lacan clearly privileges the phonetic mode here. The word "Lituraterre", then, owing to its association with literature, stands for "writing deletion [on the] ground", or "writing erasure [on] earth". It has a relation to writing on a surface in terms of an erasure rather than a deposit, such as writing on a foggy glass or on the sand with a finger. More pertinently, the mark of the erasure as the letter has an edge, which Lacan calls the littoral condition of the letter, as littoral stands for shore, coast, and edge. In the final analysis, therefore, although the word "Lituraterre" literally means "erasure-earth", in the Lacanian sense, the word means "writing erasure having an edge, on the ground".

Joyce and Beckett: Two Types of Literary Wastes and Two Types of Ends of Analysis

Lacan states that his point of departure is "the equivocation by which Joyce . . . slides from *a letter*[3] to *a litter*"[4] (Lacan, 2007, p. 113).[5] This is Lacan's first reference to Joyce in his annual public seminar. Lacan had mentioned Joyce once before, in passing, in his 1956 essay on "The Seminar on 'The Purloined Letter'" in terms of this very expression of Joyce, but he had not mentioned any of it in his 1954–1955 seminar on *The Ego in Freud's Theory and in the Technique of Psychoanalysis*, where he spoke on Poe's story for the first time, on the text of which the essay is based. Notably, on both these occasions, Lacan misquotes Joyce's "The letter! The litter!" as "A letter, a litter" (Lacan, 1957/2006, p. 18) and thus makes litter of Joyce's letter. While Joyce speaks of "the" letter in relation to "the" litter, Lacan stripped off the particularity of the letter and the litter in his distorted rendition and reduced them to just "a" letter and "a" litter, even as he elevated them to the status of any or every interrelated letter and litter conceivable. Going by the footnote to Joyce's expression in the essay (ibid., p. 47, fn. 11), Lacan had in mind Vladimir Dixon's "letter" of protest to Joyce dated 9th February, 1929, in which he described his own letter rather than any work of Joyce as "a litter" (Beckett et al., 1929/1961, p. 89). Perhaps Dixon's letter as "a letter" and "a litter" at the same time had induced Lacan's slip of the pen.

In this seminar, "letter" and "litter" denote the two forms of the letter itself: "The letter!", or the letter as meaning and semblance, and "The litter!", or the letter as an edge of the hollowed-out letter. As such, letter and litter represent two types of writing: the literal, or a writing with the help of letters that has a meaning, and the littoral, or a writing with the help of the letter as an edge that separates knowledge from jouissance. In terms of his equivocation with letter and litter, Joyce slipped from one type to the other. His slippage represents literature's crucial turn from the letter to litter and, through it, from the literal to the littoral.

"Litter" reminds Lacan of "shower" (*douche*), though the word "shower" is used only in the essay on "Lituraterre", not in the seminar. In the essay, Lacan writes, "One will recall that a lady 'Maecenas' [*messe-haine*],[6] in wanting to help him, offered him a psychoanalysis, as one might offer someone a shower. And with Jung of all people" (Lacan, 1971/2013, p. 327). Here, Lacan recalls Joyce's temporary patroness at Zurich, Edith Rockefeller McCormick, the fourth daughter of Standard Oil tycoon John D. Rockefeller and an analytic psychologist analysed by Jung at Zurich from 1913 to 1921.[7] In September 1919, McCormick offered Joyce a "shower" in the form of a psychoanalysis with Carl Jung, most probably upon Jung's request, and had offered to pay for it. Going by Joyce's report to his friend Claud Sykes, he found it "unthinkable" and refused straightaway (Thurston, 2004, p. 130). Joyce was furious when Jung diagnosed his daughter Lucia as schizophrenic, for he regarded it as a blunder. He declared that Lucia was as extraordinarily brilliant as him and that Jung had completely misunderstood her and her writings. He sarcastically stated in *Finnegans Wake* that Lucia was "yung and easily freudened" by the "grisly old Sykos" (Joyce, 1939/1975, p. 115). Joyce resented the idea of an analysis with Jung partly because he anticipated the same diagnosis as his daughter and deeply detested the idea. McCormick responded to Joyce's refusal by promptly terminating Joyce's stipend, most probably following Jung's advice. Unlike Jung and Joyce, however, Lacan thinks Joyce would have gained nothing from a psychoanalysis, for he had already managed to achieve the best one could expect from psychoanalysis at its end (Lacan, 2007, p. 113). What is more, Joyce had arrived there all by himself, without the assistance of a psychoanalyst! Here, the end of analysis is related to Joyce's act of writing, especially *Finnegans Wake*, with the help of litter. Lacan would clarify in his 1975–1976 seminar on *The Sinthome* that Joyce's end of analysis is related to his construction of and identification with his *sinthome* as a supplementary fourth ring to hold his otherwise disintegrating three-ring Borromean chain, Real-Symbolic-Imaginary, together.

Lacan briefly wonders whether Joyce's writing as "litter" could have a relation to Saint Thomas Aquinas' writing as "chaff": "In making litter of the letter, is it Saint Thomas again—you may remember, if you ever knew it, *sicut palea*—who returns to Joyce, as his work testifies throughout its whole length?" (ibid., p. 113). While Joyce's aesthetic theory is consistently and avowedly Thomistic in nature,[8] Aquinas himself described his *Summa Theologica* as "*sicut palea*", or chaff, while explaining why he stopped writing the book after having spent eight years on it, referring to his mystical experience of December 1273 which impelled him to terminate his work on the book: "All the things I have written are like chaff (*sicut palea*) to me, compared with what I have seen and what has been revealed to me" (Quoted in Nobus, 2013, p. 328).[9] However, since chaff and litter are not identical matters—unless we read *sicut palea* as dung, which is another meaning of the term—and since the composition and publication of *Finnegans Wake* are vastly different from the writing and abortion of *Summa Theologica*, Lacan is not sure whether Aquinas had indeed informed Joyce's slippage, which is why his remark on Joyce qua Aquinas is in the interrogative mode.

Lacan then states that Joyce at once contained and spilled the literature of litter. He contends that Joyce's work introduced the literary dustbin that consigned polluted literature to it, which made him Saint Joyce in Lacan's eyes because, unlike Aquinas, who considered the saint's business to be *caritas*, or charity, Lacan considered the saint's business to be *trashitas*, or to act as trash, which is why he remarked in *Television*: "A saint's business, to put it clearly, is not *caritas*. Rather, he acts as trash [*déchet*]; his business being *trashitas* [*il décharite*]" (Lacan, 1974/1990, p. 15). And at the same time, Joyce allowed a spill-over and re-circulation of the contents of the dustbin, which made him a heretic. Such re-circulation of litter was, in fact, enabled not only by the publication of Joyce's later literary works, especially *Finnegans Wake*, as Lacan indicates, but also by the posthumous publication—or, better still, "*poubellication*", or publication as trash, as Lacan says in his 1968–1969 seminar on *From an Other to the other* (Lacan,

2006, p. 11) and elsewhere—of Joyce's private correspondence with Nora called "the dirty letters" that was not meant for publication.

Lacan spoke on the relationship between sewerage and civilisation with great emphasis both before and since. In "Lituraterre" itself, Lacan alludes to his lecture entitled "My Teaching, its Nature and its Ends", addressed to interns in psychiatry at Bordeaux's Hôpital Psychiatrique Charles-Perrens on 20th April, 1968,[10] where he had enthusiastically spoken on "the great anal circuit of culture" and "the prodigious analogy that exists between sewage and culture":

> [U]nlike what happens at every level of the animal kingdom . . . man is naturally characterized by the extraordinary embarrassment he feels about . . . the evacuation of shit. . . . A great civilization is first and foremost a civilization that has a waste-disposal system. So long as we do not take that as our starting point, we will not be able to say anything serious. . . . when it comes to the equation *great civilization = pipes and sewers*, there are no exceptions. There were sewers in Babylon, and Rome was all sewers. That's how the City began, with *Cloaca maxima*.
>
> (Lacan, 2005/2008, pp. 64–66)

Lacan would return to this theme in reply to Willard von Orman Quine's question following his lecture at the Massachusetts Institute of Technology on 2nd December, 1975:

> Waste (*les déchets*) comes from inside, perhaps, but it is characteristic of man that he doesn't know what to do with his waste.
> Civilization is waste, *cloaca maxima*.
> Waste is the only thing that testifies to our having insides.
>
> (Lacan, 1976/2022, p. 94)

Since "litter" denotes both rubbish and excreta in Joyce, it invokes both the dustbin and the sewerage, respectively, as functions to keep them contained and controlled, thereby opening up the possibility of leakages from them as well. Joyce is the placeholder of the sewerage in literature. He inaugurated and embodied that place before others joined him. As the holder of this place, Joyce both contained excreta and leaked it out, which ought to be understood precisely in terms of the anal drive in psychoanalysis. The anal drive urges the subject to control and contain its excreta until a proper place to be relieved is found, which is due to its toilet training in terms of a series of demands of the Other, usually the mother, as the trainer. Since the anal drive is thus a matter of compliance or non-compliance with the Other's demand, the subject, at times, wants to frustrate rather than fulfil it, which it does by expressing its own anal desire, usually by relieving itself at what the Other would consider a wrong place. Leakage or relieving oneself at a wrong place is thus a form of assertion of one's own desire that is also a subversion of the demand of the Other. In his 1960–1961 seminar on *Transference*, Lacan explains that children generally comply with but occasionally revolt against the demand of the Other to express their own desire through deliberate defecation or urination at the wrong place (Lacan, 1991/2015, pp. 203–204).

Joyce made litter of the letter by describing the anal drive of his characters, such as Bloom in *Ulysses*. At the end of the "Calypso" episode in *Ulysses*, Bloom defecates in the unclean outhouse and then checks his trousers to make sure that there is no stain on them, especially as he has to attend a funeral shortly thereafter: "he eyed carefully his black trousers, the ends, the knees, the houghs of the knees" (Joyce, 1922/2000, p. 85). Throughout "Sirens", Bloom feels the need to defecate but holds back the urge. He keeps reminding himself that he really must do Sandow's Exercises. The chapter closes with Bloom letting out a loud fart but concealing it under the noise of a passing tram. Thus, while Bloom's anal desire complies with the Other's demand in the "Calypso" episode, he at once defies and complies with the Other's demand in the "Sirens" episode by farting at the wrong place and cleverly masking the sound of the fart respectively, which is in perfect consonance with the nature of the expression of Joyce's own anal desire as a writer:

Prrprr.
Must be the bur.
Fff. Oo. Rrpr.
Nations of the earth. No-one behind. She's passed. *Then and not till then*. Tram. Kran, kran, kran. Good oppor. Coming. Krandlkrankran. I'm sure it's the burgund. Yes. One, two. *Let my epitaph be*. Karaaaaaaa. Written. I have.
Pprrpffrrppfff.
Done.

(Ibid., pp. 374–375)

By composing his epitaph with the combination of solemn words and sounds of farting, Joyce writes not only with the help of letter and litter but with the help of litter as letter. Apart from the word "farting" itself, derivatives of the word "fart"— such as "farther", "fartoomanyness", "farth", "fartas", "pienofarte", "Grandfarthring", "farthing", "breakfarts", "farthingales", "farternoiser", "farthest", "farth", "fartykket", and "Afartodays"—occur throughout *Finnegans Wake* (Joyce, 1939/1975). Therefore, in the final analysis, Joyce was paradoxically protecting and damaging literature by containing and leaking out polluted literature at once.

At the broadest level, Lacan views Joyce's act of writing with litter in two ways. In 1971, in "Lituraterre", he sees it as a form of hollowing out of the letter, thereby reducing the letter to an edge with which is produced the discourse of the littoral that serves to separate knowledge from jouissance. And in 1975–1976, in the seminar on *The Sinthome*, Lacan views Joyce's act of writing with litter or *lalangue* as the construction of his unanalysable *sinthome* that produced jouissance.

Speaking on the relation between civilisation and the sewer, Lacan "avows", "I was a little weary of the dustbin (*poubelle*) to which I have riveted my fate" (Lacan, 2007, p. 114). A psychoanalyst's fate is riveted to the dustbin not only in the sense that he constitutes the place where analysands dump their trash but also in the deeper sense of the analyst's becoming the waste product at the end of every analysis. Lacan spoke on the relation between the psychoanalyst and trash in the former sense in the seminar on *The Psychoses*:

> The life of a psychoanalyst—as I was reminded by my analysands [*analysés*] several times on the one day—isn't rosy.
> The comparison that can be made between the analyst and a rubbish dump is justified. All day long in fact he has to endure utterances that, surely, are of doubtful value to himself and even more so to the subject who communicates them to him. This is a feeling that the psychoanalyst, if he is a real one, has not only been accustomed to overcoming for a long time, but, to be honest, it's one that he purely and simply abolishes within himself in the exercise of his practice.
> (Lacan, 1981/1993, p. 29)

But in the seminar on "Lituraterre", Lacan equates the psychoanalyst to trash in the additional sense that, when an analysis is completed, the analyst, as the catalyst that had initiated and facilitated the analytic act, is left behind as the waste-product or residue or remainder of the analysis that Lacan termed the object small *a*.

After avowing his relation to waste as a psychoanalyst, Lacan says that he is neither the only person who is related to waste nor the only person to admit such a relation. To illustrate this, he invokes Samuel Beckett's avowal of his relation to waste as an author. Lacan made a passing remark on *Waiting for Godot* (Beckett, 1953/2003) in 1956 while explaining why the number two is odd—"the two numbers that have no equal are waiting for Godot" (Lacan, 1956/2006, p. 395)—after Beckett had come into prominence following the staging of this play in Paris in 1953. He made another passing remark in 1962 in the context of his discussion on God: "echoing Beckett who one day called him Godot" (Lacan, 2002, p. 324). More pertinently, however, Lacan mentions Beckett in conjunction with the dustbin in the opening session of the 1968–1969 seminar on *From an Other to the other*:

> [A] certain number of us [those labelled "structuralist" by the publisher], by the grace of this agency ["the publisher"], find ourselves together in the same dustbin (*poubelle*) . . . I cannot, in any case, feel bad about it. Especially since we know a little bit about what is involved in dustbins in this time dominated by the genius of Samuel Beckett.
> (Lacan, 2006, p. 11)

Here, Lacan describes Beckett as the dominant figure of a period whose "dustbins" he and the other so-called structuralists had a little bit of knowledge of. Taking the argument further in the seminar on "Lituraterre" two-and-a-half years later, Lacan highlights Beckett's crucial admission of the relation of being to trash: "the admission [*l'avouère*], to pronounce it in the old fashioned way, the 'asset' [*l'avoir*] which Beckett balances with the 'owed' [*doit*] which wastes [*déchet*] our being" (Lacan,

2007, p. 114). Beckett's admission or confession is the asset or credit [*l'avoir*] with which he settles the debt or debit [*doit*] that, when not settled, wastes our being. Insofar as Beckett's admission balances "debit" and "credit", it is akin to an act of accounting. However, "*l'avoir*" also means "the having", whereby Lacan's word-play with *l'avouère* and *l'avoir* suggests a relation between "owning up" and "owning". Beckett owned up to the waste that he owned in order to settle the debt that otherwise reduces our being to trash. Moreover, the word "*doit*" also means "must", and therefore Lacan's sentence also means "the admission . . . or the having with which Beckett must (*doit*) balance what makes waste of our being". In this rendition, *l'avouère* relates to *l'avoir* by underlying it, in the sense that we can only avow what we have, which necessarily includes the waste or excreta that we cannot exclude when we "must" avow all that we have. The allusion to filth is strengthened by the fact that *l'avoir* is phonetically similar to *lavoir*, which means laundry.

In both these later references dated 1968 and 1971, Lacan was most probably alluding to Beckett's 1957 play *Endgame*, whose title bore a fortuitous resonance of the "end" (of analysis)—as does "*Fin*"*negans Wake* in another sense—and throughout which its protagonist Hamm kept his parents, Nagg and Nell, "bottled" in two dustbins, thus making them human trash who literally lived in trash[11] (Beckett, 1957/2003). As if to indicate a relation of contiguity between excreta and trash as the two forms of human refuse, the play which premiered as a curtain raiser to *Endgame* at London's Royal Court Theatre in 1958 was *Krapp's Last Tape*, the protagonist of which, whose name contains a pun on "crap", suffered from a "bowel condition" in the form of an "unattainable laxation", owing to which he abstains from consuming a fourth banana (Beckett, 1958/2003, pp. 217–218). Not only that, in his 1951 novel *Molloy*, Molloy's first sexual encounter with an old woman called Ruth or Edith takes place in a rubbish dump:

> We met in a rubbish dump, unlike any other, and yet they are all alike, rubbish dumps. . . . Anyway it was she who started it, in the rubbish dump, when she laid her hand upon my fly. More precisely, I was bent double over a heap of muck, in the hope of finding something to disgust me for ever with eating, when she, undertaking me from behind, thrust her stick between my legs and began to titillate my privates.
>
> (Beckett, 1951/1959, p. 57)

Whether or not Lacan was aware of it while writing "Lituraterre", it is noteworthy that Beckett's thirty-five-second play on "littered . . . rubbish", *Breath*, was written and staged in Paris in 1969, only two years before "Lituraterre" was written. *Breath* turned out to be an extremely successful play for Beckett since, according to Acklerley and Gontarski, between 1974 and 1989, "85 million people saw 1314 performances [on Broadway] making it easily Beckett's most viewed play" (Ackerley & Gontarski, 2006, p. 73).

The play depicts "Faint light on stage littered with miscellaneous rubbish. . . . Faint brief cry and immediately inspiration . . . Expiration and . . . immediately cry as before". In the stage directions, Beckett mentions, "Rubbish. No verticals, all scattered and lying" (Beckett, 1969/2003). The play is about human life, from the beginning to the end, and about its brevity—life is the duration of a single breath. Beckett wrote in his 1977 play *A Piece of Monologue*: "Birth was the death of him" (Beckett, 1979/2006, p. 425). In *Breath*, human life is reduced to its fundamental function, sound or cry; its fundamental acts, breathing and littering; and its fundamental metaphor, breath. The play possibly means we breathe in and we breathe out, and that's it. In between, we wait and produce rubbish as we do so, but our waiting proves futile because nothing happens in the end. Life is rubbish. But "No verticals", because time is needed for rubbish to pile up at one place vertically. The play thus equates human life, which is as short as a single breath, to a brief moment of littering situated in the interval between two cries. As such, the play is a pithy comment on life in terms of a ruthless depiction of the history of the human spirit insofar as breath and spirit are related and have common connotations. Beckett thus glorifies rubbish, first by elevating it to the status of the only thing, apart from babies, that life produces; second, by equating it with breathing and articulating; and third, by making it consubstantial with life itself. Lacan states that Beckett's avowal relieved him of the need to believe that the psychoanalyst alone was privileged to know a little bit about the dustbin (Lacan, 2007, p. 114). He was relieved to see that there were others who were equally sincere and vigilant about the dustbins of civilisation.

Above all, Lacan thinks that Beckett's act of balancing the debt through his avowal, or owning up, "saved the honour of literature" (ibid., p. 114). The honour of literature is salvaged by Beckett's insistent admission that its true object is trash in terms of repeated graphic depictions of the same. This remark is, moreover, to be understood in the light of Lacan's own definition of literature as "leftovers" that follows. Lacan states that the textbooks of literature have always displayed that "literature is nothing but a way of accommodating oneself to leftovers (*des restes*). Is it a matter of collecting in a writing, what at first, primitively, was song, spoken myth, dramatic procession?" (ibid., p. 114). In other words, insofar as literature is marked by a transition from the oral to the written, from the whole to its fragments, and from the great many to the few surviving, it is, properly speaking, a matter of satisfying oneself with the crumbs left behind. Literature thus being the leftovers of what once was, its honour is saved only by the avowal of that truth in the body of literature itself, which Beckett had faithfully carried out. Joyce and Beckett thus bring out the two types of relations that literature has with trash. While Beckett's writings depict life as trash, Joyce reduced language to trash and then wrote with it. This would explain why Lacan defines literature as leftovers following Beckett and emphasises the weight of the word literature in terms of the letter as litter following Joyce: "And to underscore the weightiness of the word literature, I shall utter the equivoque that Joyce often plays on—letter, litter. The letter is litter" (Lacan, 1982/2016, p. 145). Above all, Lacan was not talking about this or that literary work or about the works of this or that author any more in "Lituraterre". For him, literature itself is to be understood in terms of litter and waste following the works of Joyce and Beckett.

Beckett and Joyce moreover provided support for Lacan's discussions on two types of ends of analysis that began in 1967 and 1975–1976, respectively. We may call them the end of the analysis of the neurotic subject, which Lacan describes partly vis-a-vis Beckett, and the end of the analysis of the ordinary psychotic subject—a classification introduced by Miller—which Lacan describes largely vis-a-vis Joyce. So, what does the end of analysis mean in the case of neurosis? Well, the end of the analysis of the neurotic subject is that stage of analysis when the subject has gradually emptied its subjectivity in speech and has nothing more left to say at the analytic level. The subject thus attains a state of subjective destitution and comes to realise the truth that he is nothing but an empty subject of the signifier. The neurotic subject's end of analysis is marked by the sensations of un-being, emptiness, exhaustion, and destitution. It is also marked by the dis-being of the subject supposed to know in terms of the liquidation of the Other through analysis of the transference. The dis-being of the Other compounds the destitution of the subject. Thus, the subject's own field and the field of his Other are both emptied at the end of the analysis. In general, this gives the subject a glimpse of the real of his being as waste, like Oedipus before his passing away at Colonus, for the subject finds himself as a scrap in the real at the end, as a piece of Beckettian trash in the dustbin of life. This realisation produces beneficial effects because it is attained long before the real end of life. Having exhausted the gradual construction of his fantasy in the course of the analysis, the subject crosses it at the end and finds himself reduced to a particular object. This has an effect on his desire in the sense that the neurotic's end of analysis is marked by relation to lack, by the birth of a decided desire, by the feeling of having something to say and to do, and by the blending of desire, duty, and destiny, all of which may have contributed to making Beckett the kind of author of waste and minimalism that he did become. It often leads to the reconstitution of the subject from the ashes of destitution in terms of the subject's procurement of himself through extraction from the real order and thus to the birth of a new subject, such as a new psychoanalyst or a new author. While it is certain that Beckett was psychoanalysed by Wilfred Bion at the Tavistock Clinic in London for two years, from 1934 to 1935, around the beginning of their respective careers,[12] and Beckett's writings do indicate that he is likely to have experienced the effect of the end of analysis of a neurotic subject, we do not know for sure whether he had experienced that effect with or without the assistance of his analysis. If the latter is true, then he is somewhat like Joyce, his countryman and master, who represents to Lacan the other type of end of analysis.

While Lacan describes the end of the analysis of the neurotic subject in terms of an emphasis on fantasy, object, and desire, he describes the end of the analysis of the ordinary psychotic subject in terms of an emphasis on the symptom, or, better still, the *sinthome*, the One, and jouissance. As Miller explains in his unpublished "Course" of 2011, especially in Lessons Eleven through Fourteen, while the former notion of the end of analysis is related to Being as waste and to the identification with an object of desire beyond the fantasy, the latter notion of the end of analysis is related to Existence as the One-all alone, and to the subject's assumption of the

One beyond the fantasy that Miller terms "the ultra-pass" (*l'outrepasse*) or beyond the pass (Miller, 2011). Joyce experienced the ultra-pass by identifying with the singular, unanalysable *sinthome* he had painstakingly constructed without the support of an analysis.[13]

In this manner, the instances of Joyce and Beckett that are suggestive of two forms of affinity between the letter and the litter in two types of ends of analysis indicate how literature appeared to tend towards lituraterre with the help of litter functioning as waste or as an edge. Lituraterre, which is otherwise veiled by literature—"'lituraterre' . . . is what literature veils", said Miller in 1995 (Miller, 1999/2013, p. 43)—is unveiled by this.

The Apologue of the Siberian River and Its Embankment

Lacan then offers a "literal demonstration" (*démonstration littérale*) of the idea that "literature may be turning towards lituraterre" (Lacan, 2007, p. 119) in terms of a little by little construction of an apologue that constitutes the most perfect, because "literal", illustration of lituraterre in Lacan. While flying back to Europe from Tokyo at the end of his second visit to Japan shortly before writing the essay, over the otherwise barren Siberian Plain, the only thing that he could see through the window of the aircraft—and from between the clouds—was rivers. He calls these solitary traces in view "shimmering" (*ruissellement*), and writes:

> That's how it invincibly appeared to me in a circumstance which is worth remembering, namely from between the clouds, there appeared to me the shimmering which is the only trace to appear by operating there . . . in what is called the Siberian plain, a plain truly desolate, in the literal sense of the term, of any vegetation, except for reflections, reflections of this shimmering, which pushes into the shadow that which does not shimmer.
>
> (Ibid., pp. 120–121)

Lacan would ratify in his 1972–1973 seminar *Encore: On Feminine Sexuality, The Limits of Love and Knowledge* that the clouds and the rivers or streams described in "Lituraterre" metaphorically denote writing: "'The cloud of language,' I expressed myself metaphorically, 'constitutes writing.' . . . [and] that we can read (*lire*) the streams I saw over Siberia as the metaphorical trace of writing" (Lacan, 1975/1998, p. 120). Signifieds as rain pour down from the clouds of signifiers, forming furrows filled with flowing water on the ground that appear as shimmerings from the place of the clouds above. In the seminar on "Lituraterre", Lacan describes the two constituents of the shimmering viewed as writing:

> What is this shimmering? It is a bunch. It acts like a bouquet, of the first stroke and what effaces it, that I have distinguished elsewhere. . . . I said it in connection with the unary trait, it is by the erasure of the trait that the subject is

designated. It is marked, then, in two stages. It is therefore necessary that the erasure be distinguished there.

(Lacan, 2007, p. 121)

Later, when the aeroplane swerved to sustain itself in isobars, Lacan saw "traces which are of the order of an embankment" (ibid., p. 122). The literal demonstration ends here, with Lacan's emphasis clearly placed on the first stroke and its effacement, and the embankment or the edge of the shore designating the effacement as a form of lituraterre.

Lacan had indeed distinguished the first stroke and what effaces it in his seminar on *Identification* where, in order to explain the manifestation of the subject, he differentiated "the unary trait" from "the relationship of the sign to the thing [that] should be effaced":

> It will first of all be necessary for us to distinguish the signifier from the sign and for us to show in what sense the step taken is that of the effaced thing: the different effacer (*effaçons*) . . . in which the signifier comes to birth, will give us precisely the major modes of the manifestation of the subject.
>
> (Lacan, 2002, pp. 44–45)

Simply put, Lacan defines the sign, following Charles Sanders Peirce, as what "represent[s] something for someone", and he differentiates the signifier from the sign by describing the signifier as "the presence of difference as such and nothing else", as well as by defining the signifier as that which represents the subject for another signifier. Lacan explains that the subject, better still the barred subject ($\$$), comes into being as a result of the operation of alienation, in the gap between two signifiers, S_1 and S_2, when S_1, the first signifier or the first stroke, represents it for S_2, or the rest of the signifiers. Lacan writes this as $S_1 \rightarrow \$ \rightarrow S_2$. Thus, in order to explain how the subject is designated by the signifier, Lacan distinguishes the signifier from the sign and effaces the relationship of the sign to the thing (ibid., pp. 44–45). Alternatively, it may be argued, as Jean-Pierre Klotz does, that the unary trait, in fact, symbolises the gap between S_1 and S_2 (Klotz, 2012, p. 199), which the barred subject erases by coming into being there. In any case, Lacan consistently describes the subject of the first operation, of alienation, in terms of its representation by the signifier S_1 for the signifier S_2 throughout *Écrits* and in all his early works. This idea that the place of the subject is in the gap between two signifiers is indicated by others as well, such as Lao-tzu, for a part of verse 42 of his masterpiece *Tao te Ching* that Lacan read and discussed with François Cheng goes as follows:

> The original Tao engenders the One
> The One engenders the Two
> The Two engenders the Three
> The Three produces the Ten-thousand beings

The Ten-thousand beings lean on the Yin
And embrace the Yang
Harmony is born of the breath of the Median-Void.
(François Cheng's translation quoted in
Roudinesco, 1993/1997, pp. 351–352)

The subject is born in the "breath of the Median-Void" between Yin and Yang, between One, or S_1, and the rest, or S_2. However, since the first stroke or the unary trait or the letter in "Lituraterre" is already an erasure, we may also read Lacan's expression "a first stroke and of what effaces it" awry, defying Lacan's intended meaning, by reading it in terms of an *après-coup* or retroaction. Thus, if the first stroke is a furrow on the ground, an empty riverbed, an erasure written on earth, then the shimmering indicates its partial effacement in terms of the water that filled up the furrow. This means that a letter is essentially a hollow and empty shell that is filled up with meaning and significance later on. However, the more pertinent point in the present context is that the effacement of the furrow is only partial insofar as the shimmering water does not efface the edges of the erasure. Rather, the water establishes the edges as the two banks of the river, which thereby continue to distinguish and highlight the erasure. A river always consists of a single furrow and a single flow of water that invariably produces two edges or two banks: "The One engenders the Two". Now, if we read the relation of the letter to its erasure in this passage in the light of an *après-coup*, we may say that the letter is retroactively posited from an erasure. If we were to thus view the letter not as that which is erased but rather as that which is retroactively posited from an erasure, then we can regard this remark as Lacan's definition of the subject of separation. To consider the subject as an entity made out of the conjunction of an erasure and a hollowed-out letter produced by that erasure is to describe the subject of the operation of separation insofar as the subject may be said to have been defined here in terms of its act of procuring itself from the real order by way of its separation or extraction from it. Notably, Éric Laurent aligns the edge of the hollowed-out letter "*a*" representing the "object *a*", or the littoral condition of the letter that situates jouissance beyond the limit of knowledge, with the operation of separation (Laurent, 1999/2007, pp. 38–39).

Lacan clarifies that the only decisive thing he saw in the Siberian Plain was the littoral condition: "The only decisive condition here is precisely the condition of the littoral" (Lacan, 2007, p. 119). The letter as erasure, in the form of the shimmering river, stood out for the onlooker due to the absolute barrenness of the Siberian Plain, where neither any vegetation nor any litter was to be seen. Lacan further clarifies that he did not perceive the littoral condition in the Siberian Plain so strongly on his flight *to* Japan but that he did so while flying back to Europe *from* Japan thanks to the appropriate sensitisation of his perception in the course of his stay in Japan in terms of the excess created by Japanese writing that was necessary to prepare him to perceive it. This detail, which brings out one of the important effects of Japanese writing on Lacan, has been completely missed out by Thelma

Sowley who, in her 2008 book chapter titled "Crossing Boundaries", claims that Lacan saw the Siberian rivers on his way *to* Japan and consistently maintained this erroneous position throughout the chapter:

> He tells us of his voyage to Japan . . . we can visualize the borders he must have crossed, the borders that divide Europe to begin with, but also that singular boundary that 'separates' two continents, Europe and Asia.
> (Sowley, 2008, p. 352)

This constitutes a misreading of Lacan because, as Lacan states in his seminar on "Lituraterre", as well as in his essay on the same, that although he had already flown over Siberia on his way *to* Japan during his second visit to that country in 1971, much unlike his first visit, in 1963, during which the flights took a different route both times and did not fly over Siberia due to "the distrust of Soviets" (Lacan, 2007, p. 119), he had failed to read the littoral condition during that flight because, being a little hard of hearing, he needed the excess of tickling that he was to receive from the Japanese letter during his stay in Japan in order to be properly prepared to read it on his way back home. Therefore, it was only while flying over Siberia for the second time, on his way back to Europe from Japan, that an adequately sensitised Lacan was able to read the littoral condition:

> I have to admit that it was not on the outward journey . . . that I managed to read [the littoral]. . . . For me, because I am a little hard of hearing, it only operated on the return journey as being literally what Japan, with its letters, had without doubt done to me, probably tickled me a little too much, which is just what it takes for me to feel it.
> (Ibid., pp. 119–120)

This concept of the hollowed letter as an edge, or of the littoral condition of the letter enabled Lacan to speak about all those things that are situated beyond one another along an edge or a frontier but did not form binary oppositions, such as knowledge and jouissance: "between knowledge (*savoir*) and jouissance, there is the littoral that turns towards the literal only in so far as you can take this turn in the same way at all times" (ibid., p. 121). In this wordplay in French and English, "littoral" means the edge and "*littéral*" means literal or something pertaining to the letter. Here, the littoral is the edge or the bank of a river where the water touches its limit. It is not a border for a number of reasons. First, because it separates two non-equivalent elements, such as water and earth, rather than two equivalent domains, such as two nations, as a border does. Lacan says: "The littoral is what sets up an entire domain as forming for another domain, if you will, a frontier, but precisely because they do not have absolutely anything in common, not even a reciprocal relation" (ibid., p. 117). Second, because it is a naturally inscribed mark rather than a letter—as in a line—that is artificially inscribed by the speaking being between two territories, that a border usually is. Third, because, as a furrow or a hollowed inscription, it is indicative of the littoral condition of the letter, unlike a border that indicates the letter's literal condition. And fourth, it is an indicator of the limit of an element and its beyond rather than a third element mediating between two other elements. The littoral is the edge of the erasure that writes the erasure, and thereby also writes the shimmering or the river as the letter, for what indicates or "writes" a river for someone viewing it from above are its banks or edges. When Lacan says, "[b]etween jouissance and knowledge, the letter would constitute the littoral" (ibid., p. 117), "between" once again does not denote a border in the form of a third element that separates the first and second elements, in the form of knowledge and jouissance. Rather, it denotes a limit that is indicative of beyond the limit, in terms of which jouissance, as something situated beyond the limit of knowledge, refers to itself through the littoral. Jouissance is situated beyond knowledge in the sense that jouissance, pertaining to the real, is incompatible with knowledge, pertaining to the symbolic. The littoral that stands for the edge that the hole in knowl-edge always has, illustrates the limit that marks jouissance as what is situated beyond that edge of the hole in knowledge. Finally, Lacan says that we might take the turn to the literal "in the same way at all times" at the end of the excerpt because, when the littoral is viewed literally, it remains unchanged at any instant, for, as a letter, it may be read in the same way every time.

In the final analysis, the Siberian river and its embankment together constitute the most perfect illustration of "lituraterre" in Lacan because the element of "terra" is perfectly accounted for in this instance alone. A riverbed constitutes a perfect example of writing erasure on the ground by its prominent edges. In all the other instances presented by Lacan, "lituraterre" stands for an edge that writes an eras-ure-as-a-letter. None of them indicate any direct relation to the ground or earth as such. Although this illustration of "lituraterre" is too literal to explain literature's turn towards lituraterre all by itself, when taken figuratively, the edge of the river that denotes the littoral condition of the letter, explains the status of the letter in the writings of Joyce and the avant-garde literature inspired by him. In the works of Joyce and his followers, the letter is hollowed out and, as such, it is littoral, not literal. Literature takes a step towards "lituraterre" when it begins to be produced by the littoral instead of the literal condition of the letter.

Is the Discourse of the Littoral Not a Semblance?

Lacan asks: "Is it possible in sum to constitute with the littoral a discourse that is characterized . . . as not based on a semblance?" (ibid., p. 124). Simply put, can there be a discourse of the littoral that is not produced by a semblance? But, first of all, what does Lacan mean by a "semblance"?

The word semblance or semblant means being like, resemblance, imitation, feign, make believe, seem, and external appearance. Lacan uses the word "sem-blance" several times in *Écrits* and a few times in the 1956–1957 seminar on *The Object Relation* where the word primarily stands for resemblance or appearance. In the 1964 seminar on *The Four Fundamental Concepts of Psychoanalysis*, where

Lacan describes a semblance as a "paper tiger" (Lacan, 1973/1998, p. 7), a semblance offers a substitute for a lost object that is gratifying despite being known to be false, such as the object a that substitutes for the lost maternal phallus. A semblance is opposed to the reality of which it is a semblance, insofar as it is not the real thing, and at the same time, it exists purely in relation to reality, insofar as all that it does is denote a relation to something real. Thus, a semblance has the ability to offer satisfaction out of nothing or in terms of something that merely seems to be, for one does not need to mistake it for the real thing in order to receive satisfaction from it. Semblance is seductive not only because it is the only available source of gratification but also because its removal forces one to encounter the loss it fills up, which in turn evokes anxiety. A semblance is also often preferred over what it replaces because it can be a replacement for a fearful object or for a void. According to Miller, a semblance is "a veil that hides nothing" and posits something in the place of nothing in terms of the very act of veiling (Miller, 1997/1999, p. 12). This is akin to the locked door in Strindberg's 1901 play, *A Dream Play*, that makes the characters think of the existence of various things behind it, although, as revealed at the end, nothing was ever there behind it. Thus, owing to the function of a semblance, something is produced by nothing. As a veil, a semblance veils and points to the act of veiling. In the seminar on *On a Discourse that Might not be a Semblance* in 1971, Lacan elevated semblance to the status of an extremely important concept of psychoanalysis. In this seminar, he used the term in the broader sense of a substitute for something and, more importantly, extended its use to radically redefine as semblances some of his important concepts originally not defined thus, such as the Other, the Name-of-the-Father, language, and the phallus in the main. Lacan would go on to point to the relations of *objet petit a*, love, and jouissance to semblance in the seminar on *Encore: On Feminine Sexuality, The Limits of Love and Knowledge*. In 1971, or the stage of his teaching that we are concerned with in this chapter, a semblance represents a truth that cannot express itself. It makes possible the presence of something at a place where it is not present. A semblance is also the negation of what it represents. And finally, a semblance is not identical to, not-all of, what it represents. Therefore, a discourse that is not emitted by a semblance is a discourse that is emitted by the truth.

In reply to the question, can there be a discourse of the littoral that is not produced by a semblance? Lacan says: "This is the question that obviously arises only with regard to what is called avant-garde literature, which is itself a littoral fact, and, therefore, is not sustained by a semblance" (Lacan, 2007, p. 124). Avant-garde literature is a discourse of the littoral because it sustains itself by the hole and not by the semblance. Of the two levels at which Lacan describes writing in the seminar on "Lituraterre"—"Writing, the letter, is in the real, and the signifier, is in the symbolic" (ibid., p. 122)—writing the letter in the real or writing as "the furrowing of the signified" in the real (ibid., p. 122) was of greater importance to him at this stage, especially because he was looking for a discourse that might not be a semblance. This is the reason that he states that, whereas literature aspires to turn to lituraterre by ordering itself from a scientific movement, where writing "has done wonders", he lituraterres himself, or he himself lands on the terrain of erasure (*lituraterrir*), by pointing out that "writing is this furrowing (*ravinement*) [itself]" (ibid., p. 124).

Although the Joyce-inspired French avant-garde literature alluded to by Lacan—some of whose important exponents are Philippe Sollers, Alain Robbe-Grillet, Nathalie Sarraute, and others—largely rejected traditional notions of character, plot, psychology, and narrative style, and therefore was a "littoral fact", or made of the littoral, it was not completely unanchored or unstructured. Much of it was concerned, in different ways, with the need to attack the conventional notion of philosophy and its theories of knowledge; the propensity to question the conventional understanding of meaning and the metaphysical bent of language towards expressivity; the tendency to severely criticise the time and expose the systems of control; the impulse to ruthlessly undermine the obscurantism of the bourgeois state; the urge to inscribe what was as it was, as announced by the title of the Parisian literary journal *Tel Quel* (1960–1982); the inclination to radically break free from the conventional notions of chronology, teleology, transcendental humanism, psychological mystification, writing, textuality, culture, reality, and subjectivity; as well as to reinterpret the role of politics, religion, art, literature, sex, and the media. The highly abrasive socio-political edge of the French avant-garde literature came from these tendencies. However, in terms of its radical departure from traditional forms of narration—by way of unconventional narrative styles, wordplay, condensation, neologism, displacement, pun, riddle, allusion, ideogram, misspelling, combination of incongruous words and phrases, use of words from different languages, absence of punctuation, stress on the sounds of words, the bent toward escaping the signifier-effects of metaphor and metonymy, the fading status of the self, et cetera—avant-garde literature comprised texts that were hallucinatory, chaotic, and situated at the very edge of meaning. By creating holes in meaning and thus eluding sense, it directed the attention of the readers to the very materiality of the letters and their sounds on the one hand and the limit of meaning and the impossible void beyond it as the site of jouissance on the other. Thus, avant-garde literature comes closest to a form of a discourse that might not be a semblance because, being made of the littoral instead of the literal, it is sustained by the holes in the semblance. As Lacan says of the littoral: "[T]he letter that erases is distinguished by being a rupture therefore, of the semblance, which dissolves whatever pretended to be a form" (ibid., p. 122). However, there is no discourse that is not a semblance, for the organising point of every discourse begins with a semblance without which it is impossible to qualify what is involved in a discourse. Besides, every discourse, lituraterre included, draws upon the signifier, which is a semblance par excellence. As Miller points out, "the Lacan of 'Lituraterre' . . . puts the signifier in the clouds of the semblant . . . , the phenomenon of illusion" (Miller, 1999/2013, p. 46). Avant-garde literature is no exception, for, in the final analysis, though it is a discourse of the littoral, it is not a discourse that is not a semblance because it only establishes the break that can be produced by a discourse that is a semblance. In Lacan's own words, "all that proves nothing, other than to show the break that only a discourse can produce ..., with an effect of production", much like all the other discourses discussed by Lacan in the previous year that are semblances (Lacan, 2007, p. 124).

The Writing Effect in the Japanese Tongue

Lacan then turns to the "writing effect" included in the Japanese tongue for the "resources" it offers "to produce an example of lituraterre" (ibid., p. 124).[14] In the fifth session of the seminar *On a Discourse that Might not be a Semblance*, Lacan singles out the Japanese language for revealing the extraordinary degree to which "a writing can work upon a tongue" (ibid., p. 91) and explains its speciality:

> What is called the monème, there, in the middle, you can change it. You give it a Chinese pronunciation, quite different from the Japanese pronunciation, so that, when you are in the presence of a Chinese character, you pronounce it *on-yomi* or *kun-yomi* depending on the case, which are always very precise ... Anyway, it teaches you a lot—a lot about this, that the Japanese tongue, it is nourished by its writing.
>
> (Ibid., pp. 91–92)

In the session on lituraterre that followed, Lacan further explains:

> If there is included in the Japanese language ... a writing effect, the important thing is ... that the writing effect remains attached to writing. What carries the effect of writing there is a specialised writing in that in Japanese this specialised writing can be read with two different pronunciations. In *on-yomi* ... its pronunciation as characters is distinct from that which is done in *kun-yomi*, which is the way in which the meaning of the character is said in Japanese.
>
> (Ibid., pp. 124–125)

Simply put, the kanji consists of Chinese characters that can be pronounced in two different ways: the *on-yomi*, or the "*on*" reading, and the *kun-yomi*, or the "*kun*" reading. *On-yomi* concerns the Chinese pronunciation of the Chinese character, while *kun-yomi* concerns the Japanese pronunciation of what it means in Japanese. The writing effect in Japanese language remains attached to writing because it is perpetually borne by this duplicity in pronunciation. It also divides the Japanese subject in a way whereby "one of his registers is satisfied with the reference to writing and the other with the exercise of speech" (ibid., p. 125). This makes the Japanese-speaking subject different from the subjects speaking, say, the Indo-European languages. Now, insofar as the Japanese tongue sustains itself as the edge of the erasure of Chinese characters, the writing effect in the Japanese tongue is an instance of lituraterre in language.[15] Above all, the writing effect illustrates how Chinese characters, or writing in Chinese, or Chinese "literature" in the broadest sense of writing with letters, tend to be converted into the Japanese tongue in the course of any verbal enunciation in Japanese. This makes the Japanese tongue a perfect instance of lituraterre in speech.

Taking the discussion a step further in his 1974–1975 seminar on *R.S.I.*, Lacan remarks on the clinical ramifications of this, with due reference to "Lituraterre":

> On returning from a trip to Japan, I believed myself to see a certain duplicity in pronunciation, doubled by the duplicity of the system of writing, a special difficulty of the language to operate at the level of the unconscious, and precisely in what would appear to make it easier.
>
> (Lacan, 1975, p. 31. Translation modified)

The duplicity in pronunciation concerning *on-yomi* and *kun-yomi* compounded by the duplicity in writing concerning *hiragana* and *katakana* as its two syllabaries, made the Japanese language resist—rather than making it conducive to—the unconscious. What does that mean? Well, Lacan had already clarified in his 1972 "Preface to the Japanese Edition of the *Écrits*" that the gap between the unconscious and speech, which is not open in any of the languages pertinent for psychoanalysis, is rendered open and "tangible at every moment" in Japanese due to its dependence on Chinese writing (Lacan, 1972/1981, p. 3). In other words, although this gap posited by the double duplicity characterising the language should have made it easier for the Japanese language to operate at the level of the unconscious, the perpetually open nature of this gap makes such an action difficult. Simply put, psychoanalytic effects are produced by opening up the gap between unconscious and speech extremely cautiously, a gap that is present but remains closed in the case of the speakers of the other dominant languages. Since this gap remains perpetually open among the speakers of Japanese by contrast, it is hard to produce meaningful psychoanalytic effects on them, effects like the crucial recovery of the subject through the object *a*. Pointing to its most pertinent consequence for psychoanalysis, Lacan remarked that "no one who inhabits this language needs to be psychoanalyzed" (ibid., p. 3). As we have seen, Lacan said in the seminar on "Lituraterre" that Joyce, and presumably others like him, did not need psychoanalysis; he says here that speakers of Japanese do not need to be psychoanalysed; and he would go on to say in the eighth session of his seminar on *The Sinthome* that "a [practising] Catholic is unanalysable" (Lacan, 2005/2016, p. 106) even though these are different types of non-analysability. Shin'ya Ogasawara argues with the support of two clinical examples that Lacan's assessment of the analysability of the Japanese subject should be read theoretically as a "limit-case of 'psychoanalysability'", not literally, for "in the Japanese unconscious the instance of the letter is made in hiragana" (Ogasawara, 1999, pp. 2–3). While it is true that psychoanalysis is practised in Japan with the presupposition that the Japanese unconscious is structured in hiragana, Ogasawara's observations neither address nor dispute the problem of the open gap caused by the double duplicity characterising the Japanese language, on which Lacan's assessment is based.

Psychoanalytic Literary Criticism

Since Lacan's essay on "Lituraterre" was meant for a volume devoted to the theme of literature and psychoanalysis, he offers some valuable advice to the exponents of this interdisciplinary area, especially in terms of an idea of the direction in which they ought to be headed. Lacan begins by pointing out that Freud's reference to the myth of Oedipus in terms of the Oedipus complex is not to be mistaken for an analysis of Sophocles' *Oedipus Rex,* as these are two different texts (Lacan, 2007, p. 114).[16] In other words, there is nothing literary about Freud's invocation of Oedipus. Referring to Freud's 1928 essay "Dostoevsky and Parricide", in which Freud read Dostoevsky's *The Brothers Karamazov* psycho-biographically, in terms of the creative artist, the neurotic, the moralist and the sinner in Dostoevsky's personality (Freud, 1928/2001), Lacan adds that Freud failed to offer textual criticism any fresh air with the help of psychoanalysis (Lacan, 2007, p. 114). Lacan rightly says that textual criticism up to that time was the preserve of the university discourse from which the psychoanalytic literary criticism of Freud and the Freudians completely failed to free it owing to the psycho-biographical bent of their work coupled with their acute lack of "literary judgement" (ibid., pp. 114–115).

On the question of what the primary concern of psychoanalytic literary criticism should be in order for it to free itself from the grip of the university discourse and for it to try to come closer to the psychoanalyst's discourse, Lacan suggests that it should concern itself with the unreadable and the impossible in literary and psychoanalytic works. Lacan states that unlike the unsatisfactory psychoanalytic literary criticism of Freud and Marie Bonaparte, his own writing on Poe—the 1956 "Seminar on 'The Purloined Letter'"—could serve as a better example of literary criticism. He thinks this could be best understood in terms of what his critique of Poe bears on. Lacan says his reading of Poe may be considered literary criticism only insofar as it bears on "what Poe does, being a writer himself, in forming such a message about the letter" (ibid., p. 115). What does Poe make of being a writer—a letter-user—as the writer of this story on the letter? Citing Poe, Lacan claims that a "writer" is one who avows it all the more rigorously by not saying it as such: "It is clear that by not saying it as it is, as I do, he is admitting it not insufficiently but all the more rigorously" (ibid., p. 115).

According to Lacan, "what is essential" in Poe's story is that "we will never know what is inside [the letter]" and yet be able to follow its trajectory in its entirety (ibid., p. 93). Insofar as Poe's story is about how a letter belonging to the Queen underwent two detours before finally, possibly, returning to her, it shows us how a story can depict in great detail the complete trajectory of a letter, including a detour within a detour, as well as the extremely precise effect of the letter on sets of characters along the way, without the need "to take any recourse to the contents of the letter" (ibid., p. 115). As Miller rightly points out, the letter, thus disjoined from the message, that is, from both the signifier and the signified, becomes "a leftover object" (Miller, 1999/2013, p. 46). This hollowed-out or emptied letter is, moreover, akin to a frame in terms of which Lacan describes the object *a*. Lacan specifies here that since the "elision of this message" cannot be accounted for in terms of Poe's psychobiography, Poe's psycho-biographical critic Marie Bonaparte "doesn't touch" this story (Lacan, 2007, p. 115) in her 922-page mammoth two-volume *Edgar Poe* in French published in 1933, and translated into English in 1949 by John Rodker as *The Life and Works of Edgar Allan Poe: A Psychoanalytic Interpretation*, in which most of Poe's other works have been discussed in detail[17] (Bonaparte, 1933/1949). The absence of any detailed discussion of this story in Bonaparte's book thus demonstrates a glaring limitation of psycho-biographical literary criticism in general. Similarly, readers of Lacan's writing on Poe will not find any mention of the term phallus in it—"what is not said" there is "the phallus" (Lacan, 2007, p. 97)—and yet, they will be able to view the "effect of feminisation" as the consequence of holding the letter or the phallus demonstrated rigorously (ibid., p. 103 and p. 115). As a letter in sufferance, as a letter doubly detoured, the purloined letter moreover brings out the "failure" of the letter in that state—in terms of its non-usability, its effeminising effect on the holder, the castrating import of its loss and, above all, the delay in its arrival at its destination. This failure of the letter in Poe helped Lacan point to the holes in psychoanalysis and thereby illuminate the field:

> As for myself, if I offer the text of Poe, together with what is behind it, to psychoanalysis, it is precisely because psychoanalysis can only approach it by showing its failure. This is how I shed light on psychoanalysis . . . However, I illuminate psychoanalysis by showing where it makes a hole.
> (Ibid., p. 116)

He further states that following the instance of the letter in Poe that "takes on its significance from the fact that it is unreadable" (ibid., p. 105)—where the unreadable content of the letter constitutes an unbridgeable gap in the narrative—one should read the structure of Freud's as well as his own teachings in their "impossibilities" (ibid., p. 97). Just as the signifiers in the Freudian unconscious are completely silent on the crucial contents of primal repression (*Ur-Verdrängung*), so is Poe's story completely silent on the crucial contents of the letter, while Lacan's seminar on the latter nowhere directly mentions the phallus. Psychoanalytic literary criticism ought, therefore, to learn from the way in which Poe and Lacan shed light on the letter and the phallus, respectively—dealing with their failures and impossibilities at their limits—by not bringing them out of their hiding. As Lacan pointed out in that seminar, truth offers itself most truly in hiding. Lacan thinks "[i]t is by this method that psychoanalysis could better justify its intrusion into literary criticism" (ibid., p. 116).

Partly in relation to the elements of failure and impossibility concerning the letter, Lacan announces for the first time in *On a Discourse that Might not be a Semblance* what would become one of his most significant later teachings, namely, that the sexual relationship between man and woman cannot be written.

He stresses this impossibility throughout the seminar, especially so in the sessions following the one on Lituraterre. Pointing to this impossibility in Poe's story, Lacan states that there is no sexual relationship in "The Purloined Letter" because the King is an imbecile, the Minister realises his castration perfectly, and the Queen as the owner of the letter does not exist in terms of the law. This means the King, as the destination of the letter, is "the subject" who is "distinguished by its very special imbecility". He "manifests himself as this function [of imbecility] of subject" and knows nothing. If he got his hands on the letter, however, the one thing he would understand despite knowing nothing is that the contents have a sense, which explains why the letter arrives at its destination because of the message it carries (ibid., p. 102). The Minister's castration at the hands of the Queen would be "perfectly realised" if he opened the facsimile letter, which would be "the most perfect castration that is demonstrated" (ibid., pp. 103–104) by Poe, or "the castration", due to the words from Crébillon's play inscribed in it by Dupin that would make "castration succeed in producing a being-there [*Dasein*]" for the Minister to swallow and digest on top of his political downfall (ibid., p. 77). And the Queen and her letter did not exist qua the law in two overlapping senses. First, as a secret document, the letter did not officially exist with respect to the law of the King and the law of the land. Transmitted only outside the field of the law, the letter was at once non-existent and unreadable within the legitimate symbolic order. If questioned about it, the Queen would be the first person to deny its legitimacy. Lacan rightly points out in "The Seminar on 'The Purloined Letter'" that we are told nothing about the message of the letter. Instead, all the emphasis is placed on the criterion that the Queen cannot let the King know about it, which, according to Lacan, "take[s] on an eminent meaning", since she is doubly bound to the King "by pledge of loyalty" and by "the role of guardian of the power that royalty by law incarnates, which is called legitimacy" (Lacan, 1957/2006, p. 19). Therefore, Lacan continues:

> [W]hatever action the Queen has decided to take regarding the letter, the fact remains that this letter is the symbol of a pact and that, even if its addressee does not assume responsibility for this pact, the existence of the letter situates her in a symbolic chain foreign to the one which constitutes her loyalty. Its incompatibility with her loyalty is proven by the fact that possession of the letter is impossible to bring forward publicly as legitimate, and that in order to have this possession respected, the Queen can only invoke her right to privacy, whose privilege is based on the very honour that this possession violates. . . . Hence, the responsibility of the letter's author takes a back seat to that of its holder: for the offence to majesty is compounded by high treason.
>
> (Ibid., pp. 19–20)

Second, somewhat like the Lévi-Straussian notion of the woman who circulates as a signifier outside patriarchy, the letter is transmitted outside the field of the law, making it non-existent from the legal perspective.

Lacan adds that the fictive promotion of the sexual relationship in Poe's story indicates the letter's relationship with a deficiency from which it gets its value (Lacan, 2007, pp. 132–133).[18] In this context, Lacan states in the fifth session of *On a Discourse that Might not be a Semblance*:

> That there is no sexual relationship, I have already fixed it in this form, that there is no mode of writing the relationship currently. Who knows, there are people who dream that one day it will be written. Why not?
>
> (Ibid., p. 83)

Following from this remark, Lacan concludes the seminar on "Lituraterre" by stating that the writers who dream of installing the sexual relationship one day might be able to do so in terms of "an asceticism of writing . . . joining up . . . with this impossible 'it's written'" (ibid., p. 127). That is to say, writers might try to write the impossible-to-write sexual relation by attempting to get it written in terms of an ascesis of writing, which is at once related to Lacan's notions of writing with the impossibility of the letter, of writing by letting the letter make edge-bearing holes in writing, and of getting something rigorously articulated in writing by not stating it at all.

Lacan further explains that Poe gave Dupin the task of throwing dust into our eyes to make us believe that the "cleverest of the clever . . . does exist", who "really understands, knows everything", for whom nothing is unreadable, even though that is patently untrue (ibid., p. 103).[19] Rather, the important point here is that Poe was able to demonstrate the effects of the letter at its limit so thoroughly because he had effaced its content and thus converted it and the narrative on it into the edges or frames of an unreadable hole, which brings out the letter's littoral condition in the story. Lacan suggests that psychoanalytic literary criticism ought to compare the impossible and the unreadable in literary and psychoanalytic works with an aim to enable the former to shed light on the edge of knowledge. Since both Poe and Lacan functioned as "writers" in this special sense of writing with the help of the failure of the letter and of writing something with greater rigour by not writing it at all, Lacan states: "Poe . . . had been guided in his fiction by the same aim (*dessein*) as mine" (Lacan, 1957/2006, p. 46).

Lacan thinks, partly following Freud, that psychoanalysis has a great deal to receive from literature, especially on the question of the letter. He states about "The Purloined Letter" in the essay on "Lituraterre": "It is certain that, as always, psychoanalysis is receiving here, from literature" (Lacan, 1971/2013, p. 329). Accordingly, he thinks that Poe's depiction of the letter in sufferance from where it showed its impossibility and failure, and Joyce's depiction of the letter tending towards the littoral by way of litter, could assist in illuminating the letter at its limit for psychoanalysis. Therefore, he states that "psychoanalysis is there [since Freud] so that literary works could measure themselves against it"—and thus help "literary criticism . . . renew itself"—with "the enigma belonging to the side of psychoanalysis" and the source of illumination belonging to the side of literature (Lacan,

2007, p. 116). With the help of these remarks on psychoanalytic literary criticism and his own psychoanalytic critique of Poe, Lacan at once indicates how literature appeared to tend towards lituraterre where it showed the hollowed-out letter reduced to an object making holes in writing, urges literary criticism, in general, to shed light on this aspect of literature, and advises psychoanalytic literary criticism in particular to compare the nature of the holes made by the letter in literary and psychoanalytic writings respectively.

Notes

1 An earlier version of this chapter has been published as Biswas, 2012.
2 Unless otherwise mentioned, all translations are mine.
3 In English in the original.
4 In English in the original.
5 After saying "Joyce", Lacan clarifies, "this is James Joyce I am talking about" (Lacan, 2007, p. 113), not in order to prevent his audience from mistaking James Joyce for the American writer Joyce Carol Oates who was in the news in 1969 for the National Book Award for her novel *Them*, but rather in order to ensure that his audience did not mistake James Joyce for Joyce Mansour, the English-born French surrealist poet of Jewish-Egyptian origin who published several volumes of poetry and a few plays and essays in French after moving to Paris in the early 1950s.
6 "*Messe-haine*" homonymically stands for several things at once, such as, "*Mécène*", meaning "*Maecenas*" or a generous patron, especially of literature or art; a hater of the Christian Mass; and "*Messire*" or a title of honour meant for special individuals.
7 See also Cambray and Carter (1977, p. 240), Thurston (2004, pp. 104–148), and McLynn (1996, p. 324).
8 Even though Joyce's aesthetic theory is predominantly Thomistic, he litters or makes a mess of the crucial concept of "*claritas*" in Aquinas on which that theory is based, as Lacan points out:

> You know that Joyce had slaved quite enough over this *saint homme*. . . . This doesn't prevent Joyce from not really making head or tail of it with respect to the thing by which he sets such great store, namely what he calls Beauty. On this point, have a look at Jacques Aubert's book and you'll see that in the *sinthomasaquinas* there is goodness knows what exactly which he calls *claritas*, which Joyce replaces with something along the lines of the *radiance* of Being, which is really the weak point at issue. Is this a personal weakness? I don't find the radiance of Being to be all that striking.
>
> (Lacan, 2005/2016, p. 6)

9 The phrase "*sicut palea*" appears several times in *The Holy Bible*; such as in the Book of Isaiah, Chapter 29, verse 5: "Moreover the multitude of thy strangers shall be like small dust, and the multitude of the terrible ones [shall be] as chaff that passeth away: yea, it shall be at an instant suddenly" (*King James Version of the Holy Bible*, 1611/2004, p. 428).
10 The date mentioned in the volume by Jacques-Alain Miller under the "Bio-Bibliographical Notes" of "20 April 1967" is incorrect (Lacan, 2005/2008, p. 115).
11 *Endgame* provides neither the first nor the only instance of characters being bottled up in repulsive containers in Beckett's plays. In his 1961 play *Happy Days*, for instance, Winnie gets buried deeper and deeper in mud in the course of the play as Willie crawls up the mud mound on all fours towards her (Beckett, 1961/2006). In his 1963 one-act play *Play*, the bodies of the three protagonists, M, W1, and W2—or man, wife and

mistress—are situated right up to their necks inside three urns from where they speak throughout the play (Beckett, 1963/2006). Beckett used a similar method much earlier in his fiction, in the form of Mahood's jar in his 1953 novel *L'Innommable* (*The Unnameable*), in which the narrator is a disembodied being living inside a large jar situated by the window of a restaurant in Paris (Beckett, 1953/1959).

12 Anzieu rightly states, "For two years, during 1934–5 Samuel Beckett (or Sam to those who knew him well), aged 28 to 29, underwent a course of psychoanalysis with Bion at the Tavistock Clinic in London, meeting perhaps four times a week" (Anzieu, 1989, p. 163). More precisely, Beckett had a total of roughly one hundred and fifty sessions of analysis with Bion from January 1934 to December 1935. The details of Beckett's analysis may be found in his letters written to his cousin Morris Sinclair, and especially to his friend Thomas McGreevy during his analysis (Beckett, 2009), and in his biography by Knowlson (Knowlson, 1996).

13 These two types of ends of analysis may be seen in different ways: The first type may be related to neurosis and the second type to ordinary psychosis; the second type may be seen as a modification of rather than an addition to the first type; the first type may be described as Freudian and the second type as Lacanian; and the first type may be situated within psychoanalysis while the second type may be situated beyond psychoanalysis.

14 In order to minimise misunderstanding, Lacan clarifies fairly early in the seminar on "Lituraterre" and more succinctly so in his essay on "Lituraterre", from where the following is cited, that although his "teaching . . . is advertised by a slogan that promotes the written form [*l'écrits*]", he is "more in tune" with the "displacement of interests" suggested by the fact "that it is only now that Rabelais is finally being read" (Lacan, 1971/2013, p. 328). As Laurent explains, Lacan wished to promote not the written but reading, which he did in this case by hailing the interest in reading Rabelais in this epoch. Laurent clarifies that although Rabelais was already a major figure who had, moreover, been made into "the great man of the Renaissance" by Jules Michelet, it is the work of Mikhail Bakhtin, who depicted the "laughter of the people of the Renaissance" in Rabelais, on the one hand, and that of Michael Screech, who showed that it was rather "the laughter of the humanists and that Rabelais's most smutty jokes are derived in general . . . from a piece of writing by Erasmus" on the other, that has drawn the attention of readers and critics from all over Europe to Rabelais's laughter in this epoch (Laurent, 1999/2007, p. 29). Nobus further informs us:

> Lacan seems to have in mind, here, the efforts by the Tel Quel group, especially Julia Kristeva, to promote the notion of intertextuality and to re-read Rabelais with the notions and methodologies advanced by Mikhail Bakhtin, whose doctoral thesis on Rabelais was translated into French in 1970. See Mikhail Bakhtin, *L'Œuvre de François Rabelais et la culture populaire au moyen âge et sous la Renaissance* (1965), trans. Andrée Robel, Paris: Gallimard, 1970.
>
> (Nobus, 2013, p. 340)

15 Rabaté explains that contrary to Roland Barthes's depiction of Japanese calligraphy as a pure void in the *Empire of Signs* (Barthes, 1970/1983), Lacan thought that "letters do not point to a pure void of signification but produce a 'hole' in which enjoyment [jouissance] of the most excessive type can lurk" (Rabaté, 2001, p. 34).

16 In Freud's conception of the Oedipus complex, boys harbour an unconscious wish to kill their father and marry their mother, yet they generally don't act upon this wish. In Sophocles' play, Oedipus does kill his father and go on to marry his mother, which he never experiences as the fulfilment of an unconscious wish, on the contrary. As such, Oedipus himself indeed didn't have an Oedipus complex. And when it comes to *Oedipus Rex*, there is only one sentence in the entire play that bears a resonance of the Freudian discovery, namely, Jocasta's remark to Oedipus, "Nor need this mother-marrying

frighten you;/Many a man has dreamt as much" (Sophocles, 429 BC/1947, p. 52). Therefore, like the myth of Oedipus, Sophocles' play, too, was not particularly conducive to a Freudian analysis.

17 Lacan's claim is not entirely correct. Bonaparte refers to the story in passing at three places in her book (Bonaparte, 1933/1949, p. 430 fn. 1, p. 484, and p. 653) and also offers a brief analysis of the story at one place where she describes the letter as the "very symbol of the maternal penis" (ibid., p. 483), which is partly akin to Lacan's own reading of the letter as a symbol of the phallus. Thus, Bonaparte does pay attention to a few details in the story and makes certain observations that must be taken seriously. Perhaps one could argue that "The Purloined Letter" doesn't receive the same degree of attention as some of the other stories in her book.

18 However, Lacan will go on to state in his 1975–1976 seminar on *The Sinthome*: "So, what is Joyce's relationship to Nora? Oddly enough, I would say that it's a sexual relation, even though I say that such a thing doesn't exist, but it's a funny old sexual relation" (Lacan, 2005/2016, p. 68). It is a funny old sexual relation because:

a) Joyce used the very lack of sexual relationship, which he calls "exiles", in order to remain bound to Nora (ibid., p. 56).
b) In Joyce's play *Exiles*, Richard introduces irremediable "jealousy" and "doubt" in the mediatory place of the third to found his sexual relationship with Bertha around it (Joyce, 1918/1962).
c) Joyce conjures up the character of "any old other man" and opened for him the choice of "the one-woman" with Nora (Lacan, 2005/2016, p. 56).
d) It is a rapport only from Joyce's side, as Nora is entirely reduced to a tightly fitting inverted glove of his. "She is absolutely pointless" apart from being his glove (ibid., p. 68).

19 Lacan's frequent criticism of Poe as an author who sought to fool his readers with the help of the deceiver Dupin, in addition to unjustifiably holding the latter in high esteem, is not a correct view of Poe. Rather than trying to deceive the readers with the help of the character of Dupin, Poe sought to depict the narrator in the act of unreasonably magnifying his friend's analytic acumen to at once expose the gullibility of the narrator and the fraudulence of Dupin before the readers. There are several indications of this. To begin with, Poe deliberately names him "Dupin", which is homonymically associated with "duper" or "duping". Besides, in a letter to his friend Philip Pendleton Cooke dated 9th August, 1846, Poe writes,

> [P]eople think them [the Dupin stories] more ingenious than they are—on account of their method and air of method . . . The reader is made to confound the ingenuity of the supposititious Dupin with that of the writer of the story".
>
> (Quoted in Quinn, 1998, p. 354)

The expression "supposititious", meaning "not genuine" and bearing connotations of "fraudulent", clearly indicates that, unlike the narrator, Poe was conscious of Dupin's trickery and never mistook that for his brilliance. He was also critical of the readers who considered these stories "more ingenious than they are" and mistook the "air of method" for a valid method. Moreover, insofar as Poe was aware that some of his readers would mistake his ingenuity for the ingenuity of Dupin, he had in a way pre-empted Lacan's mistake of regarding Dupin's quality as the quality of the author. Above all, this is one of the reasons that after inventing the genre of the detective story in 1841—without being aware of it though, for he called them tales of ratiocination—and providing evidence of having mastered it in "The Purloined Letter" in 1844, Poe completely discarded the genre forever and returned to writing stories of the "grotesque and the arabesque", as he called them. He explains his disenchantment with such tales of ratiocination in the same letter to

Cooke: "where is the ingenuity of unravelling a web which you yourself (the author) have woven for the express purpose of unravelling?" (ibid., p. 354). In fact, the unreliability of Poe's narrators in his own eyes, and his attempt to maintain a distance from them as well as from the characters described by them, are well-documented in Poe criticism. For instance, James W. Gargano points out in his essay "The Question of Poe's Narrators":

> The structure of Poe's stories compels realization that they are more than the effusions of their narrators' often disordered mentalities. Through the irony of his characters' self-betrayal and through the development and arrangement of his dramatic actions, Poe suggests to his readers ideas never entertained by the narrators. Poe intends his readers to keep their powers of analysis and judgment ever alert; he does not require or desire complete surrender to the experience of the sensations being felt by his character.
>
> (Gargano, 1963, p. 178)

References

Ackerley, Chris J. and Gontarski, Stanley E. (Eds.) (2006). *The Faber Companion to Samuel Beckett*. Faber and Faber.

Anzieu, Didier (1989). Beckett and Bion. *International Review of Psycho-Analysis*, 16, 163–169.

Barthes, Roland (1983). *Empire of Signs*. In Richard Howard Trans. Hill and Wang (Original work published 1970).

Beckett, Samuel (1959). Molloy. In *Molloy. Malone Dies. Unnameable*. John Calder, 7–178 (Original work published 1951).

Beckett, Samuel (1959). Unnameable. In *Molloy. Malone Dies. Unnameable*. John Calder, 293–418 (Original work published 1953).

Beckett, Samuel (2003). Breath. In *The Complete Dramatic Works*. Reprint, Faber and Faber, 369–372 (Original work published 1969).

Beckett, Samuel (2003). Endgame. In *The Complete Dramatic Works*. Reprint, Faber and Faber, 89–134 (Original work published 1957).

Beckett, Samuel (2003). Krapp's Last Tape. In *The Complete Dramatic Works*. Reprint, Faber and Faber, 213–223 (Original work published 1958).

Beckett, Samuel (2003). Waiting for Godot. In *The Complete Dramatic Works*. Reprint, Faber and Faber, 7–88 (Original work published 1953).

Beckett, Samuel (2006). A Piece of Monologue. In *The Complete Dramatic Works*. Reprint, Faber and Faber, 423–429 (Original work published 1979).

Beckett, Samuel (2006). Happy Days. In *The Complete Dramatic Works*. Reprint, Faber and Faber, 135–168 (Original work published 1961).

Beckett, Samuel (2006). Play. In *The Complete Dramatic Works*. Reprint, Faber and Faber, 305–429 (Original work published 1963).

Beckett, Samuel (2009). *The Letters of Samuel Beckett: Volume I: 1929–1940*. In Martha Dow Fehsenfeld and Lois More Overbeck (Eds.). Cambridge University Press.

Biswas, Santanu (2012). A Literary Introduction to 'Lituraterre'. In Santanu Biswas (Ed.), *The Literary Lacan: From Literature to Lituraterre and Beyond*. Seagull Books, 173–195.

Beckett, Samuel, Brion, Marcel, Budgen, Frank, Gilbert, Stuart, Jolas, Eugene, Llona, Victor, McAlmon, Robert, McGreevy, Thomas, Paul, Elliot, Rodker, John, Sage, Robert, Williams, William Carlos, Slingsby, G.V.L. and Dixon, Vladimir (1961). *Our Exagmination Round His Factification for Incamination of Work in Progress*. Faber and Faber (Original work published 1929).

Bonaparte, Marie (1949). *The Life and Works of Edgar Allan Poe: A Psychoanalytic Interpretation*. In John Rodker Trans. Imago (Original work published 1933).

Cambray, Joseph and Carter, Linda (1977). *C. G. Jung Speaking: Interviews and Encounters*. Princeton University Press.

Ernout, Alfred and Meillet, Alfred (2001). *Dictionnaire Étymologique De La Langue Latine: Histoire Des Mots*. Klincksieck (Original work published 1932).

Freud, Sigmund (2001). Dostoevsky and Parricide. In James Strachey (Ed.), *The Standard Edition of the Complete Psychological Works of Sigmund Freud*, Vol. XXI. Vintage, Hogarth Press and the Institute of Psychoanalysis, 173–196 (Original work published 1928).

Gargano, James W. (1963). The Question of Poe's Narrators. *College English*, 25(3), 177–181.

The Guardian (1930, September 1). *From the archive, Obituary: Dr WA Spooner*. Available at www.theguardian.com/theguardian/2010/sep/01/archive-obituary-dr-wa-spooner (Accessed on 7th January, 2024).

Joyce, James (1962). *Exiles, including Joyce's Notes on the play*. New English Library (Original work published 1918).

Joyce, James (1975). *Finnegans Wake*. Faber and Faber (Original work published 1939).

Joyce, James (2000). *Ulysses*. Penguin Classics in association with The Bodley Head (Original work published 1922).

King James Version of the Holy Bible (2004). Pdf Version, www.holybooks.com (Original work published 1611). Available at www.holybooks.com/wp-content/uploads/2010/05/The-Holy-Bible-King-James-Version.pdf (Accessed on 21st July, 2023).

Klotz, Jean-Pierre (2012). The Littoral Condition of the Letter. In Santanu Biswas (Ed.), *The Literary Lacan: From Literature to Lituraterre and Beyond*. Seagull Books, 196–204.

Knowlson, James (1996). *Damned to Fame: The Life of Samuel Beckett*. Simon & Schuster.

Lacan, Jacques (1971, Octobre). Lituraterre. In Jean Bellemin-Noël, Claude Duchet, Pierre Kuentz, Jean Levaillant (Rédactions), *Littérature*, N°3, Larousse, 3–10.

Lacan, Jacques (1975). The Seminar of Jacques Lacan. Book XXII. R.S.I., 1974–1975. Unpublished translation by Jack W. Stone of Le Séminaire de Jacques Lacan. Livre XXII. R.S.I., 1974–1975. In *Ornicar? Bulletin périodique du champ freudien*, Lyse, N°2, 1975, 87–105; N°3, 1975, 96–110; N°4, 1975, 92–106; and N°5, 1975, 17–66. Available at www.scribd.com/doc/33124001/10724-TheSeminar-of-Jacques (Accessed on 17th July, 2023).

Lacan, Jacques (1981, Octobre). Préface à l'édition japonaise des *Écrits*. In *La lettre mensuelle de L'École de la cause freudienne*, N°3, 2–3 (Original work published 1972).

Lacan, Jacques (1987, Avril-Juin). Lituraterre. In Danièle Silvestre (Rédaction) *Ornicar? Revue du champ freudien*, XII Année, N°41, Navarin, 5–13 (Original work published 1971).

Lacan, Jacques (1990). *Television: A Challenge to the Psychoanalytic Establishment*. In Denis Hollier, Rosalind Krauss and Annette Michelson Trans. W.W. Norton (Original work published 1974).

Lacan, Jacques (1993). *The Seminar of Jacques Lacan. Book III. The Psychoses, 1955–1956*. In Russell Grigg Trans. Routledge (Original work published 1981).

Lacan, Jacques (1998). *The Seminar of Jacques Lacan. Book XX. Encore: On Feminine Sexuality, The Limits of Love and Knowledge, 1972–1973*. In Bruce Fink Trans. W.W. Norton (Original work published 1975).

Lacan, Jacques (1998). *The Seminar of Jacques Lacan. Book XI. The Four Fundamental Concepts of Psychoanalysis, 1964*. In Alan Sheridan Trans. W.W. Norton (Original work published 1973).

Lacan, Jacques (2001). Lituraterre. In Jacques-Alain Miller (Rédaction) *Autres écrits*. Seuil, 11–20 (Original work published 1971).

Lacan, Jacques (2002). The Seminar of Jacques Lacan. Book IX. Identification, 1961–1962. Unofficially translated by Cormac Gallagher from the unedited French typescripts of the unpublished seminar Le Séminaire de Jacques Lacan. *Livre IX. L'Identification, 1961–1962.* Karnac Books.

Lacan, Jacques (2006). *Le Séminaire de Jacques Lacan. Livre XVI. D'un Autre à l'autre, 1968–1969.* Seuil.

Lacan, Jacques (2006). Seminar on 'The Purloined Letter'. In Bruce Fink Trans., in collaboration with Héloïse Fink and Russell Grigg, *Écrits: The First Complete Edition in English.* W.W. Norton, 6–48 (Original work published 1957).

Lacan, Jacques (2006). The Situation of Psychoanalysis and the Training of Psychoanalysts in 1956. In Bruce Fink Trans., in collaboration with Héloïse Fink and Russell Grigg, *Écrits: The First Complete Edition in English.* W.W. Norton, 384–411 (Original work published 1956).

Lacan, Jacques (2007). Leçon Sur Lituraterre. In *Le Séminaire de Jacques Lacan. Livre XVIII. D'un discours qui ne serait pas du semblant, 1971.* Texte Établi par Jacques-Alain Miller, Seuil, 113–127.

Lacan, Jacques (2008). *My Teaching.* In David Macey Trans. Verso (Original work published 2005).

Lacan, Jacques (2013). Lituraterre. Dany Nobus Trans. In *Continental Philosophy Review*, Vol. 46, N°2. Springer, 327–334 (Original work published 1971).

Lacan, Jacques (2015). *The Seminar of Jacques Lacan, Book VIII: 1960–1961: Transference.* In Bruce Fink Trans. Polity Press (Original work published 1991).

Lacan, Jacques (2016). *The Seminar of Jacques Lacan, Book XXIII: 1975–1976: The Sinthome.* In Adrian Price Trans. Polity Press (Original work published 2005).

Lacan, Jacques (2016). Joyce the Symptom. In *The Seminar of Jacques Lacan, Book XXIII: 1975–1976: The Sinthome.* In Adrian Price Trans. Polity Press, 141–148 (Original work published 1982).

Lacan, Jacques (2022, April). MIT Lecture on Topology, 2 December 1975. In Jack W. Stone and Russell Grigg Trans. *The Lacanian Review: Hurly-Burly: Journal of the New Lacanian School and the World Association of Psychoanalysis. American Lacan*, Issue 12, 87–95 (Original work published 1976).

Laurent, Éric (2007). The Purloined Letter and the Tao of the Psychoanalyst. In Véronique Voruz and Bogdan Wolf (Eds.) and Marc Thomas and Victoria Woollard Trans. *The Later Lacan: An Introduction.* State University of New York Press, 25–52 (Original work published 1999).

McLynn, Frank (1996). *Carl Gustav Jung.* St Martin's Press.

Miller, Jacques-Alain (1999). Of Semblants in the Relations Between Sexes. In Veronique Voruz and Bogdan Wolf Trans. *Psychoanalytical Notebooks of the London Society*, N°3, London Society of the New Lacanian School, 9–26 (Original work published 1997).

Miller, Jacques-Alain (2011). *Unpublished Cours, janvier—juin, Année 2011.* Available at https://jonathanleroy.be/wp-content/uploads/2016/01/2010-2011-LUn-tout-seul-JA-Miller.pdf (Accessed on 28th October, 2023).

Miller, Jacques-Alain (2013, May). L'or à gueule of Lituraterre. In Adrian Price Trans. *Hurly-Burly: The International Lacanian Journal of Psychoanalysis*, Issue 9, New Lacanian School, 39–50 (Original work published 1999).

Nobus, Dany (2002). Illiterature. In Luke Thurston (Ed.), *Reinventing the Symptom: Essays on the Final Lacan.* Other Press, 19–43.

Nobus, Dany (2013). Annotations to Lituraterre. In *Continental Philosophy Review*, Vol. 46, N°2, Springer, 335–347.

Ogasawara, Shin'ya (1999, January 19). L'instance de la lettre dans l'inconscient japonais. Ornicar? Digital, N°67, Asociación Mundial de Psicoanálisis, 1–4.

Quinn, Arthur Hobson (1998). *Edgar Allan Poe: A Critical Biography.* Johns Hopkins University Press.

Rabaté, Jean-Michel (2001). *Jacques Lacan: Psychoanalysis and the Subject of Literature*. Palgrave.

Roudinesco, Elisabeth (1997). *Jacques Lacan*. In Barbara Bray Trans. Columbia University Press (Original work published 1993).

Sophocles (1947). King Oedipus. In E.F. Watling Trans. *The Theban Plays*. Penguin Books, 25–68 (Original work published 429 BC).

Sowley, Thelma (2008). Crossing Boundaries. In Ann Banfield, Robert S. Kawashima, Gilles Philippe and Thelma Sowley (Eds.), *Phantom Sentences: Essays in Linguistics and Literature Presented to Ann Banfield*. Peter Lang, 351–376.

Thurston, Luke (2004). *James Joyce and the Problem of Psychoanalysis*. Cambridge University Press.

Chapter 6
James Joyce

Of all the littérateurs commented on by Lacan, James Joyce engaged him for the longest period of time, over two decades to be precise, enabling him to produce his most elaborate psychoanalytic discourse in relation to the works of a creative writer.[1] Lacan had, in fact, met the Irish author twice. He first met Joyce as a teenager in 1918, and three years later, on 7th December, 1921 to be exact, he heard Valéry Larbaud's lecture on Joyce's *Ulysses* with readings from the text at an event organised by *La maison des amis des livres* at which Joyce himself was present. Describing these two incidents, Lacan writes in "Joyce the Symptom":

> [I]t so happens that at seventeen, thanks to the fact that I used to drop by Adrienne Monnier's shop, I met Joyce. So too did I attend, when I was twenty, the first reading of the French translation of *Ulysses* that came out.
> (Lacan, 1982/2016, p. 142)

Lacan mentioned Joyce or his works in passing in the following eight texts: The 1956 essay, "The Seminar on 'The Purloined Letter'"; the 1971 essay, "Lituraterre"; the 1972–1973 seminar on *Encore: On Feminine Sexuality, The Limits of Love and Knowledge*; the 1973 interview, "Television"; the 1975 lecture, "Geneva Lecture on the Symptom"; the 1975 "Yale University: Kanzer Seminar"; the 1975 "Yale University: Interview with Students, Answers to Their Questions"; and the 1977 lecture at Brussels, "Remarks on Hysteria". However, Lacan's more sustained discussions on Joyce and his writings figure in Sessions 1, 4, 5, 6, 7, 8, and 10 of his 1975–1976 seminar on *The Sinthome* (*Le sinthome*), and in three separate lectures, namely, the June 1975 lectures at the fifth International Joyce Symposium in Paris, entitled "Joyce the Symptom" and "Joyce the Symptom II" respectively, at the invitation of Jacques Aubert, the renowned Joyce-expert of France, and the 1976 lecture at Nice, "On James Joyce as Symptom".

In his discussion, Lacan's focus is primarily on Joyce's four novels—the posthumously published abandoned novel *Stephen Hero*, *A Portrait of the Artist as a Young Man*, or the form in which the abandoned *Stephen Hero* was rewritten, *Ulysses*, and *Finnegans Wake*—and his play *Exiles*.[2] There is a brief mention of Joyce's letters and his critical essays in the seminar and of the collection of poems,

Chamber Music, in "Joyce the Symptom". Lacan does not ignore the Joyce-scholars in his discussion. He mentions that he has "been busy soaking up the vast literature around Joyce's work, to which it has given rise", with the assistance of "Jacques Aubert, who . . . every now and then . . . sends me up from Lyon hints on a few further authors" (Lacan, 2005/2016, p. 62) This must be true, for we find Lacan commenting on the works of Jacques Aubert, Philip Sollers, Maurice Beebe, Hugh Kenner, Robert M. Adams, Mark Schechner, Clive Hart, Richard Ellmann, Herbert Sherman Gorman, James S. Atherton, Thomas E. Connolly—whom Lacan had met—and Stuart Gilbert in the course of his discussion. Lacan even gave the floor to Aubert to speak on Joyce in the session dated 20th January, 1976 of his seminar on *The Sinthome*.

Lacan's engagement with the works of Joyce helped him shape his later teaching by enabling him to offer a deep insight into a large number of crucial concepts of that teaching, as well as by facilitating the decisive displacement of emphasis from the Freudian unconscious to the Lacanian symptom, and from Freud's symbolic unconscious to Lacan's real unconscious that characterise that teaching. Moreover, his engagement with Joyce made it possible for him to offer its due importance to the word "literature", recommend a fresh direction to the psychoanalytic readers of literature and art, and make a singular contribution to Joyce studies by shedding valuable light on Joyce's littering of the letter.

"The letter! The litter!" in Joyce

Lacan had singled out the expression "The letter! The litter!" from *Finnegans Wake* for special attention in his seminar on "The Purloined Letter", seminar on "Lituraterre", and his lecture on "Joyce the Symptom". How far was Lacan justified in doing so? In order to answer the question, let us examine the expression in its context.

"The letter! The litter!" was an absolutely unthinkable expression in the domain of literature prior to its first appearance in print in Joyce's novel *Finnegans Wake* in 1939. At crucial moments in the narratives of European fiction before *Finnegans Wake*, the protagonist is shown to exclaim, "The letter! The letter!". For instance, in chapter fourteen of Balzac's 1841 novel *Ursula*, the dying Doctor Minoret impatiently cries out to his godchild Ursula, "The letter! the letter!" referring to the crucial letter concerning her marriage to Savinien (Balzac, 1841/1911, p. 223. My translation). And again, in chapter thirteen of Flaubert's 1856 novel *Madame Bovary*, the seriously ill Emma suddenly awakens from her sleep and exclaims, "The letter! the letter!" referring to Rodolphe's letter that made her fall ill (Flaubert, 1856/1919, p. 215). And yet again, in Proust's 1920–1921 novel *The Guermantes Way*, desperately hoping for a letter from his estranged mistress, Robert starts at every sound and murmurs, "the letter! the letter!" (Proust, 1920–1921/2014). Joyce could not have been unaware of these masterpieces of French literature. In this context, his "The letter! The *litter!*" constitutes a sacrilegious departure from established literary convention, a jarring distortion of what the readers of canonical literature expected to find in a literary work, and a shocking parody, or a savage mockery, of the diction employed in literary classics until then.

The relation between writing and rubbish is an old one in Joyce. For instance, in his short story "The Encounter", written in 1905, when Father Butler says, "What is this rubbish?", he was referring to a collection of stories called *The Halfpenny Marvel* found in Leo Dillon's possession. By the term "rubbish", he meant the "wretched stuff" that the boys of the college should not be reading. Here, "rubbish" stands for only one kind of writing, namely, a kind of juvenile writing based on sensationalism that was meant for school boys (Joyce, 1914/1996, p. 20). Taking the relation further ahead in his novels, Joyce describes all the junk of everyday life in minute detail to preserve them vividly. In *Ulysses*, the characters talk, gossip, debate, think, recall, read, walk, eat, drink, sleep, urinate, defecate, et cetera, and all these particulars are described with an intense acuteness. In this sense, Joyce preserves the detritus and ephemera of life and glorifies rubbish. No wonder then that Stephen Dedalus compares the rubbish-strewn heavy sands of Sandymount Strand to the "language tide . . . wind have silted here" (Joyce, 1922/2000, p. 55). Thus, the rubbish-heap seems to be Joyce's desired site for the erection of his letter or fiction. Moreover, writing is frequently thrown away as waste in this novel. For instance, Bloom repeatedly tells Bantam Lyons, who wanted to have a look at his copy of the *Freeman's Journal*—the leading Irish newspaper of the time—that he could keep it if he wanted as he was "going to throw it away" (ibid., p. 106), and does so later on. Handbills are usually described as "throwaways" in the novel. Bloom crumples and throws away the one that the "sombre Y.M.C.A. young man" placed in his hand (ibid., p. 190): "He threw down among them a crumpled paper ball" (ibid., p. 192). But letter and litter are combined most powerfully perhaps in the "Calypso" episode where Bloom not only offers a precisely worded commentary on his bowel movement but cleans himself with the pages torn from the widely known British weekly magazine *Tit-Bits* bearing Mr Philip Beaufoy's story *Matcham's Masterstroke*, which he was reading while defecating—a story for which the author had received the enviable amount of "[t]hree pounds thirteen and six": "He tore away half the prize story sharply and wiped himself with it" (ibid., pp. 83–85).

In his last novel, Joyce took the connection between writing and rubbish far deeper by converting the letter and literary writing itself into a form of litter. It is no accident that in some of his letters written at the time of the composition of *Finnegans Wake*, Joyce often describes the early drafts of the novel as a disordered rubbish-heap. In one such letter, written on 18th February, 1931 to Harriet Shaw Weaver, to which Joyce had attached a few chapters of the *Work in Progress*, he writes: "I enclose some rubbish found in a sack, that lay in the house that Joyce leaves" (Joyce, 1957/1966, p. 301).

Even though distorting languages and disrupting conventions came naturally to Joyce, who must have thought about the idea of "The letter! The litter!" at a reasonably early stage of the composition of *Finnegans Wake*, the fact of the matter is that this particular instance of distortion of language and literary convention through it did not figure in Joyce's notebooks in the course of the first fifteen years of his work on *Finnegans Wake*. Going by volume VI.B.44, page 31, of his notebook, the expression "The letter! The litter!" first appeared in Joyce's notebook as late as 1937, merely two years before the publication of the novel. At the bottom of the page, Joyce writes, "the letter the litter the texte" (Joyce, 1977–1979, p. 295), implying in shorthand that the "*texte*", which is the French word for written work or writing, will emerge from the "litter" into which the "letter" has been converted.

So, what does the expression "The letter! The litter!" mean in *Finnegans Wake*? Joyce uses the expression "litter" and coinages based on it twenty-two times across *Finnegans Wake*, almost always with reference to writing, usually literary writing, of which only three describe the relation between the letter and litter.[3] The first one of these is: "But by writing thithaways end to end and turning, turning and end to end hithaways writing and with lines of litters slittering up and louds of ladders slettering down" (Joyce, 1939/1975, p. 114). Here, the movement of the first two clauses in opposite directions, in the form of a chiasmus, is indicative of a crossed writing or a crossed letter, which is further reinforced by the up and down movement described in the last part of the sentence denoting another form of crossing. Referring to this very idea only a few lines earlier, Joyce wrote: "One cannot help noticing that rather more than half of the lines run north-south . . . while the others go west-east" (ibid., p. 114). "Crossing" or the "cross" also refers to Christ, as does the letter "Chi" designated by the symbol "X", which is the first letter in the Greek word for Christ. That apart, three pages earlier, Joyce uses the expression "zogzag" (ibid., p. 111), meaning "zigzag", to point to a writing that moves back and forth. Gordon states that "zogzag" moreover refers to a brand of extremely thin cigarette paper named "Zig-Zag" found in Joyce's time. Due to the thinness of the paper, if it is written on, the ink would seep and cross over to the reverse side and thus enact yet another kind of crossed writing (Gordon, 2020, p. 217). The lines also contain a reference to the crossing out movement in the game of snake and ladder, where the participants rise up with the help of the ladder and fall down owing to the snake. Joyce reverses the order here to reinforce the idea of crossing doubly, for, in Joyce, litters slither up, like a snake, while ladders sletter down. This also implies that the litter rises as the letter falls. Thus, the first excerpt is about crossing a letter to convert it into litter.

A shorter version of the second description is, "the heroticisms, catastrophes and eccentricities transmitted by the ancient legacy of the past; type by tope, letter from litter, word at ward, with sendence of sundance" (Joyce, 1939/1975, pp. 614–615). Going by the complete passage from where this is excerpted, the letter is recycled litter. In that passage, Joyce mentions "mill-wheeling vico-ciclometer" (ibid., p. 614) to refer to the transmission of the past through Vico's cycles, planetary revolutions, and political revolutions. Here, letter from litter describes literary writing as a form of recycling of what has been already written, or the "dialytically separated elements of precedent decomposition for the verypetpurpose of subsequent recombination" (ibid., p. 614). Such work of literary recycling is carried out "type by tope", meaning "type for type" as well as "trope for trope", "word at ward", meaning "word for word", and "sendence of sundance", meaning "sentence for sentence" as well as "semblance of substance". Among the literary themes chosen for recycling, Joyce identifies "heroticisms", meaning heroism and eroticism, as well as "catastrophes" and "eccentricities" that have been "transmitted by the ancient legacy of the past". A broader implication of the passage is that the very novel *Finnegans Wake* is created by first breaking down all the elements received from literature and history and then recombining the fragments in a new form. Moreover, the cycle of life concerns rebirth following death. While "Fin" and "Wake" are related to the end and death respectively, "negan" sounds like "again". The expression "Finn, again!" (ibid., p. 628) figures at the very end of the novel for this very reason. Thus, the title is indicative of a re-beginning following the end or of a resurrection following death and the Wake. In the Irish-American ballad of unknown authorship named "Finnegan's Wake", published in 1864 in New York, the alcoholic protagonist Tim Finnegan, who fell from a ladder, broke his skull, and is considered dead, returns to life when the mourners at his wake accidentally spill whiskey over his corpse.

The third and arguably the most important depiction of the relation between letter and litter is, "And so it all ended. Artha kama dharma moksa. Ask Kavya for the kay. And so everybody heard their plaint and all listened to their plause. The letter! The litter! And the soother the bitther!" (ibid., p. 93). In other words, it all ended with the four objectives or goals of human life according to the Vedas and other sacred Hindu texts. These are "Dharma" or righteousness, as a moral value; "Artha" or prosperity, as an economic value; "Kama" or sensual pleasure, as a psychological value; and "Moksha" or the soul's liberation, as a spiritual value. The order of the goals is extremely important in the scriptures because prosperity and pleasure ought to be sought in a righteous manner, according to this lesson. Turning the sacred letter into literary litter, Joyce changes the order of the four goals and, notably, places prosperity and sensual pleasure before righteousness, implying thereby that pleasure and prosperity need not necessarily be attained in a righteous manner.

"Kavya" means poetry in Sanskrit. Therefore, "Ask Kavya for the kay" means look up these sacred verses for the "key" to life, as the word "key" is at times pronounced like "kay" by the Irish. "Kay" also stands for the letter "K" with which the word "Kavya" is spelt. It is also the initial for "Kate", the incarnation of the protagonist Anna Livia Plurabelle or ALP, who has the "passkey" (ibid., p. 8) or the "Key" (ibid., p. 421) before ALP herself has "The keys" (ibid., p. 628). And so everybody heard their "plaint", meaning lamentation or complaint, and everybody listened to their "plause", variously meaning "applause" in English, "flattery" from "plausy" or "*plás*" in Anglo-Irish, and "play" from the French "*plauser*". It is not by chance that the acronym for "*e*verybody *h*eard their [*com*]*plaint*" is EHC, a variation of HCE, while the acronym for "*a*ll *l*istened to their *p*lause" is ALP!

Most pertinently, Anna Livia Plurabelle's letter, which describes the crucial story concerning her husband Humphrey Chimpden Earwicker or HCE, the two young women, and the three soldiers, can be seen as a microcosm of the entire novel. This letter, which is torn, stained by tea—in Joyce's parlance, "tache of tch" (ibid., p. 111)—and found in a rubbish heap, is literally a piece of trash. And since it is referred to or alluded to in bits and pieces throughout the novel, the novel is well and truly littered with fragments of this letter. This very letter that is scratched out of a dung or rubbish heap by Biddy the Hen is, above all, *Finnegans Wake* itself! Thus, the key lies in the letter, whether sacred or mundane, and especially in the letter's inextricable link with litter. "And the soother the bitther!" The sooner this is realised, the better, even though the realisation will soothe her and bite her, for it is at once sweeter and bitter. "The letter! The litter!" is, therefore, not a random play on words in the novel. Rather, the expression is constitutive of and, therefore, has a foundational place in the narrative of *Finnegans Wake*.

Having examined the meaning of the expression "The letter! The litter!" in *Finnegans Wake*, let us now turn to its significance in Joyce's writing. What have the Joyce-scholars who looked at it from a purely literary point of view had to say about the importance of this expression in Joyce? Well, what is remarkable about the literary commentary on Joyce's expression is that it is quite sparse, even though the handful of Joyce-scholars who have commented on it considered it central to *Finnegans Wake* if not to literature, history, or the course of life itself.

William York Tindall explains the significance of the expression in his 1959 *A Reader's Guide to James Joyce* by bringing out how the three most important strands of the plot of *Finnegans Wake* are, in fact, woven around the motif of the letter and the litter. He rightly states that the most important strand of the plot of the novel concerns Tim Finnegan's death in terms of his fall from the ladder and his rise again, or Finnagain, at his wake. Equating the ladder with "latter", he writes, "From latter comes 'litter' and from the litter the letter" (Tindall, 1959, p. 257). Moving on to the second most important strand of the novel's plot, ALP's letter, Tindall correctly points out that all the members of the Earwicker family, or all four protagonists of the novel, are inextricably linked to this letter: It is uttered by ALP, uttered for HCE, written by Shem, and its delivery to HCE attempted by Shaun. This letter, its contents, its loss and rediscovery, and the repeated unsuccessful attempts to deliver it constitute the bulk of the novel's narrative. This letter, found by the hen in a dump, is the "[e]ssence of dump" and bears "all the muddled affairs of Earwicker's family, from alpha to omega, in a page" (ibid., p. 257). The third major strand of the novel's plot is Kate's conducted tour of "the museum" that describes the battle of Waterloo and several other European battles in terms of the battle between the members of the Earwicker family, especially that between ALP and HCE. At the end of the battles, a bird, or ALP, picks up the pieces so as to renew them. In this context, Tindall points out that "the museum is a dump"; that ALP picks up the litter at the end of the battles; and that "the hen's letter" comes from "the litter of battle" (ibid., p. 266). Not pointed out by Tindall, though it must have been present in Joyce's mind, "Waterloo" could easily be a euphemism for a toilet. In his 1969 *A Reader's Guide to* Finnegans Wake, Tindall goes on to equate the pattern in *Finnegans Wake* to that of life and death itself: "Dump, litter, letter, letters, and *Wake* are depositories and vestiges of our living and dying, and part of their rhythm" (Tindall, 1969, pp. 90–91). Therefore, Tindall concludes that "a major concern of the book is: time, process, the fall and rise of man, conflict and its litter, and the creation from litter of children, cities, and books" (ibid., p. 29).

John Gordon makes two important observations regarding the letter and litter in his 1986 Finnegans Wake: *A Plot Summary*. First, HCE's relationship with his wife, in terms of the letter that she wrote for him and in terms of their children, points to the two Shakespearean antidotes to mortality, namely, literature or the letter, and children or the litter (Gordon, 1986, p. 143). And second, referring to the gossip of the two washer-women about ALP's letter, her sexual transgressions in youth, HCE's guilt published in the newspaper, and so on, while washing clothes in the Liffey, Gordon states that the episode brings out "the redemptive power of litter-ature" (ibid., p. 152).

In her 1980 book *Alchemy and* Finnegans Wake, Barbara DiBernard argues that "*Finnegans Wake* is a rubbish heap yet a work of art" (DiBernard, 1980, p. 26), a litter and yet a letter. She argues how, like an alchemist who transforms the vilest substance into the Philosopher's Stone, Joyce transformed a garbage heap into an ordered art. She concludes, "to be more exact, *Finnegans Wake* is both rubbish and gold" (ibid., p. 16). In other words, the literature produced by Joyce is at once precious and trash. Neither of the two statuses is strong enough to neutralise the other.

Explaining the relation between the letter and litter in his 1997 *The Role of Thunder in* Finnegans Wake, Eric Mcluhan states that, insofar as letters are employed to produce manuscripts that become trash or litter after the publication of the work, the acts of writing and publication necessarily involve turning the letter to litter and the litter to the letter in a new form. He adds that literature, created in this manner out of the littering of letters and the lettering of litter, is then "dumped onto the market as goods" (Mcluhan, 1997, p. 123).

Arguably, the most astute literary commentary on Joyce's expression "The letter! The litter!" comes from Vincent Cheng. Cheng explains the relation between the letter and the litter in a number of overlapping ways in his 1979 *Shakespeare and Joyce*. To begin with, he explains the connection between literature and excreta by stating that a defecator, a father, a poet, and God are all equivalent "because they each create, or produce, something" (Cheng, 1979/1984, p. 17). Thus, both letter and litter are creations of the defecator poet. Cheng further states that, insofar as the Latin word for "letter", namely "*litterae*", which stands for letters of the alphabet, epistolary letters, and belles-lettres, corresponds with the word "litter" that stands for shit and birth, poetic creations in general "are at once bi-labial speech, biological offspring, and biodegradable waste. Each implies the others" (ibid., p. 17).

Turning to the hen's act of digging out the letter from the litter, Cheng states that it symbolically represents littering the letter in a number of ways, such as: that *Finnegans Wake* is "a creatio ex shitpile" (ibid., p. 17); that attempts are made to dig out the truth (or letter) from the midden heap of possibilities (or litter) (ibid., p. 29); that the digging and mis-readings involved in scholarship and historical investigation never end (ibid., p. 27); that some scratching scholar-hen will one day rescue *Finnegans Wake* from the midden pile and truly appreciate it (ibid., p. 17); that it represents Joyce's own question as to whether he should "dig . . . into the graveyard of past literature and history for his style and his subject matter" (ibid., p. 29); and that all new scholarly works on *Finnegans Wake* (or letter) are re-tellings of old works, or new plagiarised versions (or litter) of Shakespeare and Joyce (ibid., p. 106).

Expanding on the last point, Cheng then argues that "The letter! The litter!" denotes that literature as such is forgery, or a recycling of earlier literature, or plagiarism, maintaining that this is at once true of the works of Shakespeare, the works of Joyce, and even of ALP's letter supposedly written by Shem. Thus, Cheng points to Shaun's direct accusation against Shem, saying that the latter was a forger and a plagiarist because he had plagiarised ALP's letter from him. Cheng then claims that all literature written after Shakespeare, including those by Joyce, is forged from the works of Shakespeare, pointing to Shaun's allegation in the novel that Shem-Joyce's tales are all forged (ibid., p. 98). Above all, pointing to Shakespeare's forgery, Cheng states: "Shakespeare has also often been accused of fakery, either by plagiarizing other authors (according to Greene) or by not actually authoring the plays, which were supposedly written instead by Francis Bacon or others" (ibid., p. 101). Similarly, Shaun concludes that behind Shakespeare's manuscripts lay *The Odyssey* of Homer (Joyce, 1939/1975, p. 123). Cheng rightly thinks that, according to Joyce, all literature and history are Viconian cycles in which nothing is really new. Therefore, he concludes by foregrounding Joyce's view that all new works of scholarship and literature are merely "re-tellings, re-combinations, and re-workings of the same forged letter" (Cheng, 1979/1984, p. 243).

Thus, there is nothing arbitrary or excessive about Lacan's isolation and highlighting of the expression "The letter! The litter!" because, as an extraordinarily discerning reader of Joyce, he was able, unlike many Joyce-scholars, to fathom the absolute centrality and unsurpassable value of this expression not only in Joyce's philosophy of composition in general, and in the text of *Finnegans Wake* as evidence of the former, but in the progression of European literature itself.

Lacan's Discourse on "The letter! The litter!"

Both letter and litter have a relation to writing, or, in Joyce's case, to the inscription of distorted speech sounds in the form of writing. Miller rightly points out that, unlike speech sounds that dissipate soon after their articulation and can stay on thereafter only in the unconscious of those who heard them, the written letter remains in the form of tangible material and, by remaining, creates the possibility of litter (Miller, 1987/2012, p. 2).

Lacan indicates that Joyce converted letter into litter in order to irreparably deform the English language and English literature so as to avenge the English for invading and colonising his country, oppressing his countrymen, and annulling his own language, Gaelic. The composition and, more importantly, the publication of *Finnegans Wake* enabled him to achieve this. Lacan states in "Joyce the Symptom":

> [Joyce] did use one particular tongue among others, one that is not his own—for his own is precisely a tongue that had been wiped off the map, to wit, Gaelic,

of which he had a smattering, enough to get by, but hardly much more—not his own, then, but the tongue of the invaders, the oppressors.

(Lacan, 1982/2016, p. 146)

Philippe Sollers had made a similar point, as Lacan mentions: "even though Ireland was involved . . . Joyce had to write in English . . . However, as . . . Philippe Sollers . . . has remarked in *Tel Quel*, Joyce wrote in English is such a way that the English language no longer exists" (Lacan, 2005/2016, p. 3). Lacan moreover states that Joyce had changed the nature of literature forever: "literature after him can no longer be what it was before" (Lacan, 1982/2016, p. 146). Following Lacan, Miller rightly points out that *Finnegans Wake* was the fruit of Joyce's attempt to corrupt the language of the enemy of his people:

> James Joyce had a tongue, but he was enough of an enemy to this tongue, which was in fact the tongue of the Other that was oppressing his people, the tongue of the English, to work it over, to corrupt it, to lace it with others, and thus to rip through the veil of the idea and bring us its fruit, the monster of the written, this *Finnegans Wake* upon which the psychoanalyst Lacan spent one or two of the last years of his life.
>
> (Miller, 1999/2013, p. 45)

However, Joyce himself claimed, "I have put the [English] language to sleep" (Ellmann, 1959/1982, p. 546), whose meaning is best understood in terms of what he had said to Max Eastman later: "When morning comes of course everything will be clear again . . . . I'll give them back their English language. I'm not destroying it for good" (Eastman, 1931, p. 101). At a broader level, not mentioned by Joyce, Lacan, Sollers or Miller, by littering fifty-two languages in all, major and minor (Sandulescu, 2012, pp. 6–8), Joyce was trying to write a literature of litter on an unthinkable scale, as well as trying to write the last word in literature with the help of a work that would destroy all existing notions of literature itself. His aim was thus to redefine almost all languages and all literature in the course of disrupting the English language and English literature.

An important aspect of Joyce's slippage from the letter to litter is that its magnitude kept on increasing as he progressed from one work to the next. Offering an explanation for this in the seminar on *The Sinthome*, Lacan says that Joyce's torturing of speech sounds more and more in his writings that ended in breaking or dissolving language itself in his last work, *Finnegans Wake*, where phonatory identity is almost lost and gone, is really his response to a certain relation to speech that the place of his lacking father was increasingly imposing on him. Lacan wonders whether, by decomposing speech in this manner, Joyce was able to free himself from speech or whether, paradoxically, he had exposed himself to a greater invasion of speech by thereby empowering its polyphony:

> In his efforts dating back to his first critical essays, then in *A Portrait of the Artist*, and ultimately in *Ulysses* and ending in *Finnegans Wake*, in what is in some

sense the continuous progress that his art constituted, it is hard not to see how a certain relationship with speech is increasingly imposed upon him—namely, this speech that comes to be written while being broken apart, pulled to pieces—to the point that he ends up dissolving language itself . . . He ends up imposing on language itself a sort of fracturing, a sort of decomposition, which makes it so that there is no longer any phonatory identity.

There is undoubtedly a reflection here at the level of writing. It is through the intermediary of writing that speech is decomposed by imposing itself as such. This occurs through a warping, and it is ambiguous as to whether this warping lets him free himself from the parasite of speech I was speaking about earlier, or whether it leaves him on the contrary open to invasion from the essentially phonemic properties of speech, from the polyphony of speech.

(Lacan, 2005/2016, p. 79)

What exactly was Joyce's method of converting the letter into litter? Lacan answered the question from several perspectives. Let us focus on the three most important ones among them. Lacan's first response to the question, in his seminar on *Encore: On Feminine Sexuality, the Limits of Love and Knowledge*, is that Joyce converted the letter into litter in *Finnegans Wake* by making his signifiers stuff the signified. Shedding light on this aspect of Joyce's language, Miller writes, "It is not that the monster of the written [*Finnegans Wake*] no longer carries any meaning. On the contrary, it has no *common sense*, but rather a sense that multiplies, that becomes infinite, that spurts, overflows, and invades everything" (Miller, 1999/2013, p. 45). However, when Lacan says that the signifiers stuff the signified, he means, more precisely, that Joyce's signifiers are like slips of the tongue that can be read in an infinite number of ways. Notably, Joyce had not only read Freud's *The Psychopathology of Everyday Life*, a book that he owned, but also declared in *Ulysses*, somewhat like Freud, that "errors . . . are the portals of discovery" (Joyce, 1922/2000, p. 243). Lacan adds that, since the signifiers thereby tend to produce an enigmatic meaning, they are difficult to read, difficult to read in any one way, difficult not to read awry, and difficult to decide to read:

What happens in Joyce's work? The signifier stuffs (*vient truffer*) the signified. It is because the signifiers fit together, combine, and concertina—read *Finnegans Wake*—that something is produced by way of meaning (*comme signifié*) that may seem enigmatic, but is clearly what is closest to what we analysts, thanks to analytic discourse, have to read—slips of the tongue (*lapsus*). It is as slips that they signify something, in other words, that they can be read in an infinite number of different ways. But it is precisely for that reason that they are difficult to read, are read awry, or not read at all.

(Lacan, 1975/1998, p. 37)

Illustrating one of the many ways in which the signified is stuffed by the signifier, Lacan states in "Joyce the Symptom" that in *Finnegans Wake*, there is a very peculiar kind of a pun in which three or four words flash in a single word, such as the word "*pourspère*", which is fascinating even though meaning tends to get lost in the absence of an anchoring point (Lacan, 1982/2016, p. 144). *Pourspère* is a coinage by Lacan that sounds like a cluster of words in French that means "to spoil/rot in hoping/waiting" (*pourrir espérer*), "for father" (*pourpère*), "prosper" (*prospère*), "imitator" (*pasticheur*), "pastiche" (*pasticher*), and "rottenness" (*pourriture*). Owing to an excess of meaning, the exact meaning of such words is always hard to determine and therefore they are always difficult to read satisfactorily.[4]

In this context, Lacan further clarifies that this very peculiar kind of punning brings out Joyce's "*cancellation of subscription to the unconscious*" (ibid., p. 146, emphasis in original). The expression has at least three meanings. First, Joyce did not prescribe any one meaning in the unconscious. Second, Joyce's writing neither endorses the view that the unconscious is structured like a language—for he delinks language from the unconscious and meaning—nor subscribes to an unconscious structured like English, as Lacan points out in this essay:

> I've said that the unconscious is structured like a language. It's odd that I'm also able to speak in terms of a *cancellation of subscription to the unconscious* for someone who plays strictly on language, though he did use one particular tongue among others, one that is not his own.
>
> (Ibid., p. 146)

Third, Joyce's *Finnegans Wake* is that kind of a symptom that does not tell the readers anything at all, as it does not allow anything in it to hook on to something in the unconscious of its readers: "It is the symptom inasmuch as it stands no chance whatsoever of hooking anything of your unconscious" (ibid., p. 145). Therefore, as Lacan states in the same essay, Joyce the symptom is Joyce's singular symptom, for it does not concern anyone else and is completely unanalysable, due to which literature itself is forever altered by it:

> Joyce lifts the symptom to the power of language, without for all that any of it being analysable. This is what strikes you, and literally renders you . . . *speechless*. . . . That is what makes for the substance of what Joyce brings us, whereby, in a certain way, literature after him can no longer be what it was before.
>
> (Ibid., p. 146)

Lacan's second response to the question figures in "Joyce the Symptom", where he explains with the help of an example how Joyce was able to convert the letter into litter by making use of the peculiarity of English orthography, which tends to support translinguistic homophony in a special way:

> Now, were it not for this very special kind of spelling [letter-litter] that is specific to the English language, a good three quarters of the effects of *Finnegans Wake* would be lost. The most extreme case, I can tell you, and I owe this to

Jacques Aubert, is—*Who ails tongue coddeau, aspace of dumbillsilly*? Had I come across this piece of writing on my own, would I have perceived or not—*Où est ton cadeau, espèce d'imbécile?*' Where's your present, you imbecile? What is unprecedented in this is that the homophony, translinguistic homophony on this occasion, is sustained only by letters that conform to English-language spelling.

(Ibid., p. 145)

Another example, pointed out by Hart, is that "Sevastopol", the name of the Crimean city implied in the "Butt and Taff" episode, though not explicitly mentioned therein, also denotes "see a vast pool" and through it "the horrors of the Flood", the "apple" as the cause of the "original Fall", as well as "the name of Siva, the destroyer-god [in Hinduism]" (Hart, 1962, p. 33). In other words, Joyce littered the letter on the way to composing *Finnegans Wake* essentially in terms of the prodigious exploitation of the accidents of history, such as of the translingual homophony that the orthography and phonetics of the English language could accommodate.

In the form of his third response, which may be found in the "Additional Session" to Session 4 of the seminar on *The Sinthome*, Lacan mentions how, from *Ulysses* onward, Joyce turned the letter into litter by subtly breaking up the sentences to give language another, usually unconventional, use:

Joyce writes English with these peculiar refinements that mean that he disarticulates the tongue, the English tongue on this occasion. Don't imagine that this only begins with *Finnegans Wake*. Long before, notably in *Ulysses*, he had a way of chopping up sentences [*les phrases*] that already inclined that way. It is truly a process that is exerted in the direction of finding another use for the language in which he writes, in any case, a use that is far from ordinary. This is part and parcel of his *savoir-faire*.

(Lacan, 2005/2016, p. 59)

Lacan's expression "*les phrases*" stands for both "sentences" and "phrases", and his remark is valid for both these levels of Joyce's language. At the level of the phrase, for instance, Joyce distorts the expression "tongue-tied" into "Tung-Toyd" (Joyce, 1939/1975, p. 123) to allude to "Jung-Freud" as two doctors whose "tongues toyed" with their patients and with each other, as well as to point to the "split" between them with reference to the context of "Schizophrenesis" (ibid., p. 123), or "schizophrenia", in which the expression is used. All of the instances are highly unusual uses of the original expression.[5] While at the level of the sentence, for instance, we find the following broken sentences in the penultimate line of the novel: "Lps. The keys to. Given! A way" (ibid., p. 628). Here "Lps" is "lips", "The keys" also stands for "the kiss", and the set of fragmented sentences together mean, "The kiss given away [by ALP's lips]". Gordon rightly states, "ALP's letter always ends with kisses; this is the last one" (Gordon, 2020, p. 119). Moreover, as

Tindall explains, "The keys to" refers to "the keys of me heart" (Joyce, 1939/1975, p. 626); "The keys to. Given!" also means "the keys to heaven"; and "Given. A way" stands for both "the given away" and "the given or whatever is", the latter reaffirming ALP's earlier remark, "What will be is. Is is" (ibid., p. 620) (Tindall, 1969, p. 328), whereby "given" is "a way" of dealing with the events of life. Such "chopping up" of sentences makes unconventional uses of language possible by introducing a charged impulse for reintegration or re-combination at different levels among the fragments, thereby creating the possibility of textual intertwining and the production of multiple novel meanings.

Regarding Joyce's act of writing *Finnegans Wake*, Lacan clarifies that the act provided Joyce with jouissance. Lacan repeatedly states that we do not know what *Finnegans Wake* means, insofar as it is an unreadable and unanalysable work, but we can clearly sense as readers that Joyce enjoyed writing every word in it. Lacan believes that this enjoyment was Joyce's whole purpose for writing *Finnegans Wake*; that Joyce is, as his name suggests, joy, enjoyment, "joyssance". As Miller puts it, "Joyce . . . handl[ed] the letter outside of signified effects, for the purpose of pure jouissance" (Miller, 1987/2012, p. 4). This would explain why Lacan considers jouissance to be situated beyond knowledge, where the ridge between the two is marked by the letter functioning as an edge that Lacan calls the littoral in "Lituraterre".

Lacan mentions another detail while making this very point in "Joyce the Symptom": "this *jouissance*, is the sole thing in his text on which we can get a purchase" (Lacan, 1982/2016, p. 146). In other words, that Joyce enjoyed writing *Finnegans Wake* is the only thing that we can understand as readers of the novel. Lacan relates this to Joyce's unanalysable symptom. Going a step further, Lacan adds that this very jouissance of Joyce is what enables the readers to go through this otherwise unreadable novel without understanding anything of it at all: "Read a few pages of *Finnegans Wake* without striving to understand it. It's quite readable . . . because one can sense the presence of the jouissance of he that wrote it" (ibid., p. 144). The novel is Joyce's symptom because we are unable to understand anything of it other than the fact that Joyce enjoyed writing it.

Lacan further explains that the readers are unable to understand anything more than the fact that Joyce enjoyed writing it because the language of the novel that is generated by littering the letter represents Joyce's *lalangue*, or a kind of meaningless speech sounds, with which the novel is written. Mentioned for the first time in his lecture on *The Knowledge of the Psychoanalyst* dated 4th November, 1971, the term *lalangue*, or "thelanguage" as a single word, is a coinage by Lacan that contains an allusion to Pierre André Lalande, author of a dictionary of critical and philosophical terms in French, and stands for the nonsensical articulation or absurd babble indicative of an elementary phenomenon that often characterises the language of the psychotic subject. Although *lalangue* is not a structure like a language, it is nonetheless capable of producing the polysemic, homophonic, and equivocal effects of the latter. It is a kind of phonation that predates language, meaningful speech, and subjectivity itself. While language captures the unconscious's meaning effect, *lalangue* captures its jouissance effect. Joyce's meaningless littering in *Finnegans Wake* thus constitutes a unique instance of the creation of literature with the help of *lalangue*. *Finnegans Wake* is a symptom, according to Lacan, because no meaning connects to the *lalangue* in terms of which it is composed. In this context, the letter stands for language and meaning, while litter stands for *lalangue* and jouissance.

Lacan considers *Finnegans Wake* unreadable, unanalysable, completely meaningless, and the destroyer of the English language and literature. For these very reasons, however, he thinks that the novel paradoxically exemplifies a kind of perfection of language. He says in the seminar on *Encore: On Feminine Sexuality, the Limits of Love and Knowledge* that language attains such perfection when it is enabled to litter writing properly: "You must sit down and read a little work by writers, not of your era . . . but you could read Joyce, for example. You will see therein how language is perfected when it knows how to play with writing" (Lacan, 1975/1998, p. 36). Here, "perfection" stands for perfection in converting the letter into litter and perfection in creating a new letter out of that litter without ever departing from the fundamental rules of language and writing. Language is perfected in the process of such play with writing in terms of speech sounds because it is thus enabled to expand and incorporate what was missing in it until then. Therefore, Joyce represents that moment in history when literature and the English language were perfected in terms of the conversion of littering into writing with extraordinary subtlety and finesse.

Joyce the Symptom

According to Lacan, Stephen in *A Portrait of the Artist as a Young Man*, who represents Joyce, "doesn't get very far because he believes in all his symptoms. This is very striking" (Lacan, 2005/2016, p. 54) For instance, he believes in the uncreated conscience of his race:

> [H]e believed in such things as *the uncreated conscience of my race*. You find that at the end of *A Portrait of the Artist as a Young Man*. It's plain to see that this doesn't reach very far. . . . To believe, however, that there is an uncreated conscience of any race is a great illusion.
>
> (Ibid., pp. 55–56)

In addition, "[h]e . . . believes that there is a *book of himself*. What an idea! To make oneself be a book! Really, such a thing can only occur to a stunted poet, a confounded poet" (ibid., p. 56). Following from these illusions, Lacan discusses a number of other symptoms of Joyce. In the first place, with reference to Sollers' designation of Joyce's work with the English language as "something like . . . elation", Lacan states that "Joyce's last work [*Finnegans Wake*] looks like" what "in psychiatry we call mania" (ibid., p. 4).

Another symptom of Joyce is that he renounced his father even as he remained attached to him. Thus, even though Joyce's father—an alcoholic incapable of supporting his family—was "an unworthy father, a failing father", Joyce addresses the following prayer to him at the end of *A Portrait of the Artist as a Young Man*: "*27 April: Old father, old artificer, stand me now and ever in good stead*". Similarly, in *Ulysses*, Stephen looks for Bloom but in places where he cannot be found. While Bloom "is trying to find himself a son", Stephen thinks, "*After the father I had, I've had my fill. No more father*". And yet, "it's quite peculiar how Bloom's ponderings and Stephen's orbit each other and are pursued throughout the novel". In fact, "Blephen and Stoom" in *Ulysses* "clearly shows that they are made not only of the same signifier but truly of the same matter". Thus, Lacan concludes, "*Ulysses* is the testimony of how Joyce remains deeply rooted in his father while still disowning him. That's precisely what his symptom is" (ibid., p. 55).

However, Lacan thinks that Joyce's core symptom is related to the shortcoming in his sexual relation with Nora, as borne out by the play *Exiles*:

Exiles is really an approach to something that for him is the core symptom, which is formed from the specific shortcoming of sexual relation. . . . There can be no better term to express non-relation than *exile*, and all that transpires in *Exiles* revolves precisely around this non-relation.

(Ibid., p. 56)

Here, non-relation is to be understood in terms of the fact that "there is really no reason to hold one-woman-among-others to be *one's* woman", while "[o]ne-woman-among-others is also she who has a relationship with just any old other man", namely the character of Robert in the play who "knows how to open up the choice of the one-woman in question" (ibid., p. 56). At the end of *Exiles*, Richard is irredeemably uncertain as to whether his wife Bertha had been disloyal to him with his friend Robert.

Furthermore, with reference to the facts that Joyce "remains stuck, attached, to examining Vico", and "worse still, to conversing with spirits"—which Lacan terms "Spiritism" instead of "Spiritualism"—Lacan states that these are at times "a contributing factor in *Finnegans Wake* in the guise of the symptom" (Lacan, 1982/2016, p. 147).

Regarding Joyce's symptom, Lacan informs us that it does not concern the reader in any respect whatsoever because it cannot latch on to anything whatsoever in the reader's unconscious and thereby become meaningful to him (ibid., p. 145). Lacan further clarifies that the only thing the reader can understand in Joyce's works embodying his symptom is that he enjoyed writing them, as we have already seen. His works constitute his symptom precisely because, even though the symptom is conditioned by *lalangue*, it does not shed any light on the latter, and despite the fact that Joyce lifts the symptom "to the power of language", it continues to remain unanalysable (ibid., p. 146).

Above all, Lacan states that Joyce "earned the privilege of having reached the extreme point of embodying the symptom in himself". He says so because the symptom, by tying itself to Joyce's idea of the body, which is the imaginary, and thereby tying itself to the real, and at the same time tying itself to the unconscious as a third term, is able to take on its limits by engaging all three orders at the same time (ibid., pp. 147–148).

Was Joyce Mad?

But we must answer a prior question first: Did Lacan contradict himself by asking this question after having emphatically declared earlier that there is no question of psychoanalysing a dead author? Well, the answer is no, because Lacan was merely trying to frame his argument on a somewhat novel clinical problem—one that some Lacanians would go on to call "untriggered psychosis" later—with the help of the instance of Joyce's writing. Lacan's aim was to be able to think through the idea of the *sinthome* as a fourth Borromean ring with the help of Joyce's writing rather than to psychoanalyse Joyce, for Joyce's writing would remain unanalysable to Lacan till the end. This is the reason the title of Lacan's discussion is interrogative rather than affirmative. Apart from that, after having questioned psychoanalysis on the basis of speech all this while, Lacan wanted to question psychoanalysis on the basis of writing, choosing Joyce's writing for the purpose. As Miller rightly points out, Lacan invokes Joyce in order to "question psychoanalysis in the field of language on the basis of writing" (Miller, 1987/2012, p. 4). Miller specifies that rather than try to psychoanalyse Joyce, Lacan turned to the Irish writer in order to question the analyst's discourse with the help of the unanalysable symptom that he represented. In other words, whereas psychoanalysis is in no position to analyse Joyce, and Joyce had managed to reach the best possible end of an analysis by identifying with his symptom without the support of a psychoanalysis, his writing could help Lacan question the psychoanalyst's discourse as well as find an instance of the best possible end of an analysis:

> Evoking psychosis was in no way applied psychoanalysis; on the contrary, it was *with* the Joyce-symptom held to be unanalyzable, calling the analyst's discourse into question, in so far as a subject who is identified with his or her symptom is closed off to the artifice of analysis. And perhaps an analysis has no better end.
> (Ibid., pp. 4–5)

Lacan begins by stating that since the question of madness tends to suck one in, it is not surprising that he had turned to Joyce in 1975 after having started out by writing the piece called "*Écrits inspires: Schizographie*" in 1931 (Lacan, 2005/2016, p. 63). As a matter of fact, Lacan had written on "Structures of paranoid psychoses" (*Structures des psychoses paranoïaques*) before that in the same year and on "Encephalitic Hallucinatory Psychosis" (*Psychose hallucinatoire encéphalitique*) in the previous year, not to mention his doctoral thesis on paranoid psychoses written in 1932.

Lacan says, "the dreadful thing is that I'm reduced to reading him, because surely enough I didn't analyse him, which I regret" (ibid., p. 64). If Lacan regrets that he is reduced to reading Joyce or to reading Joyce without having analysed him, then that is understandable. But if he regrets that he had not analysed Joyce, then Lacan is contradicting himself here, for he had stated in 1971 that Joyce did not need an analysis as he had reached its end all by himself and followed it up in the present seminar with the remark that Joyce and his symptom/*sinthome* are unanalysable. On the question of madness, Lacan indicates that Joyce had a deficiency in the place of the Name-of-the-Father owing to his paternal lack, which had the effect of a foreclosure (*Verwerfung*) that forms the basis of psychosis. Moreover, one witnesses two elementary phenomena in Joyce that are often indicative of psychosis. These are his compulsive distortion of language, in the form of his use of *lalangue* to write his last novel, and his hallucinations in the form of what literary critics call his epiphanies. Lacan clarifies that "every single epiphany is invariably characterized by the . . . consequence that results from the mistake in the knot, namely, that the unconscious is tied to the real" (ibid., p. 134). Apart from these, the endless proliferation of meaning in Joyce that does not know how to stop and be meaningful is another lesser indicator of a psychotic structure.

In addition to these, Lacan mentions Joyce's hint in his earliest novel that he is becoming a redeemer, which may be thought of as an instance of "Grandiose Delusion" or "Delusion of Grandeur", though Lacan did not use any of these expressions. He merely asks Aubert: "Isn't there in Joyce's writings what I shall call the *hint* that he is, or is turning himself into, what in his language he terms a *redeemer*?" And Aubert replies, "*In* Stephen Hero*, there are traces. . . . In the first version, there are very sharp traces*" (ibid., pp. 64–65). Apart from that, Lacan points out that despite being very close to each other, every time Nora gives birth to a child, there is a scene because it did not fit into Joyce's programme:

[W]hen they are in Trieste, whenever she drops a sprog . . . it causes a scene. It wasn't part of the programme. Unease sets in between Nora and the one called Jim [Nora wrote to him using this name], who are thick as thieves. . . . With each new rug rat, things go awry between them. Always, in each case, it causes a scene.
(Ibid., p. 68)

Lacan then states that Joyce's father "neglected pretty much everything, save for relying on the good Jesuit fathers, the *Church diplomatic*", while Joyce compensated as it were for this "paternal abdication, this de facto *Verwerfung*" with the feeling of having "imperiously received his calling" (ibid., pp. 72–73). Lacan moreover highlights that while defending his daughter, Lucia, who had been diagnosed a schizophrenic, Joyce claimed that she was miraculously telepathic, and in making such a claim, he attributes to her his own symptom by introducing the point of the failing of the father that he himself had to deal with:

His daughter, Lucia . . . is what is commonly known as schizophrenic. . . .
Joyce, who put up a fierce defence on her behalf against the grip of the doctors, affirmed one thing, namely, that she was telepathic. In the letters he

wrote about her he says that she is far more intelligent than everyone else, that she informs him—*miraculously* is the word that is implied—about everything that happens to a certain number of people, that for her these people hold no secret.

Isn't this something quite striking? . . . [T]hat Joyce attributed this virtue to her, through a number of signs and declarations that he understood in a particular way, is precisely where I can see how, in order to defend, as it were, his daughter, he attributes to her something that is an extension of what I shall for the time being call his own symptom.

[For] Joyce testifies to at this very same point, which I designated as being the point of the failing of the father.

. . . Is there something that belongs to the realm of the slip in the initial fault that Joyce puts forward so strongly?

(Ibid., pp. 78–80)

Furthermore, Lacan points to Joyce's act of decomposing language. He states that Joyce writes speech while breaking it apart to the point of dissolving language itself (ibid., p. 79). Finally, referring to the incident in which four or five of his classmates, led by a certain Heron, pinioned Joyce up against a barbed-wire fence and gave him a hiding with a cane, Lacan draws our attention to Joyce's unusual reaction to the offence and what that indicates about the psychology of his relationship with his body, especially the sliding of the Imaginary and the consequent failure of the Borromean knot:

After the escapade, Joyce wonders how it is that, once the thing was over, *he bore no malice* to him. He . . . metaphorizes his relationship with his body. He observes that the whole business was divested of, like a fruit peel.

. . . He had a reaction of disgust. . . . In sum, this disgust has to do with his own body. . . .

To have a relationship with one's own body as though it were foreign is certainly a possibility, one that is expressed by the use of the verb *to have*. . . . The form that this *dropping* of the relationship with the body takes for Joyce is, however, altogether suspicious for an analyst.

All that remains to this capital I [Imaginary] is for it simply to clear off. It slides away, in just the same way as what Joyce feels after his hiding.

It slides, and the imaginary relationship has no locus.

(Ibid., pp. 128–131)

To this, Lacan adds the detail that, in Joyce's case, the "*Ego* [is] . . . of enigmatic functions, of reparatory functions" (ibid., p. 133).

Notably, in spite of all these signs of psychosis, Joyce never experienced a psychotic breakdown because he was able to supplement for the lack in the place of the Name-of-the-Father in terms of his writing. Joyce's writing of *Finnegans Wake* was his own way of creating this supplement in the form of the *sinthome* that, as the fourth Borromean ring, held together his disintegrating R.S.I. and thus prevented it from falling apart. Differently put, Joyce never experienced a psychotic breakdown because he had been successful in creating a *sinthome* for himself. Miller went on to name this type of un-triggered psychosis "Ordinary psychosis" (*La psychose ordinaire*) in 1996 so as to differentiate it from the classical or full-blown psychosis of the kind we find in the case of Daniel Paul Schreber, where the breakdown does take place. Thus, Lacan read Joyce's writings in conjunction with Borromean rings, not with the trivial aim of psychoanalysing Joyce but rather with the more profound aim of clearing fresh grounds for the clinic of the psychoses.

Joyce the *Sinthome*

Lacan's most original observation on Joyce's writing is that Joyce wanted to compensate for his deficient Name-of-the-Father caused by paternal lack by making a name for himself, with the help of academics, in terms of the publication of his writings. Joyce's composition and publication of especially his last novel, *Finnegans Wake*, helped him create a *sinthome*, or a fourth Borromean ring, as well as identify with it so as to hold together his otherwise disintegrating Real-Symbolic-Imaginary as a three-ring Borromean knot and thus help him avoid a psychotic episode. Thus, the sinful act of writing *Finnegans Wake* made it possible for Joyce to construct his *sinthome*, even though he is converted into a *synth-homme* or a synthetic, as in artificially constructed, man in the process.

Lacan specifies that Joyce had a paternal lack and a phallic lack to compensate for with the help of his art. Regarding Joyce's phallic lack, or his lack in the signifier borne out of the combination of his sexual organ and speech, Lacan says:

> [S]ince his dick was a bit lax, as it were, his art supplemented his phallic allure. And this is always the way. The phallus is the conjunction between . . . the little scrap of a dick in question, and the function of speech. And it is in this respect that his art is the true guarantor of the phallus.
> (Lacan, 2005/2016, p. 7)

Regarding paternal lack, Lacan first mentions that Joyce was "born in Dublin with a boozing father who was more or less a . . . fanatic" (ibid., p. 7), and then states that he supported his father who burdened him, as well as the family, through his art. In his art, he moreover illustrated this very act of supporting as a writer the burden of a lacking father, of a deficient family, and even of a race whose conscience had not been properly formed:

> [A]ll in all, he [Joyce] is tasked with a father. To the extent that he must support this father for him to subsist, as is borne out by *Ulysses*, Joyce, through his art—this art which is always that which, down through the ages, comes to us as emanating from the artisan—not only makes his family subsist, but *illustrates* it, as it were. By the same token he *illustrates* what somewhere he calls my

country, or better still, *the uncreated conscience of my race*, on which he ends *A Portrait of the Artist*. This is the mission Joyce sets himself.

(Ibid., pp. 13–14)

In *Ulysses*, Joyce illustrates his very act of writing novels so as to sustain his family by making the protagonist do the same. Notably, the deficiency of the father we are concerned with here is not his deficiency in the family but rather his deficiency in the Oedipus complex, as Lacan already explained in the seminar on the *Formations of the Unconscious* when he said that "[s]peaking of his deficiency in the family isn't the same as speaking of his deficiency in the complex" (Lacan, 1998/2017, p. 153). Lacan clarified in that seminar that what concerns a psychoanalyst is the father's deficiency in the Oedipus complex because such deficiency alone tends to have a direct bearing on the clinical structure of the child in the form of neurosis, psychosis, or perversion. In Joyce's case, the paternal deficiency is rather more pertinent at the level of the Oedipus complex than at the level of the family, and it takes the shape of a foreclosure (*Verwerfung*) of the Name-of-the-Father that Joyce had to compensate for with his writing. Lacan then states that in order to make up for his paternal lack, Joyce valorises his proper name, or S_1, which is the master signifier, to the extent of making it the S_2, or the rest of the signifiers, or knowledge, by piling up proper nouns until they became common nouns:

> The name that is proper to him is what Joyce valorizes at the expense of the father. It is to this name that he wanted homage to be paid, a homage that he refused to anyone else.
>
> It is in this respect that one is able to say that the proper noun does all it can to make itself more than the S_1, the master's signifies which heads towards the S that I've labelled with the index of a subscript 2, which is that around which the gist of knowledge accumulates.
>
> $S_1 \rightarrow S_2$
>
> It's quite clear that the fact that there are two names that are proper to the subject was an invention that spread as the story unfolded. That Joyce was also called James links up in a succession only with the use of the alias—James Joyce also known as Dedalus.
>
> The fact that we can pile up a whole stack of them ultimately leads to one thing—it introduces the proper noun back into the common nouns.
>
> (Lacan, 2005/2016, p. 73)[6]

The Name-of-the-Father is the master signifier that tends to hold together the Real, Symbolic, and Imaginary as a stable three-ring Borromean knot. Figure 6.1 represents the R.S.I. stably knotted together in a Borromean way.

Lacan had already explained in the seminar on *Encore: On Feminine Sexuality, the Limits of Love and Knowledge* that rather than being knotted together, each ring

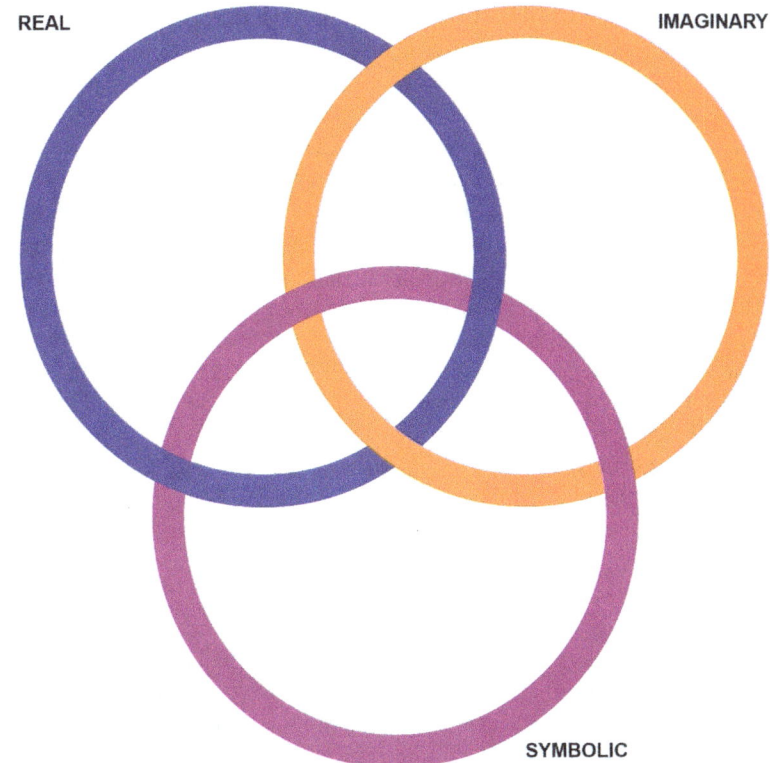

Figure 6.1 A Three-Ring Borromean Knot. Courtesy Santanu Biswas

is held in its place by the support of the other two, as may be seen in Figure 6.1: "It is easy for you to see that no two rings of string are knotted to each other, and that it's only thanks to the third that they hang together" (Lacan, 1975/1998, p. 124). This would explain why Borromean knots must consist of at least three rings, because every two rings must be held together by a third ring. This would also explain the Borromean property in that if every two rings are held in place by nothing but the third ring, then all three rings may be made to fall apart by simply disengaging any one of the rings. Lacan had spelt out in his seminar on the *R.S.I.* that the Borromean property consists of the peculiar fact that if any one ring is cut or separated, the rest of the rings fall apart regardless of the number of rings:

> The Borromean knot consists strictly insofar as three is the minimum . . . If you unknot two rings in a chain, the others remain knotted. In a Borromean knot, if you break one of the three, all three are liberated. The remarkable thing, a fact of consistency, is that you can add an indefinite number of rings—it will always

be true that, if you break one of the rings, all of the others, however numerous, will be free.

(Lacan, 1975, p. 9)

Lacan was working on Borromean knots since the late 1960s as a method of teaching psychoanalysis through writing, and he continued to do so till the end of his life in 1981. During this period, possibly in the early 1970s, he is likely to have heard about "the arms of the Milanese dynasty, the Borromeos" at a dinner party from "a young woman mathematician named Valérie Marchande", as Elisabeth Roudinesco informs us. "[T]hese consisted of three circles arranged in the shape of a clover leaf or trefoil [knot]" that stood for an alliance of the three circles representing the three main family lines (Roudinesco, 1993/1997, p. 363). Every member of the Borromean dynasty wore this ring, believing if any one circle was broken, all three circles, the entire Borromean dynasty, would fall apart.[7]

Lacan states in the seminar on *The Sinthome* that "starting with three rings, a link is made such that a break in one of the rings, the middle one, . . . sets the other two, whichever they may be, free from one another" (Lacan, 2005/2016, p. 11). When the R.S.I. as a three-ring Borromean knot tends to fall apart, it may be held together by a fourth Borromean ring that Lacan names the "*Sinthome*". Lacan clarifies that the three-ring Borromean knot remains intact in most people, as may be seen in Figure 6.1, where "the symbolic, the imaginary, and the real have become intertwined to the point that each forms the continuation of the other, for want of any operation that would set them apart as in the link of the Borromean knot" (ibid., p. 71). However, "Joyce's case corresponds to a way of making up for the knot's coming undone" (ibid., p. 71). The undone knot is held together with the help of the fourth ring called the *Sinthome* (ibid., p. 12). Figure 6.2 and Figure 6.3, respectively, depict the undone knot and how it is held together by the *Sinthome*. Figure 6.2 depicts the Real, the Symbolic, and the Imaginary as separated from one another, or an undone R.S.I., while Figure 6.3 depicts how an undone R.S.I. is bound together with the help of the *Sinthome* as the fourth ring in the form of the small sausage-shaped ring at the centre.

The "*Sinthome*", according to Rabelais, is the Latin way of spelling the Greek origin of "*Symptôme*", the French word for "Symptom". Lacan states that, according to the etymological dictionary of the French language by Oscar Bloch and Walther von Wartburg, "*symptôme* was initially spelt *sinthome*", adding that Rabelais had modernised the spelling of the word: "Rabelais was the one who turned *sinthome* into *symptomate*. It's not surprising. He was a doctor" (Lacan, 1982/2016, p. 142). In the present seminar, Lacan reiterates,

[T]he symbolic, the imaginary, and the real . . . a fourth term has to be supposed, which on this occasion is the sinthome. I'm saying that what forms the Borromean link has to be supposed to be tetradic . . . and that all in all, the father is a symptom, or a sinthome, as you wish.

(Lacan, 2005/2016, p. 11)

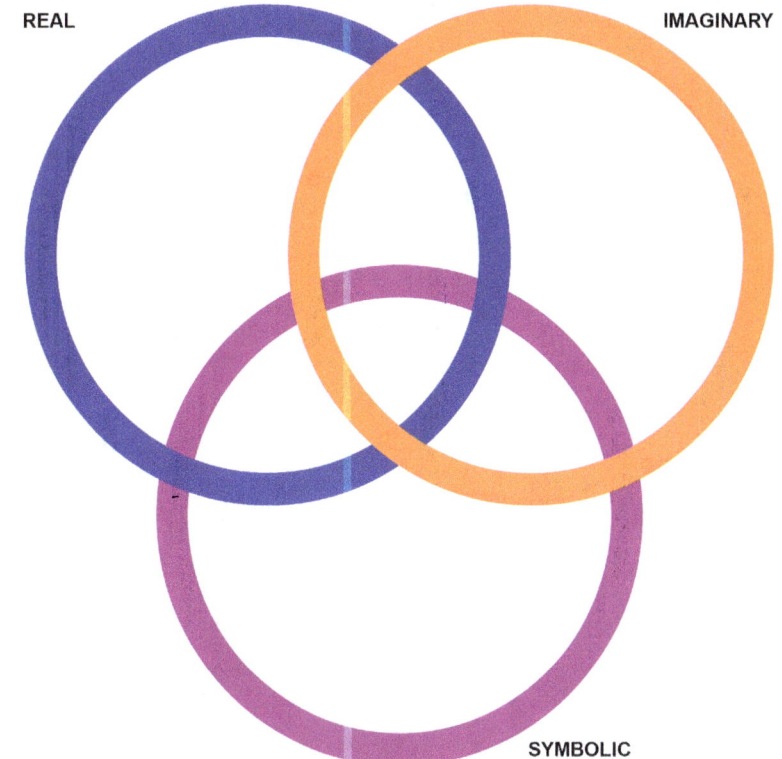

Figure 6.2 A Three-Ring Borromean Knot, Undone. Courtesy Santanu Biswas

The father is a *sinthome* because the latter compensates for the lack of and stands in for the former.[8] In other words, the *sinthome* is situated at the place of a fault, a lapsus: "What I sustain by means of the *sinthome* is . . . brought to bear at the very site where, shall we say, there is a mistake in the tracing out of the knot" (ibid., p. 80). Joyce, Lacan says, had aimed precisely at the *sinthome* in terms of his writing: "Joyce turns out to have targeted, in a privileged way, through his art, the fourth term known as the sinthome" (ibid., p. 27). He further clarifies that the father, or better still, that which is involved in the Name-of-the-Father as the fourth ring in Joyce's case, ought to be crowned with what is known as the *sinthome*:

> The father is this fourth element . . . without which nothing is possible in the knot of the symbolic, the imaginary and the real.
>
> There is, however, another term for this. This is where today I'm going to crown what is involved in the Name-of-the-Father, at the very degree to which Joyce bears it out, with what it would be most suitable to call *the sinthome*.
>
> (Lacan, 1982/2016, p. 147)

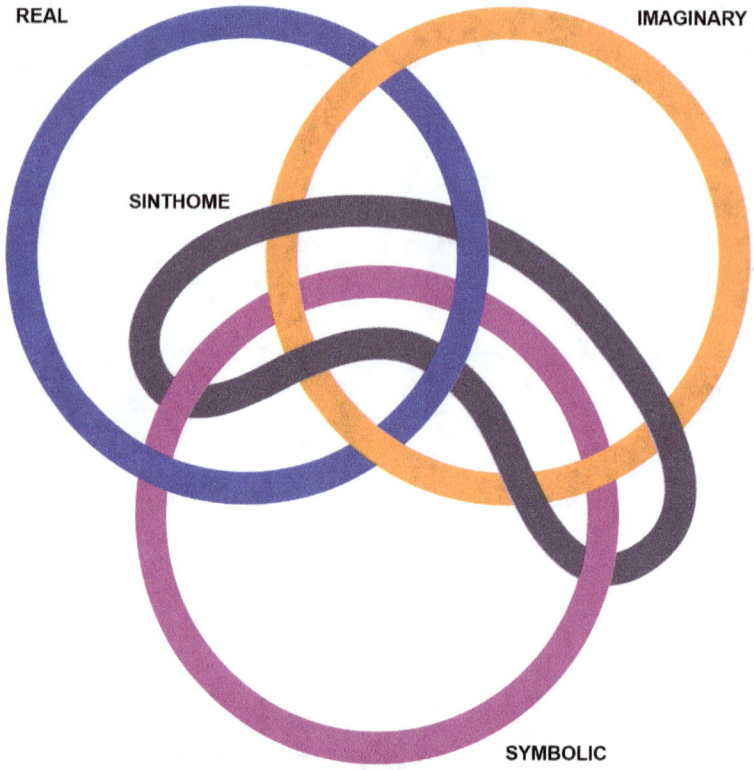

Figure 6.3 An Undone Three-Ring Borromean Knot Held Together by a Fourth Ring, the *Sinthome*. Courtesy Santanu Biswas

Thus, according to Lacan, Joyce's reason for writing is related to his desire to make a name for himself so as to compensate for his paternal failing. He asks:

> [I]sn't his desire to be an artist who would keep the whole world busy, or in any case as many people as possible, what compensates exactly for the fact that, let's say, his father was never a father for him? Not only did he teach him nothing, he neglected pretty much everything
>
> (Lacan, 2005/2016, p. 72)

Lacan finds this an unusual reason for writing: "from the very start he [Joyce] wanted to be someone whose name—very precisely the name—would endure forever. . . . No one had ever made literature like that" (Lacan, 1982/2016, p. 145). He then sums up his argument by stating:

> Joyce has a symptom that starts off from the fact that his father was a failing father, a radically failing father. He speaks of nothing but that. . . . it was in

wanting a name for himself that Joyce came up with a compensation for the paternal failing. . . . It is clear, however, that Joyce's art is something so particular that the term sinthome is really what suits it.

(Lacan, 2005/2016, p. 77)

Moving on, Lacan rightly mentions that Joyce tried to make a name for himself with the help of the academy:

The Joyceans who have enjoyment of his heresy are only to be found in academia. But Joyce quite deliberately wanted this breed to busy themselves with him. The best of it is that he managed, and beyond all measure. It has lasted, and will last further still. He expressly wanted three hundred years of it. He said he wanted to *keep the critics busy for three hundred years*, and this he shall achieve, provided God does not a-Thomize us.

(Ibid., p. 7)

Lacan repeats the same argument in his "Yale University Interview with Students, Answers to Their Questions" in 1975, adding that Joyce's avowed reason for writing was a very bad one:

The literary text, despite its appearances, has no effect. It only has an effect on academics: it stings them in the buttocks.
   When I'm interested in Joyce, it's because Joyce is trying to move beyond that; he said that scholars would be talking about him for three hundred years.
   Among the reasons [for literature's being], there are some very bad ones: Joyce's reason to become an important man, for example.

(Lacan, 1975/2022, p. 67)

Lacan is right. Joyce had said to Jacques Michel Gabriel Paul Benoist-Méchin in an interview in 1956: "I've put in so many enigmas and puzzles that it will keep the professors busy for centuries arguing over what I meant, and that's the only way of insuring one's immortality" (Ellmann, 1959/1982, p. 521). While Joyce expected his work to keep the professors busy for centuries, he expected his readers, in general, to devote their entire lives to reading his works, going by his remark to Max Eastman: "The demand that I make of my reader is that he should devote his whole life to reading my works" (Eastman, 1931, p. 100). In the same vein, Joyce wrote in *Finnegans Wake* that he expected his ideal reader to develop an ideal insomnia: "look at this prepronominal funferal to be nuzzled over a full trillion times for ever and a night till his noddle sink or swim by that ideal reader suffering from an ideal insomnia" (Joyce, 1939/1975, p. 120).
   Lacan rightly points out that "not only do academics dominate, they are pretty much the only ones to busy themselves with Joyce. This is altogether striking. . . . He hoped for nothing less than to keep them busy till the university is no more" (Lacan, 1982/2016, p. 143). Joyce has been able to produce endless work for

academics by writing extremely allusively with the help of a somewhat strange language, by leaving behind texts that are "teeming with utterly captivating problems, fascinating problems that academics can get their teeth into" (ibid., p. 143), by encouraging researchers to hunt out the enormous amount of notes and drafts he had left behind (Lacan, 2005/2016, p. 63), and by the sheer number of riddles contained in his works (ibid., p. 132).

Lacan then adds a few significant details about Joyce's *sinthome*. To begin with, he states that in Joyce's imagination, *Finnegans Wake* is a *sinthome* in the form of Jung's collective unconscious:

> Joyce slides . . . slides . . . slides to Jung, slides to the collective unconscious. There is no better proof than Joyce that the collective unconscious is a sinthome, for it cannot be said that *Finnegans Wake*, in his imagination, does not partake of this sinthome.
>
> (Ibid., p. 106)

Lacan moreover states that he became interested in Joyce precisely owing to the *sinthome* that he created, adding that this *sinthome* is perfectly unanalysable: "So, the sign of my entanglement is indeed Joyce, precisely inasmuch as what he puts forth, . . . the sinthome, and a sinthome such that there is nothing to be done to analyse it" (ibid., p. 106). Lacan had already stated in "Lituraterre" that Joyce had no need for an analysis. In the present seminar, after stating that Joyce's *sinthome* is unanalysable, he adds Joyce himself, as a Catholic brought up by Jesuits, is unanalysable: "A rock-solid catholic, as was Joyce, who never did anything to compromise his proper upbringing by the Jesuits, a catholic, a genuine article . . . well, a catholic is unanalysable" (ibid., p. 106).

Lacan is aware that Joyce had absolutely no idea of the Borromean knot aspect of his writing—"Joyce didn't have the faintest idea about the Borromean knot" (ibid., p. 123)—and he is surprised that this is so for a number of reasons. In the first place, the circular or ring-like structure of *Finnegans Wake* could have helped Joyce take note of this, though it did not:

> [H]ow can *Finnegans*, this dream, be said to be finished, since already its last word cannot help but join back up with the first, the *the* by which it ends soliciting the *riverrun* by which it starts, which indicates circularity? To spell it right out, how did Joyce manage to miss, right here, what I am at present introducing by way of the knot?
>
> (Lacan, 1982/2016, p. 148)

Besides, Joyce had no idea of Borromean rings even though his writing is replete with circles and crosses:

> It is striking that Clive Hart should lay the emphasis on the cyclic form and on the cross as being what Joyce substantially attaches himself to. Some of you

know that with this circle and this cross I have been tracing out the Borromean knot.

(Ibid., p. 147)

Not only that, in Joyce, there is no progress; there is only going around in circles. As we have already seen, the letter is recycled litter in *Finnegans Wake*, while Joyce considers literature as re-tellings, re-combinations, and re-workings of the same old letter. According to Lacan, *Finnegans Wake*, as a dream where the dreamer is the dream, brings out how the Vico myth and Madame Blavatsky's ideas are all dreams indicative of going round in circles, even though this circular movement did not enable Joyce to take note of the Borromean ring element of his work:

> *Finnegans Wake* . . . as a dream . . . denotes how Vico is a dream just as much as Madame Blavatsky's diffuse bleed, the *manvantara* and everything that ensues . . . One never *finds again*—or else, this denotes how one only ever turns round in circles—one *finds*. The only advantage of this *finding again* is to highlight what I'm indicating, that there cannot be any progress, that one only ever goes round in circles.
>
> (Lacan, 2005/2016, pp. 105–106)[9]

Finally, Lacan points out that Joyce had no idea of Borromean rings in spite of the fact that he always wrote with reference to the framing, which is akin to the ring that supports a framing:

> So, someone went to see him one day and while there asked him about a picture that depicted a view of the town of Cork. Joyce, who knew how to head his man off at the pass, replied that it was Cork. Whereupon the fellow said—*Yes, I see it's Cork. But what's that framing the image?* To which Joyce replied—*cork*.
>
> This is given as an illustration of the fact that in what he writes Joyce always goes via this relationship with framing. You just have to read the little table of points of correspondence that he provided for *Ulysses*. He gave it to Stuart Gilbert, he gave it to Linati too, albeit a slightly different one, and to a few others, including Valery Larbaud. In each thing he gathers up, each thing he recounts in order to turn it into the work of art that *Ulysses* is, the framing always bears at least a homonymic relationship with what he is presumed to be recounting as an image. For example, each of the chapters in *Ulysses* claims to be supported by a certain mode of framing, which is called, for example, *dialectic*, or *rhetoric*, or *theology*. For Joyce, this framing is linked to the very stuff of what he recounts. This is not without producing an evocation of my little rings, which are also the support of a framing.

(Ibid., p. 127)

How Reading Joyce Helped Lacan

Reading Joyce by foregrounding the expression "The letter! The litter!" proved to be highly efficacious for Lacan. In the first place, it definitely helped Lacan elaborate on some of the crucial concepts of Lacanian psychoanalysis, such as semblance, the littoral condition of the letter, lacking Name-of-the-Father, psychoses, and so on. Joyce's writing also helped Lacan frame his discussion on some of the key concepts of his later teaching, such as the real unconscious, Borromean rings, writing with holes, the symptom, the *sinthome*, jouissance, *lalangue*, et cetera, to illuminate them for the psychoanalytic community properly.[10]

Reading Joyce, moreover, helped Lacan support, and possibly even partially helped him deduce, the crucial notion of interpretation through equivocation. Although Lacan considers Carroll a "precursor of Joyce" on the question of the use of puns as portmanteau words (Lacan, 1982/2016, p. 144), he differentiates the two authors by stating that whereas Carroll's wordplay is free of equivocation—"the play on words in Carroll is always unequivocal" (Lacan, 1966/2002, p. 10)—Joyce's "The letter! The litter!" is an "equivocation" (Lacan, 2007, p. 113), and his play on words in general is equivocal (Lacan, 2005/2016). In this context, Lacan states in the seminar on *The Sinthome*:

> [W]hen all is said and done the equivoque is all we have as a weapon against the symptom. . . . The second stage consists in playing on the equivoque that might free up something of the sinthome. Indeed, interpretation operates solely through equivoques.
>
> (Ibid., p. 9)

Not only that, Lacan states in the December 1975 "Columbia University Lecture on the Symptom" that insofar as the analyst's reaction is conveyed with signifiers rather than with words, it always "lends itself to equivocation" owing to the "sonorous element" of signifiers, whose resonance with the unconscious is what the analyst should seek to ensure (Lacan, 1976/2022, p. 82). Moreover, interpretation as equivocation has the advantages of touching on jouissance, of aiming at the real unconscious, and of going against what Lacan had elsewhere called the "mirage of truth" in relation to transference (Lacan, 1973/1998, p. viii). It is not by chance that Lacan had neither spoken about interpretation through equivocation nor about interpretation being operative or possible only through equivocation, not even about equivocation being the psychoanalyst's only weapon against the symptom as well as the means to freeing up the *sinthome*—let alone about the ability of equivocal interpretation to at once address the mirage of truth, jouissance, and the real unconscious—before he had taken to reading Joyce.

Lacan is moreover able to shed valuable light on an aspect of the psychoanalytic act with the help of the following riddle of Stephen in *Ulysses*, whose answer is "*The fox burying his grandmother under a holly bush*":

> *The cock crew,*
> *The sky was blue:*

The bells in heaven
Were striking eleven.
Tis time for this poor soul
To go to heaven.
      (Lacan, 2005/2016,
           p. 57)

Trying to explain "what kind of echo might this have . . . for those . . . who are analysts", Lacan says that the analysand poses a riddle for the analyst in terms of his symptom, which is quite like Stephen's riddle. For instance, the analysand's symptom or riddle of summoning the maid to show her the stain of tomato ketchup on the table cloth discussed in the introduction. Analysis consists of the analyst's particularly silly response to the riddle in terms of a splice between the imaginary and unconscious knowledge or the symbolic with an aim to obtain a meaning:

> That's what analysis is. It's the response to a riddle. Moreover, it's a response—it has to be said, from this example—that is quite especially daft. This is precisely why one must keep a firm hold on the rope. . . .
>
> Meaning emanates from a field that lies between the imaginary and the symbolic. That goes without saying.
>
> All of this is done to obtain a meaning, which is the object of the analyst's response to what the analysand exposes at length through his symptom.
>
> (Ibid., pp. 57–58)

In addition, reading Joyce in terms of the expression "The letter! The litter!" enabled Lacan to highlight the weight of the word "literature" itself. Apart from writing with litter, in the form of hollowed out or distorted or over-stuffed letters, Joyce wrote partly by putting together fragments of conversations, writings, languages, literary works, and scraps and pieces of miscellaneous other things, always picked up and recycled in a disjointed or distorted form, very much like a rag picker stitching together his collection to form a dress. Hart writes:

> Joyce has been variously praised and reviled for filling his later books with literary rubbish—catch-phrases, clichés, journalese, popular songs, and the worst kind of gush from girls' weeklies. It is undeniable that he found considerable delight in such trash, and a delight that was not always critical.
>
> (Hart, 1962, p. 31).

As a matter of fact, Joyce's very method of collecting material for *Finnegans Wake* was a deliberately non-systematic one. Dirk Van Hulle captured this creative haphazardness of Joyce's method with the remark: "[A] note from a newspaper can end up next to a note from, say, the *Encyclopaedia Britannica*, without any distinction. This obliteration of the original context creates opportunities for new associations" (Van Hulle, 2008, p. 89). In this, Joyce's collection functions like the unconscious, in which all kinds of scraps of writings can easily coexist without any conflict or contradiction. Van Hulle rightly adds that Joyce "decomposed" external material while composing *Finnegans Wake* (ibid.). Correspondingly, Shem's house in *Finnegans Wake* is littered with a bizarre catalogue of things that contribute to his art. His house is described as "persianly literatured with burst loveletters, telltale stories, stickyback snaps, doubtful eggshells, bouchers, flints, borers, puffers, amygdaloid almonds, rindless raisins, alphybettyformed verbage, vivlical viasses, ompiter dictas, visus umbique, ahems and ahahs"; the list goes on (Joyce, 1939/1975, p. 183). In this way, Joyce turned the letter into litter and then created a new letter with its help through his writing. This is the reason that Lacan did not feel the need to look beyond Joyce's equivocation of the letter and the litter to emphasise the weight of the word "literature" itself, as he states in "Joyce the Symptom": "And to underscore the weightiness of the word *literature*, I shall utter the equivoque that Joyce often plays on—*letter, litter*.[11] The letter is litter" (Lacan, 1982/2016, p. 145). Since the letter is litter following the publication of the later works of Joyce, Lacan thinks literature itself owed its importance to the littering of the letter and must be viewed specifically in relation to this fact. Here, littering stands for both recycling that characterises almost all literature and rendering the letter enjoyable but meaningless that literature turned into at the hands of Joyce.

Not only that, Joyce's writing enabled Lacan to come across a work that is designed like a Borromean knot, and as an authentic one at that, insofar as Joyce himself had no idea of this:

> Well, I think that, thanks to Joyce, we touch upon something I hadn't thought of.
> I didn't think of it straightaway, but it occurred to me in time. Joyce's text is fashioned just like a Borromean knot. And what strikes me is that he's the only one whose notice this escaped. There's not the faintest trace in his whole life's work of anything that looks like one. This seems to me, however, to be more of a sign of authenticity.
> (Lacan, 2005/2016, p. 132)

Furthermore, Lacan's reading of Joyce undoubtedly facilitated his broad shift of focus on two levels. First, Joyce's works supported the displacement of Lacan's focus from the Freudian unconscious to the Lacanian symptom that characterises his later teaching as a whole, as well as a part of his latest teaching that followed. Accordingly, following his engagement with Joyce, whose writings often avowedly dealt with symptoms, such as "paralysis" in *Dubliners*, Lacan not only thinks that works of literature and art ought to be explained in terms of the symptom rather than the unconscious, but he stresses moreover in the seminar that he gave the following year that what marks the crucial end of analysis of the subject is not his identification with his unconscious but rather his identification with his symptom (Lacan, 1976–1977, p. 4. My translation). And second, Joyce's works helped him shift his emphasis from the Freudian unconscious, which is symbolic and must be grasped in terms of the Other, the signifier, language, and meaning, to the Lacanian unconscious, which is real and must be grasped in terms of the One, the letter, *lalangue,* and jouissance.

Last but not least, Lacan's engagement with Joyce enabled him to make a pathbreaking contribution to the field of Joyce studies by shedding valuable light on the cause, the effect, the very process, as well as the psychological ramifications of his littering the letter from a singularly original perspective.

Notes

1. Parts of this chapter have been published in Biswas, 2023.
2. Joyce wrote four plays in all, among which only the last two have survived. He wrote his first two plays—*A Brilliant Career* and *Dream Stuff*, respectively—in 1900 when he was still a young man living in Dublin. None of these plays have survived. In 1902, Joyce himself destroyed *A Brilliant Career*, his very first play, which he had dedicated to his own soul. He had sent the manuscript to William Archer, whose commentary on the play has survived and is the most important source of information on this lost play. Joyce's two published plays are *Exiles* and the "Circe" episode, or Episode 15 of *Ulysses*, written in the form of a play.
3. The nineteen relatively less pertinent instances of the use of the expression "litter" or coinages based upon it are the following, in their chronological order of appearance: "clittering up" (Joyce, 1939/1975, p. 5); "Countlessness of livestories have netherfallen by this plage, flick as flowflakes, litters from aloft" (ibid., p. 17); "the hour of the twattering of bards in the twitterlitter" (ibid., p. 37); "litterish fragments lurk dormant in the paunch" (ibid., p. 66); "a cloudletlitter" (ibid., p. 73); "ayes and neins to a litter" (ibid., p. 202); "illitterettes" (ibid., p. 284); "Concoct an equoangular trillitter" (ibid., p. 286); "jetsam litterage of convolvuli" (ibid., p. 292); "*glitteraglatteraglutt*" (ibid., p. 349); "skittered his litters" (ibid., p. 370); "Honour thy farmer and my litters" (ibid., p. 413); "The Reverest Adam Foundlitter" (ibid., p. 420), "laying out his litterery bed" (ibid., p. 422); "*artis litterarumque patrona*" (ibid., p. 495); "an absquelitteris puttagonnianne" (ibid., p. 512); "a litterydistributer in Saint Patrick's Lavatory" (ibid., p. 530); "outcast mastiff littered in blood currish" (ibid., p. 534); and "litteringture of kidlings" (ibid., p. 570).
4. Hart makes a similar though not identical point when he states that:

   > The essential value of the pun or portmanteau-word in *Finnegans Wake* lies . . . in its capacity to compress much meaning into little space. . . . A good example is the word 'paltipsypote' (Joyce, 1939/1975, p. 337) from the 'Scene in the Public', which neatly integrates 'pal', 'tipsy' and 'pote' into the idea of 'participating' in a round of Guinness.
   >
   > (Hart, 1962, pp. 32–33)

   Even though both Hart and Lacan talk about packing a lot into a single word or coinage, the examples that they gave indicate that, whereas Hart was thinking of coinages that resulted from the simple combination of a number of complete regular words, Lacan was thinking of coinages that resulted from the complex overlap of different speech sounds, or fragments of speech sounds, evoking different expressions.
5. Joyce's previous observation that Jung and Freud are "different", which he had expressed in a letter to Weaver dated 24th June, 1921, by stating that "Doctor Jung (the Swiss Tweedledum who is not to be confused with the Viennese Tweedledee, Dr. Freud)" (Joyce, 1957/1966, p. 166), culminates here in his allusion to the "split" between them. Moreover, since Jung had diagnosed Joyce's daughter Lucia as schizophrenic, much to Joyce's dismay, he seems to be pointing to the split or schizophrenia between Freud and

Jung in the form of a caustic innuendo—insofar as schizophrenia is defined in terms of a split—in addition to making the ironic suggestion: physicians, heal thyselves.

6 Lacan would go on to play on Joyce's name once again: "I would say that Joyce is an *a-Freud*, playing on the word *affreux*. Thus, he is an *a-Joyce*" (Lacan, 2005/2016, p. 101). Lacan, who played on his own name in 1975—"Jacques Lacan, they don't have a clue, *Jules Lacue* would do just as well" (Lacan, 1982/2016, p. 141)—plays on the sound of his own proper name so as to reduce it to a common noun, following the instance of Joyce:

> Well, listen now, since I've reached this point at this hour, you must have had your *claque*, your fill, and even your *Jaclaque*, because I'll add, too, the *han* that shall stand as the expression of the relief I feel for having completed this path today. So it is that I reduce my proper name to the most common noun.
>
> (Lacan, 2005/2016, p. 73)

7 Roudinesco further informs us:

> St. Charles Borromeo, one of the family's most illustrious representatives, was a hero of the Counter-Reformation. A nephew of Pope Pius IV and himself a cardinal, he introduced a stricter discipline into clerical life in the sixteenth century. He distinguished himself by his charitable works during the plague of 1576 . . . The famous Borromean islands on Lake Maggiore were conquered a century later by a Count Borromeo, who gave them their name and turned them into one of Italy's most baroque landscapes.
>
> (Roudinesco, 1993/1997, pp. 363–364)

8 In the classical teaching of Lacan, the father is a symptom because he is a metaphor. For instance, the symptom of little Hans in Freud's famous case history is the phobia of horses. The boy was afraid that the horse would bite him. Analysis revealed that the horse represented his father. Thus the horse was a metaphor of Hans' father as well as his symptom. In the 1957 essay in the *Écrits* entitled "The Instance of the Letter in the Unconscious or Reason Since Freud", Lacan defines a metaphor as a "signifying substitution" of one signifier for another: "Now we turn to metaphoric structure, indicating that it is in the substitution of signifier for signifier that a signification effect is produced that is poetic or creative, in other words, that brings the signification in question into existence" (Lacan, 1957/2006, p. 429). Accordingly, the father, or more precisely the Name-of-the-Father, as a signifying substitution of the mother's desire, is a metaphor, as Lacan explains in the seminar on the *Formations of the Unconscious*, where he describes the father as a metaphor:

> The father isn't a real object . . . [T]he father is a metaphor.
> What is a metaphor? . . . A metaphor is a signifier that comes to take the place of another signifier. That is the mainspring, the essential and unique mainspring, of the father's intervention in the Oedipus complex.
>
> (Lacan, 1998/2017, p. 158)

Lacan reiterates in his 1958 paper "The Direction of Treatment and the Principles of Its Power" that the paternal metaphor is: "[T]he substitution of one term for another to produce a metaphorical effect" (Lacan, 1961/2006, p. 519). A symptom is a metaphor for the same reason. One type of symptom-formation specified by Freud is substitute-formation. Underlying the strange symptom of Freud's female patient discussed in the introduction is her unconsciously executed signifying substitution of the stain of tomato ketchup on the table cloth for the stain of red ink, representing blood, on the bed sheet. This is the reason that Lacan writes in "The Instance of the Letter in the Unconscious or Reason Since Freud": "For the symptom *is* a metaphor, whether one likes to admit it or not" (Lacan, 1957/2006, p. 439).

9 Lacan adds in this context that Freud's imponderable death drive is another indicator of the fact that there is no progress:

> Even so, there is perhaps another way of explaining that there is no progress. It is that there is no progress but bearing the stamp of death, which Freud underscores by *triebing* this death, if I can put it like that, by making it a *Trieb*.
> The death drive is the real inasmuch as it can only be pondered qua impossible. This means that each time it rears its head it is imponderable. To approach this impossible could never constitute a hope, because this imponderable is death, whose real grounding is that it cannot be pondered.
> (Lacan, 2005/2016, p. 106)

10 For a concise account of Lacan's "later teaching", see Biswas, 2018.
11 In English in the original.

References

Balzac, Honoré de (1911). *Ursule Mirouët*. A. Perche (Original work published 1841).
Biswas, Santanu (2018, December 2015). Locating and Annotating the Expression 'The Later Teaching of Lacan'. In Russell Grigg (Ed.) *Psychoanalysis Lacan, Electronic Journal*. Vol 1, Australia, Lacan Circle of Melbourne, 28–32. Available at https://lacancircle.com.au/psychoanalysislacan-journal/psychoanalysislacan-volume-1/locating-and-annotating-the-expression/ (Accessed on 7th January, 2024).
Biswas, Santanu (2023, February). Why does Jacques Lacan Highlight James Joyce's Expression The letter! The litter!? In David Ferraro, Dominique Hecq, Jonathan Redmond (Eds.) *Psychoanalysis Lacan, Electronic Journal*. Vol 6, Australia, Lacan Circle of Australia, 51–68. Available at https://lacancircle.com.au/wp-content/uploads/2023/02/08-Why-does-Jacques-Lacan-Highlight-James-Joyces-Expression.pdf (Accessed on 7th January, 2024).
Cheng, Vincent (1984 [1979]). *Shakespeare and Joyce: A Study of Finnegans Wake*. University Park and Pennsylvania State University Press.
DiBernard, Barbara (1980). *Alchemy and Finnegans Wake*. State University of New York Press.
Eastman, Max (1931). *The Literary Mind: Its Place in an Age of Science*. Charles Scribner's Sons.
Ellmann, Richard (1982). *James Joyce*. Oxford University Press (Original work published 1959).
Flaubert, Gustave (1919). *Madame Bovary: A Study of Provincial Life*. Eleanor Marx-Aveling Trans. Brentano's (Original work published 1856).
Gordon, John (1986). *Finnegans Wake: A Plot Summary*. Syracuse University Press.
Gordon, John (2020). *John Gordon's Finnegans Wake Blog*, Book I. Available at https://johngordonfinnegan.weebly.com/book-i (Last accessed on 17th October, 2022).
Hart, Clive (1962). *Structure and Motif in Finnegans Wake*. Northwestern University Press.
Joyce, James (1966). *Letters of James Joyce*, Vol. I. Stuart Gilbert (Ed.) The Viking Press (Original work published 1957).
Joyce, James (1975). *Finnegans Wake*. Faber and Faber (Original work published 1939).
Joyce, James (1977–1979). *The James Joyce Archive*, Vol. 39. Garland.
Joyce, James (1996). The Encounter. In Robert Scholes and A. Walton Litz (Eds.), *Dubliners: Text, Criticism and Notes*, 19–28. Penguin Books (Original work published 1914).
Joyce, James (2000). *Ulysses*. Penguin Classics in Association with the Bodley Head (Original work published 1922).
Lacan, Jacques (1975). The Seminar of Jacques Lacan. Book XXII. R.S.I., 1974–1975. Unpublished translation by Jack W. Stone of Le Séminaire de Jacques Lacan. Livre XXII.

R.S.I., 1974–1975. In *Ornicar? Bulletin périodique du champ freudien*, Lyse, N°2, 1975, 87–105; N°3, 1975, 96–110; N°4, 1975, 92–106; and N°5, 1975, 17–66. Available at www.scribd.com/doc/33124001/10724-TheSeminar-of-Jacques (Accessed on 17th July, 2023).

Lacan, Jacques (1976–1977). Le Séminaire de Jacques Lacan. Livre XXIV. L'insu que sait de l'une-bévue s'aile à mourre, 1976–1977. Partly published. In *Ornicar? Bulletin périodique du champ freudien*, Lyse, N°12–13, 1977, 21–32; N°14, 1978, 33–39; N°15, 1978, 49–68; and N°17–18, 1978, 69–74. Available at http://staferla.free.fr/S24/S24%20 L%27INSU .... pdf (Accessed on 11th January, 2024).

Lacan, Jacques (1998). *The Seminar of Jacques Lacan. Book XI. The Four Fundamental Concepts of Psychoanalysis, 1964*. In Alan Sheridan Trans. W.W. Norton (Original work published 1973).

Lacan, Jacques (1998). *The Seminar of Jacques Lacan. Book XX. Encore: On Feminine Sexuality, The Limits of Love and Knowledge, 1972–1973*. In Bruce Fink Trans. W.W. Norton (Original work published 1975).

Lacan, Jacques (2002). Hommage rendu à Lewis Carroll. In *Ornicar? Revue du champ freudien*, N°50, 2003, Navarin, 9–12 (Original text delivered on French radio France Culture on 31st December, 1966).

Lacan, Jacques (2006). The Direction of Treatment and the Principles of Its Power. In Bruce Fink Trans., in collaboration with Héloïse Fink and Russell Grigg, *Écrits: The First Complete Edition in English*. W.W. Norton, 489–542 (Original work published 1961).

Lacan, Jacques (2006). The Instance of the Letter in the Unconscious or Reason Since Freud. In Bruce Fink Trans., in collaboration with Héloïse Fink and Russell Grigg, *Écrits: The First Complete Edition in English*. W.W. Norton, 412–441 (Original work published 1957).

Lacan, Jacques (2007). Leçon Sur Lituraterre. In *Le Séminaire de Jacques Lacan. Livre XVIII. D'un discours qui ne serait pas du semblant, 1971*. Texte Établi par Jacques-Alain Miller. Seuil, 113–127.

Lacan, Jacques (2016). Joyce the Symptom. In Adrian Price Trans. *The Seminar of Jacques Lacan, Book XXIII: 1975–1976: The Sinthome*. Polity Press, 141–148 (Original work published 1982).

Lacan, Jacques (2016). *The Seminar of Jacques Lacan, Book XXIII: 1975–1976: The Sinthome*. In Adrian Price Trans. Polity Press (Original work published 2005).

Lacan, Jacques (2017). *The Seminar of Jacques Lacan. Book V. Formations of the Unconscious, 1957–1958*. In Russell Grigg Trans. Polity Press (Original work published 1998).

Lacan, Jacques (2022, April). Columbia University Lecture on the Symptom. In Russell Grigg Trans. *The Lacanian Review: Hurly-Burly: Journal of the New Lacanian School and the World Association of Psychoanalysis*. American Lacan, Issue 12, 75–84 (Original work published 1976).

Lacan, Jacques (2022, April). Yale University Interview with Students, Answers to Their Questions. In Philip Dravers Trans. *The Lacanian Review: Hurly-Burly: Journal of the New Lacanian School and the World Association of Psychoanalysis. American Lacan*, Issue 12, 63–68 (Original work published 1975).

Mcluhan, Eric (1997). *The Role of Thunder in Finnegans Wake*. University of Toronto Press.

Miller, Jacques-Alain (2012). Joyce with Lacan. In Santanu Biswas (Ed.) and Russell Grigg Trans. *The Literary Lacan: From Literature to Lituraterre and Beyond*. Seagull Books, 1–7 (Original work published 1987).

Miller, Jacques-Alain (2013). L'or à gueule of Lituraterre. Adrian Price Trans. In *Hurly-Burly: The International Lacanian Journal of Psychoanalysis*, Issue 9, New Lacanian School, 39–50 (Original work published 1999).

Proust, Marcel (2014). *The Guermantes Way*. In C. K. Scott Moncrieff Trans. Available at https://gutenberg.net.au/ebooks03/0300411.txt (Accessed on 17th July, 2023) (Original work published 1920–1921).
Roudinesco, Elisabeth (1997). *Jacques Lacan*. In Barbara Bray Trans. Columbia University Press (Original work published 1993).
Sandulescu, Constantin George (Ed.) (2012). *Joyce Lexicography Volume Five: A Lexicon of Small Languages in Finnegans Wake*. Contemporary Literature Press.
Tindall, William York (1959). *A Reader's Guide to James Joyce*. The Noonday Press.
Tindall, William York (1969). *A Reader's Guide to Finnegans Wake*. Farrar, Straus and Giroux.
Van Hulle, Dirk (2008). *Manuscript Genetics, Joyce's Know-How, Beckett's Nohow*. University of Florida Press.

Index

Aletheia 29–30
alienation 154
anal drive 147–148
Antigone 2, 3, 9, 10, 78–115, 127; beautiful 98–99, 101, 102; beauty-effect 102, 104; Choral ode on man 92–93; Chthonic laws 93–95; Creon's mistake 85–90; criminal desire 96; cylindrical anamorphosis 97–99; desire for death 90–99; ethics of psychoanalysis 109–113; Hegel's reading 78–84; *kommos* 10, 91, 105; Lacan critiques Hegel 84–85; language and singular individual 95–96; limit of life 99–106
Apollinaire, Guillaume 12n4
Aquinas, Saint Thomas 102, 146, 166n8
Aristotle 84; topology 6; error of judgement 89; catharsis 102, 103, 114; ethics 90, 110
Atè 2, 89, 90, 93, 104, 128; and beauty 102, 104; and criminal desire 96; as destiny 96–97, 127, 129; as limit 91–92
Aubert, Jacques 166n8, 173, 174, 184, 189
Auden, Wystan Hugh 12n2, 118, 140

Barnacle, Nora 6, 147, 168n18, 187, 189
beauty: and anamorphic art 97, 99; beyond beauty 126, 127; and desire 101–102, 104; and Joyce 166n8; and pain 106
Beckett, Samuel 12n2, 39n6, 40, 145, 169, 170, 207; and avowal 149–151, 166–167n11; and end of analysis 152–153, 167n12
Belleforest, François de 42, 55, 59
Benoist-Méchin, Jacques Michel Gabriel Paul 197
The Bible 26, 40, 116, 166n9, 170

Binswanger, Ludwig 114, 114n1
Bonaparte, Marie 9, 12n2, 13, 162, 163, 168n17, 169
Borromean chain *see* Borromean knot
Borromean knot 6, 146, 190, 191, 192–196, 198–199, 202
Borromean ring 6, 188, 191, 194, 198, 199, 200
Bugliani, Ann 140, 140n2, 140n4

Carroll, Lewis 1, 3, 200, 206
castration 29, 43, 68, 70, 72, 138, 164
catharsis 102–104, 113
Cervantes, Miguel de 11n1
Cheng, François 154–155
Cheng, Vincent 179–180, 205
Claudel, Paul 1, 12n3, 116–119
comedy 1, 10, 13n7, 132, 133
Cooke, Philip Pendleton 168–169n19
Cornec, Gilles 118, 141
The Coûfontaine Trilogy 119–124; Oedipal father 132–134; psychoanalyst's position in transference 130–131; structural repetition of family myths 134–138; symbolic affects flesh 124–126; Sygne's "No" 127–129; Sygne's sacrifice 126–127; three stages of desire 138–140
Crébillon, Jolyot de 16, 28, 39n2, 40, 164

Dasein 27–29, 38, 164
death drive 97, 100, 105, 205n9
Derrida, Jacques 18, 35, 36, 37, 40, 84
The Dialogue of the Dogs 11n1
DiBernard, Barbara 179, 205
Dixon, Vladimir 39n6, 40, 41, 145, 169
Don Quixote 11n1
Dubliners 175, 202, 205

Duras, Marguerite 1, 2, 3, 5–6, 13, 14

Eastman, Max 181, 197, 205
Ellmann, Richard 39, 174, 181, 197, 205
end of analysis 145, 146, 152–153, 167n13, 202
erasure 143, 144, 153–154, 155, 157, 159, 160
Ernout, Alfred and Meillet, Alfred 142–143, 170
Exiles 168n18, 170, 173, 187, 203n2

fantasy 5, 46, 51; and Claudel 119; and end of analysis 152–153; of Hamlet 54, 55–61; and Klein 130; and Sade 106
Finnegans Wake 3, 14, 145–146, 148, 170, 173; and end of analysis 2, 146; and litter 5, 143, 146, 174–186, 200–207; and madness 186–187; and *sinthome* 190–199
first stroke 153–155
Fliess, Wilhelm 1, 13, 135
foreclosure *see Verwerfung*
Freud, Anna 13, 130
Freud, Sigmund: *Delusion and Dream in Jensen's Gradiva* 1, 7, 9, 13; "Dostoevsky and Parricide" 1, 71, 76, 76n1, 162, 170; *Interpretation of Dreams* 1, 3, 13, 39n3, 76n1, 77, 135; *Introductory Lectures on Psychoanalysis* 8–9, 13; *The Psychopathology of Everyday Life* 34, 60–61, 77, 182; "Some Character-Types met with in Psychoanalytic Work" 1, 7, 13; *Totem and Taboo* 68, 69, 77, 133, 141

Gargano, James W. 169, 170
Genet, Jean 1, 3, 10
Gide, André 1, 5, 14, 117, 143
Goethe, Johann Wolfgang von 1, 2, 42, 84, 90, 94, 95, 102
Gordon, John 176, 179, 184, 205
Grammaticus, Saxo 42, 55

Hamlet 2, 3, 4, 7, 9, 10, 11–12n2, 42–43, 77; dissolution of Oedipus complex 68–70, 74; father in 132–133, 140n3; Hamlet's identifications 62–68; Hamlet's relationship with Ophelia 55–62; inaction 52–55; and *Oedipus Rex* 1, 2, 70–76; Other's desire 43–48; other's time 48–52; second death 100–101

Hart, Clive 174, 184, 198, 201, 203n4, 205
Hegel, Georg Wilhelm Friedrich 27, 63, 64, 114–115, 132; on *Antigone* 78–84, 85, 90
Heidegger, Martin 27, 28, 29–30, 40, 84, 115
hole: in knowledge 5, 157; in reality 59; in the written 4–6, 158, 159, 163, 165, 166, 167n15, 200
The Holy Bible see The Bible
hysteria 7, 47, 51–52, 76n3, 173
hysteric *see* hysteria

ideal ego 62–64
identification 60; imaginary 34; with object 152; with *sinthome* 146; with symptom 202; *see also* Hamlet's identifications under *Hamlet*

Johnson, Barbara 36, 37, 40
jouissance 3, 113, 125, 132, 148, 152, 158, 200, 203; and Joyce's writing 6, 185–186; and knowledge 10, 145, 148, 155, 156, 157; and meaning 9, 10, 159, 167
Joyce, James: his daughter 145–146, 189–190, 203–204n5; his father 6, 181–182, 189–192, 195–197, 200; Lacan helped by reading 200–203; letter and litter 174–186; and madness 188–191; and *sinthome* 191–199; and symptom 186–188
Jung, Carl 145–146, 170, 171, 184, 198, 203–204n5

Kant, Immanuel 90, 106–109, 113, 115
katharsis see catharsis
King James Version of the Holy Bible see The Bible
Klein, Melanie 130
Klotz, Jean-Pierre 154, 170
knowledge 5, 72, 131, 132, 135, 192, 201; *see also* jouissance and knowledge
kun-yomi 160–161

Lacan, Jacques: *Desire and Its Interpretation* 4, 7, 14, 42–77; *The Ego in Freud's Theory and in the Technique of Psychoanalysis* 2, 4, 14, 15, 20, 27, 33, 34–35, 40, 84, 100, 115, 145; *Encore: On Feminine Sexuality, The Limits of Love and Knowledge* 153–154, 158, 170, 173, 182, 186, 192–193, 206;

Formations of the Unconscious 61, 77, 192, 204n8, 206; *The Four Fundamental Concepts Psychoanalysis* 5, 98, 114n2, 115, 131, 141, 157–158, 170, 200, 206; *From an Other to the other* 146–147, 149, 171; *Identification* 142–143, 154, 170–171; "The Instance of the Letter in the Unconscious or Reason Since Freud" 143, 204n8, 206; "Joyce the Symptom" 9, 171, 173–174, 180–183, 185, 202, 206; "Kant with Sade" 108–109, 115; *L'insu que sait de l'une-bévue s'aile à mourre* 13n6, 14, 202, 206; "Lituraterre" 4, 5, 14, 142–172, 173, 185, 198; "Logical Time and the Assertion of Anticipated Certainty: A New Sophism" 22, 41, 68, 77; "The Mirror Stage as Formative of the *I* Function as Revealed in Psychoanalytic Experience" 62–64, 77; *The Moment to Conclude* 9–10, 14; "The Neurotic's Individual Myth, Or Poetry and Truth in Neurosis" 134, 135, 141; *The Object of Psychoanalysis* 4–5, 14; *On a Discourse that Might not be a Semblance* 5, 14, 37, 41, 142–172; *The Psychoses* 149, 170; *R.S.I.* 161, 170, 193–194, 205–206; "The Seminar on 'The Purloined Letter'" 15–41, 66, 145, 164, 173; *The Sinthome* 4, 8, 14, 146, 148, 161, 166n8, 168n18, 171, 173–207; *Television* 8, 14, 146, 170, 173; *Transference* 2, 12n3, 13n7, 14, 97, 116–141, 147–148, 171; "Yale University Interview with Students, Answers to Their Questions" 7, 14, 173, 197, 206; "Yale University: Kanzer Seminar" 9, 14, 173
lalangue 6, 9, 10, 148, 185–186, 187, 189, 200, 203
Lao-tzu 154–155
Laurent, Éric 25, 41, 155, 167n14, 171
Lévi-Strauss, Claude 25, 41, 134, 140n5, 141, 164
little Hans 204n8
littoral 3, 9, 10, 143, 144, 145, 148, 155, 156–157, 165, 170, 185, 200; *see also* littoral discourse and semblance under "Lituraterre"
"Lituraterre" 142–144; literary wastes of Joyce and Beckett 145–151; littoral discourse and semblance 157–160; psychoanalytic literary criticism 162–166; Siberian river and its embankment 153–157; writing effect in Japanese tongue 160–161

McCormick, Edith 145, 146
Mcluhan, Eric 179, 206
Meno 26, 41
Miller, Jacques-Alain 2, 3, 14, 41, 141, 142, 152–153, 158, 159, 162, 166n10, 170, 171, 180, 181, 182, 185, 188, 191, 206
Milner, Jean-Claude 39n2, 41
Murray, Gilbert 103

Name-of-the-Father 68, 95, 100, 158, 189, 190, 191, 192, 195, 200, 204n8
neurosis 7, 12n2, 21, 40, 51, 54, 56, 68, 76n3, 113, 129, 134–135, 141, 152, 162, 167n13, 192
neurotic *see* neurosis
Nobus, Dany 14, 143, 146, 167n14, 171

object *a* 4–5, 55, 57, 60, 61, 62, 155, 158, 161, 162
object small *a see* object *a*
objet petit a see object *a*
obsessional 7, 8, 51–52, 54, 76n3, 134, 141
Oedipus at Colonus 84, 129, 152
Oedipus complex 1, 2, 8, 9, 10, 11n1, 11n2, 11n3, 61, 77, 116, 162, 167–168n16, 192, 204n8; *see also* dissolution of Oedipus complex under *Hamlet*; *see also* Oedipal father under *The Coûfontaine Trilogy*
Ogasawara, Shin'ya 161, 171
the One 152–153, 203
Ordinary psychosis 152, 167n13, 191
on-yomi 160–161
Orosz, István 98–99, 115

Peirce, Charles Sanders 154
phallus: Gertrude's desire for 43–47; mortal phallus 66–68; and Ophelia 58–60; there and not there 66–68; thing of nothing 74–76
Plato 13n7, 26, 40, 41, 90, 103, 130, 131, 141
A Portrait of the Artist as a Young Man 173, 181, 186, 187, 191–192
primal crime *see* primal parricide
primal horde 68, 69, 133
primal law 69–70
primal parricide 70, 133

primal repression 162
primal scene 12n4, 15, 16, 17, 19
psycho-biography 1, 4, 6, 76, 162, 163
"The Purloined Letter": address is Law
   26–27; be and not be 22–23; Eat
   your *Dasein*! 27–29; insistence and
   ex-sistence 19–22; intersubjectivity
   15, 18, 19, 20, 21, 22, 33; letter's
   arrival at destination 35–38; money
   and transference 30–32; narration
   17–18; odd or even 33–35; of a woman
   24–25; singular materiality 23; *see also*
   psychoanalytic literary criticism under
   "Lituraterre"

Rabaté, Jean-Michel 11–12n1, 14, 41, 116,
   121, 124–125, 127, 140n2, 141, 144,
   167n15, 172
Rabelais, François 1, 167n14, 194
Rat Man 134–135
The Ravishing of Lol Stein 5–6, 13
refusal *see Versagung*
Regnault, François 127, 141
repetition 15–17, 19, 21, 34, 116; *see also*
   structural repetition of family myths
   under *The Coûfontaine Trilogy*
Roudinesco, Elisabeth 29, 38, 41, 154–155,
   172, 194, 204n7, 207

Sade, Marquis de 1, 3, 78, 101, 106–109,
   115, 127
Sandulescu, Constantin George 181, 207
second death 99–100; and Antigone 100,
   109; and beautiful 101; and Hamlet
   100–101; and Polyneices 90, 100; and
   Sade 101; and Sygne 126–127, 128
semblable 62, 63–64, 67
semblance 10, 145, 157–158, 159–160, 200
separation 155
sexual relationship 163–164, 165, 168n18,
   187
Silberstein, Eduard 11n1, 13
sinthome 2, 6, 9, 10, 146, 148, 152, 153,
   188, 189, 190–191, 200, 206; *see also*
   sinthome under James Joyce
Socrates 26, 29, 90, 130–131

Sophocles 1, 2, 3, 11n1, 78–115, 134, 162,
   167–168n16, 172
Sowley, Thelma 155–156, 172
Spoonerism 143–144
Spooner, William Archibald 143, 144, 170
Steiner, George 116, 117, 118–119, 124, 141
The Symposium 130, 131, 141
symptom 152, 190; and equivocation
   200–201; and father 194, 196–197,
   204n8; and jouissance 185, 186; as
   metaphor 6, 68–69, 204n8; unanalysable
   183, 188, 189; and unconscious 7–9,
   13n6, 174, 202–203; *see also* Joyce's
   father under James Joyce; *see also*
   symptom under James Joyce

Tel Quel 159, 167n14, 181
thelanguage *see lalangue*
Tindall, William York 178–179, 185, 207
tragedy 1, 9–10, 80, 90, 99, 102, 103, 104,
   127, 132, 139
transference 3, 10, 11n1, 116, 130–131,
   141, 152, 200; *see also* money and
   transference under "The Purloined
   Letter"
truth 7–8, 18, 21, 37, 51, 56, 108–109, 151,
   152, 158, 179, 200; *see also* Aletheia

the ultra-pass 152–153
Ulysses 148, 170, 173, 175, 181, 182, 184,
   187, 191, 192, 199, 200–201, 203n2,
   205
unary trait *see* first stroke
Ur-Verdrängung see primal repression

Valente, Joseph 36, 41
Van Hulle, Dirk 201–202, 207
Versagung 116, 128–129
Verwerfung 59, 189, 192
Vico, Giambattista 176, 187, 199

Weaver, Harriet Shaw 175, 203n5
Wolf Man 31–32, 40, 41
Work in Progress 39n6, 40, 169, 175

Žižek, Slavoj 32–33, 36, 37, 38, 41

For Product Safety Concerns and Information please contact our EU representative GPSR@taylorandfrancis.com
Taylor & Francis Verlag GmbH, Kaufingerstraße 24, 80331 München, Germany

www.ingramcontent.com/pod-product-compliance
Lightning Source LLC
Chambersburg PA
CBHW061348300426
44116CB00011B/2033